cognitive development

cognitive
development

JOHN H. FLAVELL
Stanford University

PRENTICE-HALL, INC., ENGLEWOOD CLIFFS, NEW JERSEY

Library of Congress Cataloging in Publication Data

Flavell, John H. (date)
  Cognitive development.

    Bibliography: p. 257
    Includes index.
    1. Cognition (Child psychology)   I. Title.
BF723.C5F62   155.4'13   76-13238
ISBN 0-13-139774-5
ISBN 0-13-139766-4 pbk.

The Prentice-Hall Series in Experimental Psychology
James J. Jenkins, editor

Printed in the United States of America

10 9 8 7 6 5 4 3 2 1   BF
                                 723
                                 C5
                                 F62

PRENTICE-HALL INTERNATIONAL, INC., *London*
PRENTICE-HALL OF AUSTRALIA PTY. LIMITED, *Sydney*
PRENTICE-HALL OF CANADA, LTD., *Toronto*
PRENTICE-HALL OF INDIA PRIVATE LIMITED, *New Delhi*
PRENTICE-HALL OF JAPAN, INC., *Tokyo*
PRENTICE-HALL OF SOUTHEAST ASIA PTE. LTD., *Singapore*

TO ELLIE, BETH, AND JIM

contents

preface

The intended audience for this book is anyone who has reason to read about human cognitive development. I hope and expect that it will be comprehensible and interesting to readers with a very wide range of backgrounds: people interested in the topic but with little or no background in psychology; undergraduate and graduate students in general, developmental, cognitive, educational, and perhaps social psychology, various fields of education, and possibly other social sciences; perhaps even postdoctoral professionals in these areas. It certainly should be suitable as a text for either an undergraduate or a graduate course.

Several things were done in hopes of making the book useful to a wide variety of readers. Many references are cited in the text, especially secondary sources that would provide quick access to much of the primary research literature in an area. Some readers will find these quite useful; others obviously will not. On the other side, I have explained the meaning of most technical terms used, even those that people with only a little background in psychology might know. I have also tried to make the exposition straightforward and readable, and also perhaps a little lighter and less formal than textbooks sometimes are. I personally do not enjoy reading most textbooks and therefore would like this one to be, if not actually enjoyable, at least not wholly unenjoyable.

I am indebted to the following individuals and organizations for granting me permission to quote or excerpt material from their publications: Rheta DeVries, Brian Foss, Eleanor J. Gibson, Akira Kobasigawa, Jean Piaget, H. R. Schaffer, Academic Press, Inc., Meredith Corporation, Presses Universitaires de France, and Society for Research in Child Development, Inc. I wish to thank Eleanor R. Flavell, William Kessen, James J. Jenkins, Anne D. Pick, Herbert L. Pick, Philip H. Salapatek, and Adrien Pinard for their helpful comments on the manuscript. Sincerest thanks are also due to Kathleen A. Casey, Sharon Deering, Deborah Memcek, Annette F. Pinkham, and Kathleen A. Triden for typing the manuscript, and to the University of Minnesota's Institute of Child Development and Center for Research in Human Learning for numerous forms of help and support. Finally, I am especially grateful to Ellie Flavell for her patience, encouragement, and help throughout the writing process.

cognitive development

1

introduction

COGNITION

The really interesting concepts of this world have the nasty habit of avoiding our most determined attempts to pin them down, to make them say something definite and make them stick to it. Their meanings perversely remain multiple, ambiguous, imprecise, and above all unstable and open—open to argument and disagreement, to sometimes drastic reformulation and redefinition, and to the introduction of new and often unsettling concept instances and examples. It is perhaps not a bad thing that our prize concepts have this kind of complexity and instability (some might call it richness and creativity). In any event, they do seem to have these properties, and therefore we would be wise not to expend too much of our time and energy trying to fix them in formal definition.

Problems in Defining and Limiting the Concept of Cognition

So it is with that concept called *cognition*, the development of which is the subject of this book. Obviously, it is important here to communicate some ideas and images about the nature of cognition, but it

1

will be neither possible nor desirable to define it and limit its meaning in any precise or inflexible fashion.

A traditional but still current image of cognition tends to restrict it to the fancier, more unequivocally "intelligent" processes and products of the human mind. This image includes such Higher-Mental-Processes types of psychological entities as knowledge, consciousness, intelligence, thinking, imagining, creating, generating plans and strategies, reasoning, inferring, problem solving, conceptualizing, classsifying and relating, symbolizing, and perhaps fantasizing and dreaming. Although some of these activities would surely be credited to the psychological repertoires of other animals, they nonetheless have a decidedly human, mind-of-man ring to them.

While no contemporary psychologist would want to exclude any of these traditional components from the cognitive domain, he or she might feel it either desirable or necessary to add some others, perhaps reformulating ideas about the original components while going along (recall the point about the inherent instability and open-endedness of important concepts). Certain components would have a somewhat humble, less purely cerebral-intellectual cast to them. Organized motor movements (especially in infants), perception, imagery, memory, attention, and learning are possible cases in point. Others might look more social-psychological than the word "cognition" usually connotes. Instances here would include all varieties of social cognition (that is, cognition directed at the world of human versus nonhuman objects) and the social-communicative versus private-cognitive uses of language. Once embarked on this course of broadening and restructuring the domain beyond the classical *higher mental processes,* it is very difficult to decide where to stop. One is finally led to ask, what psychological processes can *not* be described as "cognitive" in some nontrivial sense, or do *not* implicate "cognition" to a significant degree? The answer is that mental processes habitually intrude themselves into virtually *all* human psychological processes and activities, and consequently there is no really principled, nonarbitrary place to stop. To be sure, this book will say little about such noncognitive-sounding things as emotions, personality, aggression, and so on. There are many *practical* reasons for slighting these and other topics, such as space limitations, lack of an adequate data base in some cases, consideration for teachers' and readers' expectations about what a book with this title should contain, and sheer personal preferences. The point to be underscored, however, is that there is no *principled* justification for excluding them. What you know and think (cognition) obviously interacts in a very substantial and significant way with how you feel (emotions), to take but one example. Depending only upon the state of existing theory and empirical evidence, a longer or shorter cognitive story could be told about virtually any phenomenon mentioned in an introductory psychology textbook. We only have a single head, after all, and it is firmly attached to the rest of the body.

The Need for a Broad and Complex
Conception of Cognition

If there is no nonarbitrary place to stop once we go beyond a narrow, purely Higher-Mental-Process image of cognition, why go beyond it at all? The answer is that we simply cannot talk coherently and realistically about the nature and development of cognition without enlarging and complicating that image. There is a deep and a not so deep reason why this is so. The latter reason is that processes like perceiving, remembering, evaluating other people, exchanging information with them, etc., are routine functions of the brain and mind; they simply are as genuinely "cognitive" by any reasonable definition as syllogistic reasoning is. Moreover, you will see in Chap. 2 that children exhibit intelligent-looking patterns of motor and perceptual behavior well before they can operate with symbols at all, let alone engage in syllogistic reasoning. It would seem arbitrary in the extreme to christen children "cognitive" only after they had achieved the ability to engage in the more exalted forms of cerebration.

The deep reason is that the psychological events and processes that go into making up what we call "thinking," "perceiving," "remembering," and the rest are in fact complexly interwoven with one another in the tapestry of actual, real-time cognitive functioning. Each process is believed to play a vital role in the operation and development of each other process, affecting it and being affected by it. This idea of mutual, two-way interactions among cognitive processes is an exceedingly important one. A paper by Frijda (1972) on current theoretical models of long term memory illustrates this point. Since memory is the topic, readers of Frijda's article are hardly surprised to encounter words like *recognition, recall, storage,* and *retrieval.* However, the idea that human memory simply cannot be meaningfully discussed without reference to all manner of other, very cognitive-sounding processes is forcibly brought home as the readers also encounter expressions like these: *idea, meanings, logical consistency, inference, knowledge, strategies, problem solving,* and *intelligence.* Lest they still be tempted to regard "memory" as a distinct and autonomous cognitive component, they are assured that "the distinction between remembering and problem solving is a gradual and imprecise one" and that "inference processes in particular play an important part in recall" (Frijda, 1972, p. 26).

Frijda's disposition to implicate a veritable host of plain and fancy cognitive processes in his account of how memory operates—all of the mind, practically—is not unusual in present-day theorizing about memory (e.g., Flavell, 1971*b*). Nor is memory in any way a special case in this respect. Single out for analysis any other process or category of processes you wish—perception, imagery, reasoning, classification, etc. —and it could readily be argued that all the others affect it and are affected by it in one way or another. What you know affects and is affected by how you perceive, how you conceptualize or classify things influences the way you reason about them and vice-versa, and so on and on. If we pretend for purposes of psychological analysis that cognitive man is a machine or device that carries out a variety of mental operations to achieve a variety of mental products, the present argument would be that he is a very highly organized device, one whose numerous "parts" are richly interconnected to one another. Man is, in short, not a collection or aggregate of unrelated cognitive components; he is a complexly organized *system* of interacting components. It would be tedious to keep pointing out these interactions throughout the book, but it would be well to bear in mind that they are ubiquitous in cognitive functioning.

MAN AS A COGNITIVE SYSTEM

What type of cognitive system might man be? Just what theoretical conception of that system should we adopt? As with all such questions, opinion varies considerably. Some psychologists would favor one or another type of behavioristic account, perhaps conceptualizing the system as a structural network of external and internal stimulus-response connections. Psychoanalytically-oriented theorists would talk about the structure and functions of the ego, psychometrically-oriented ones about the organization of intelligence in the IQ test sense, and so on. My own biases lead me to favor some combination of two other approaches, although not with the uncritical zeal of the "true believer" in either instance. One approach might be termed the *structuralist-organismic* orientation, chiefly represented by Jean Piaget's theory of the mind but with some of Heinz Werner's ideas also included. The other is the *information-processing* approach, as embodied in the writings of Herbert Simon, Allen Newell, Walter Reitman, and numerous others (the above-mentioned paper by Frijda is an example).

The Information-Processing View

Just enough will be said here about the information-processing view to suggest its compatibility with the image of cognitive man I have been trying to convey in the preceding pages; a fuller but still brief and synoptic account of this view can be found in Dember and Jenkins (1970, pp. 502–11). The information-processing theorist thinks of man as a complex machine or device, in some ways analogous to a modern electronic computer, that possesses elaborate "programs" for dealing with information in intelligent and adaptive ways. The programs consist of intricately interrelated and sequenced cognitive operations or processes that construct or create, receive, transform (recode, reduce, elaborate), store, retrieve, and otherwise manipulate units of information or knowledge.

> If we examine the fine structure of thought as it shows up in the protocols of human problem solving, we discover that even routine accomplishments appear to involve many steps integrated into complex sequences. Information-processing theories encourage us to investigate in detail the systems of cognitive structures, elementary psychological processes, and higher order strategies it seems necessary to postulate to account for the behaviors and achievements we observe . . . . the information-processing approach to the study of man follows his purposes and plans as he seeks, does, and creates things, manipulating objects and information to attain his ends. (Reitman, 1965, pp. 1–2)

The Piagetian View

One of the virtues of the information-processing conception from the present standpoint is precisely that it *does* explicitly represent human beings as complex cognitive systems, that is, as extremely rich and elaborate structures composed of interdependent cognitive processes. It is scarcely credible that cognition will ever be adequately represented by any theoretical approach that credits us with any *less* complexity than information-processing models typically do. It is also possible within such models to say a great deal about a problem that has not yet been dealt with explicitly here, namely, the nature of the cognitive system's interaction with the external world of objects and events (see, for example, Simon and Newell, 1970). Similarly, structuralist-organismic theories such as Piaget's both impute complex internal organization to the cognitive system and also make claims about how that system relates to its environment. Piaget's account of cognitive man's relationship with his milieu is probably more useful for our purposes than the information-processing account of it, however, and is accordingly summarized below. But first a few cautionary remarks about the relationship between Piaget and this book.

Piaget's contributions to our knowledge of cognitive development have been nothing short of stupendous, both quantitatively and qualitatively. Moreover, his ideas about cognitive growth are often very complex and difficult to grasp, even when presented as an integrated whole, at length and in full detail. They are particularly prone to distortion, oversimplification, and general misunderstanding when one tries to integrate brief summaries of Piaget's ideas within a more general narrative about the field such as this book aims to be. That is, the danger of misunderstanding is very great when they are presented briefly and discontinuously, one set of ideas at this point in the narrative and another set at a later point. A reasonable conclusion from these facts is that, unless they do some supplementary reading (e.g., Flavell, 1963; Furth, 1969; Ginsburg & Opper, 1969; Piaget, 1970a), readers may be destined to mislearn at least some aspects of Piaget's theory in the course of (I hope) learning something interesting and substantive about cognitive development in general. The same could be true for anyone else's work, of course, but in Piaget's case the likelihood of unavoidable misrepresentation is especially great; one always has the feeling, when writing about Piaget's theory, that brevity, clarity, and accuracy are somehow incompatible. It could be argued that a minimum of two sources is needed to attain an adequate introductory level understanding of cognitive development at this particular point in the history of the field. These would be a general survey of the field as a whole, plus a more detailed account of Piaget's contributions alone.

Assimilation-accommodation as a model of cognitive functioning. Piaget views human cognition as a specific form of biological adaptation of a complex organism to a complex environment. The cognitive organism he envisages is, however, an extremely active kind of knower. That is, the Piagetian man actively selects and interprets environmental information in the construction of his own knowledge rather than passively copying the information just as it is presented to his senses. Of course, while paying attention to and taking account of the structure of the environment during knowledge seeking, the Piagetian man always reconstrues and reinterprets that environment to make it fit in with his own existing mental framework. Thus, the mind neither copies the world, passively accepting it as a ready made given, nor does it ignore the world, autistically creating a private mental conception of it out of whole cloth. Rather, the mind builds its knowledge structures by taking external data and interpreting them, transforming them, and reorganizing them. It therefore does indeed meet with the environment in the process of constructing its knowledge, and consequently that knowledge is to a degree "realistic" or adaptive for the organism. However, Piaget makes much of the idea that the mind meets the environment in an extremely active, self-directed way—meets it more than half way, as it were.

Piaget's conception of how the cognitive system interacts with the outside world may become clearer if we examine his concept of *adapta-tion* more closely. Cognition, like other forms of biological adaptation, always exhibits two simultaneous and complementary aspects, which Piaget refers to as *assimilation* and *accommodation.* While it is con-venient to talk about them as if they were distinct and separate cognitive activities, it must be kept in mind that Piaget conceives of them as but two indissociable aspects of the same basic adaptational process—two sides of the same cognitive coin. Assimilation essentially means interpreting or construing external objects and events in terms of one's own pres-ently available and favored ways of thinking about things. The young child who pretends that a chip of wood is a boat is, in Piaget's terms, "assimilating" the wood chip to his mental concept of boat, incorporating the object within the whole structure of his knowledge of boats. Accom-modation roughly means noticing and taking cognitive account of the various real properties and relationships among properties that external objects and events possess; it means the mental apprehension of the structural attributes of environmental data. The young child who pains-takingly imitates his father's gestures is "accommodating" his mental apparatus (and thence, his motor gestures) to the fine detail of his father's behavior. Assimilation, therefore, refers to the process of adapt-ing external stimuli to one's own internal mental structures while ac-commodation refers to the converse or complementary process of adapting these mental structures to the structure of these same stimuli. In the more obviously biological adaptation of ingestion-digestion of food, organisms simultaneously accommodate to the particular structure of the food (chew hard or easy, digest with the help of this enzyme or that, depending upon what the food is) and assimilate the food to their own physical structure (transform its appearance, convert it into energy, etc.). In cognitive adaptations, we can say that individuals simultaneously accommodate to the particular structure of the object of their cognitions and assimilate that object to their own cognitive structures.

Another example may serve to point up the extreme interdepen-dence or indissociability of assimilation and accommodation, the sense in which they really are but two aspects of the same cognitive process. Suppose I show you a symmetrical blot of ink on a piece of paper, ask you what it reminds you of, and hear you say that it resembles a bat. Piaget would say that you had cognitively accommodated to certain physical features of the blot and used these as the basis for assimilating the blot to your internal concept of a bat. It is important to recognize that you did not merely accommodate to an external stimulus; that is, you did not just passively and mindlessly scan the blot and "discover" a bat "that was really there." For without a preexisting, well elaborated conception of bat in your cognitive repertoire you would certainly not have been able to detect and integrate into a whole perceptual structure the particular constellation of blot features that you did. In other words, your accommodatory possibilities were just as surely limited and constrained by your assimilatory ones as your assimilatory possibilities were by your accommodatory ones. Obviously, if there were no bat-compatible physical properties in the blot to be accommodated to, there would be no assimilation of the blot to "bat," that is, no perception of the blot as resembling that animal. If the ink blot took the form of a thin, straight line, for instance, there would naturally be no temptation to construe it as a bat. Not quite so obviously, perhaps, but just as surely, if you had no cognitive bat concept to which to assimilate the blot, your accommodation to the blot's various physical features would be entirely different. If the perceiver were a one-year-old baby, with a belfry as yet devoid of bats, the perceiver would not process the structural information contained in the blot as you did and would not see it in the same way that you did because, in a manner of speaking, the perceiver's mind's eye would differ from yours.

In Piaget's view, therefore, in any cognitive encounter with the environment, assimilation and accommodation are of equal importance and must always occur together in a mutually dependent way. His model of the human cognitive system stresses the constant interaction or collaboration of the internal-cognitive with the external-environmental in the construction and deployment of knowledge, with both factors making a vital contribution to this construction and deployment. What you know already will greatly shape and constrain what environmental information you can detect and process, just as what you can detect and process will provide essential grist for the activation of present knowledge and the generation of new knowledge. To return to our first two examples, the wood chip likely would never metamorphize into a boat if it could not float and were not vaguely boat-shaped, and the father's gestures could not be mimicked if the child could not assimiliate them to motor action patterns he already possessed.

Assimilation-accommodation as a model of cognitive development. Thus Piaget's assimilation-accommodation model provides a valuable general conception of how man's cognitive system might interact with man's external environment. However, it is also a particularly useful vehicle for thinking about cognitive development, that is, about how the child's cognitive system might gradually evolve with maturation and experience. As we have seen, the model is well set up to give an essentially nondevelopmental, atemporal description of the mind-environment interaction, a description that holds true of any mind interacting with any environment at any given moment of time. The present point, however, is that it is equally well set up to describe how a mind might gradually develop and change its structure and content through repeated interactions with the milieu, and is therefore a particularly useful model to communicate in a text on cognitive development. Let us reconsider the wood chip example to illustrate how the model might help us think about cognititve growth as well as about cognitive functioning.

In the situation we are imagining, a young child is playing with his toy boats in the bathtub and suddenly notices in the corner of the soap dish a tiny fragment of wood from a broken pencil. He picks it up, and after some deliberation (he has sailed many a boat, but nary a wood chip), gingerly places it in the water. Upon discovering that it floats, he adds it to his armada, and emerges from his bath some time later a wiser as well as a cleaner child. The question is, in what way wiser, and through what sorts of wisdom-building (cognitive-developmental) processes?

Let us credit him, at the beginning of the bath, with a certain organized body of knowledge and certain abilities concerning the concrete, functional properties of the main entities in the situation (toy boats, small, nondescript objects, and water). He knows much about their characteristic look and feel and also something of their characteristic reactions to his actions upon them. We could say that he has already achieved a certain level of cognitive development with respect to this microdomain of his everyday world and consequently, in Piaget's terms, he assimilates it and accommodates to it in specific ways that faithfully reflect this cognitive-developmental level. As a result of the new things he did and observed during this particular bath, however, that level will have changed ever so slightly, and consequently his future assimilations and accommodations within that microdomain will also have changed ever so slightly.

Let us suppose he has discovered (accommodation) some things he did not know before about what little pieces of wood can and cannot do (float rather than sink, make only a tiny splash when dropped in water, fail to move a big toy boat when they bump into it) and about what one can and cannot do with them (sail them, make them bob to the surface by holding them under water and then letting go, give them rides on top of other toy boats). Additionally, during this process of "minidevelopment," the content and structure of his mind and its capacity to construe and interpret this microdomain (assimilation) has also altered slightly. For example, his functional class of boat-like entities has now generalized to include at least certain small lightweight objects that do not closely resemble the more typical and familiar instances of this class (e.g., his toy boats). Subsequently, this small change in conceptual structure may permit him to construe (assimilate) still other kinds of objects as novel candidates for boat play. Moreover, the category of boat-like things may now be functionally subclassified for him into big, strong ones and small, weak ones, whereas it may previously have been a more or less homogeneous, undifferentiated class.

Thus, in the course of trying to accommodate to some hitherto unknown functional properties of a relatively unfamiliar sort of object, and of trying to assimilate the object and its properties to existing concepts and skills (trying to interpret them, make sense out of them, test out one's repertoire of actions upon them) the child's mind has stretched just a little, and this stretching in turn broadens slightly his future assimilatory and accommodatory possibilities. By repeated assimilation of and accommodation to a given milieu, the cognitive system evolves slightly, which makes possible somewhat novel and different assimilations and accommodations, with these latter changes producing further small increments of mental growth. Thus, the dialectical process of development continues in this gradual, leg over leg fashion. $Mind_1$ (i.e., at some arbitrary point in its development) makes possible $Assimilations_1$ and $Accommodations_1$ (i.e., assimilations and accommodations of a particular, characteristically $Mind_1$ type), the informational products or feedback from which help to generate $Mind_2$, which then makes possible $Assimilations_2$ and $Accommodations_2$, which again yield new information to provide some of the developmental raw material for $Mind_3$, etc. Figure 1-1 illustrates the developmental process just described.

Figure 1-1. An assimilation-accommodation model of cognitive growth. $Mind_1$ (i.e., of some given developmental level) is very gradually transformed into $Mind_2$ (i.e., of some arbitrarily higher level) as a consequence of correspondingly gradual changes in assimilatory and accommodatory possibilities, these changes in turn resulting from the continuous exercise of these mental functions in the course of adapting to the environment.

It is clear why such a development would be slow and gradual. Each Mind represents but a small, imperceptible departure from its immediate predecessor; it is rooted in, constrained by, and free to deviate but slightly from that predecessor. It is also clear, however, that a very, very substantial modification in the human cognitive system could eventuate from year after year of daily, virtually continuous assimilation of milieu to mind and accommodation of mind to milieu. Thus Piaget's assimilation-accommodation model seems to have the right properties to characterize the childhood evolution of our cognitive system, as well as to characterize the functioning of that system during a particular interchange with the environment. The model makes childhood cognitive growth a logical outcome of repeated cognitive functioning, suggests that it should be slow and gradual, and allows for a considerable amount of total developmental change, given a whole childhood in which to accumulate. These are the very properties we think human cognitive development does in fact possess.

It will become apparent in Chap. 7 that Piaget's model can be criticized, and that the question of how the process of cognitive growth is best described and explained is still unsettled. However, a plausible working conception of how the child makes cognitive advances is useful to have at the outset, before examining the nature of those advances (Chaps. 2–6). Piaget's assimilation-accommodation model is just such a conception.

AN OVERVIEW OF THE BOOK

The major landmarks of general mental growth from birth to adulthood are chronicled in Chaps. 2–4. The principal emphasis is on Piaget's work, although the ideas and research findings of others are also included in those chapters. The development of social cognition is also included in Chaps. 2 and 4. Chaps. 2–4 may therefore be considered the core of the book, since they describe the child's growing intellectual mastery of his social and nonsocial environment. Chaps. 5 and 6 deal with the onto-genesis of perception, communication, and memory. These three topics, together with the growth of social cognition, are currently receiving a good deal of research attention by developmental psychologists. Their inclusion reflects the book's emphasis on a broader rather than a narrower view of cognition. Finally, some major questions and problems concerning cognitive development are discussed in Chap. 7.

This book has some idiosyncrasies of which the reader is entitled to be aware. It is probably a more "personal" book than most texts. First, I did not feel as constrained as many textbook writers might to cover all the important topics in the field. In general, a topic was likelier to get included to the extent that I: (1) found it interesting to read, think, and write about; (2) already had a fairly deep, "insider's" acquaintance with it, perhaps because I had previously written or done research in that area; (3) felt I could write a coherent account of it, in the space available, that a reader unfamiliar with the field of cognitive development could ·comprehend and remember. There is, for example, no treatment of language development in the book. This important topic fully meets criterion (1), partly meets (2), but unfortunately fails to meet (3), for reasons given on pp. 172–73.

Second, the topics finally selected by these idiosyncratic criteria were also approached in an idiosyncratic fashion. My approach tends to be more description-oriented and less explanation-oriented than that of many developmental psychologists. There is, therefore, considerable emphasis on describing *what* cognitive abilities and knowledge children develop and, if known, the sequential steps involved in their formation. This contrasts with an emphasis on trying to show what factors or variables (e.g., in the child's cognitive experiences and environment) generate, facilitate, or impede these developments. While it is true that there are problems in deciding what constitutes an explanation or a cause of cognitive growth (Chap. 7), this book's emphasis on description would undoubtedly appear excessive to some developmentalists.

Finally, the book contains a fair amount of informed opinion and educated guess where (most everywhere, it sometimes seems) the facts are not solid. Those opinions and guesses are mostly my own, and others in the field would undoubtedy disagree with some of them.

In sum, this book was meant to be, and I hope is, an adequate introductory textbook on cognitive development. It is also, however, very clearly an expression of my personal views and biases as to what can and ought to be said about the field at this time.

SUMMARY

The concept of cognition favored in this book is a broad and inclusive one, covering more than such traditional, more narrowly "intellectual" processes as reasoning and problem solving. Cognitive man is conceptualized as a complex *system* of interacting processes which generate, code, transform, and otherwise manipulate information of diverse sorts. Contemporary *information-processing* approaches to the study of human cognition are therefore seen as promising and highly compatible with this conceptualization.

Piaget's *assimilation-accommodation* model describes how this cognitive system interacts with its environment, and, by means of many such interactions, undergoes developmental change. According to this model, the individual plays a very active role in his cognitive interchanges with the environment. He creates a mental construction of reality in the course of numerous experiences with his milieu, rather than simply making a mental copy of what is experienced. Each cognitive encounter with the world always has two aspects, *assimilation* and *accommodation.* Assimilation essentially means interpreting or construing external data in terms of the individual's existing cognitive system. What is encountered is cognitively transformed to fit what the individual knows and how he thinks. Accommodation means taking account of the structure of the external data. According to Piaget's model, therefore, the cognitive system simultaneously adapts reality to its own structure (assimilation) and adapts itself to the structure of the environment (accommodation). By repeatedly attempting to accommodate to and assimilate novel, previously unassimilated environmental elements, the system itself gradually changes its internal structure, i.e., cognitive development takes place (see Fig. 1-1).

The plan of the book is as follows. Chaps. 2–4 contain a Piaget-oriented account of general conceptual development during infancy (Chap. 2), early and middle childhood (Chap. 3), and adolescence (Chap. 4). The development of social cognition during infancy and during the post-infancy years is taken up in Chaps. 2 and 4, respectively. I then describe developmental aspects of perception (Chap. 5), communication (Chap. 5), and memory (Chap. 6), and conclude with a discussion of outstanding questions and problems in the field (Chap. 7). While the book obviously is intended to be an introductory text, it probably reflects the author's own personal views about the field more than is true of most introductory texts.

2

infancy

One hardly needs to read a textbook to recognize that there must be staggering differences between the cognitive system of the very young infant and that of the very young child (0–1 versus 18–30 months of age, let us say). These two organisms scarcely seem to belong to the same species, so great are the cognitive as well as physical differences between them. The very young infant is an intellectual zero to the casual observer; he or she appears to have no "mind" at all. While there is now a great deal of research evidence to show that such a judgment does not in fact do justice to the baby's capabilities, the intellectual gap between the neonate (newborn) and the two year old child nonetheless remains enormous. It is clear to casual observer and researcher that unlike the very young infant, the late-infancy and early post-infancy child can represent and communicate information by means of symbols (in speech, gesture, drawing, play, etc.), can solve a number of concrete, practical problems by the intelligent, planful use of simple tools and other means, possesses a considerable amount of practical knowledge concerning his everyday world of people, objects, and events, and much else besides.

This marked contrast between newborn and early childhood cognitive systems can perhaps be brought home more forcefully by considering the following "oddity problem," as the specialist in learning would call it. We are presented with a newborn infant, a two year old child, and an adult. After watching each of these three "stimuli" behave for a while, our task is to pick the one that seems most different from or unlike the other two as a thinking and knowing creature, that is, as a cognitive organism. I would definitely select the neonate as the odd one out in this comparison, and suspect you might do the same. For despite the obvious and undeniable intellectual differences between the two older members of the trio, they both strike us as being endowed with "minds," and with decidedly human ones at that. The young infant just does not give such an impression to most people (the infant's mother is, of course, mercifully excused from this oddity problem), notwithstanding what is really a rather trifling gap in chrononogical age between it and the two year old.

The objective of this chapter is to convey some of the highlights of the truly momentous cognitive transformation that takes place during this brief interval between early infancy and early childhood. The first section of the chapter describes the major landmarks of infant cognitive growth, using Piaget's six stage model of the development of sensory-motor intelligence as the basic framework. Special attention will be paid to the eventual attainment of the capacity to use and comprehend symbols, possibly the most significant and far-reaching outcome of the sensory-motor period.

The second section concentrates on a very special acquisition that takes place within this general process of sensory-motor development, namely, the acquisition of the all important object concept or concept of object permanence. The pioneering ideas and observations of Piaget will, of course, dominate both of these sections. However, important work also has been done by other psychologists on these same topics, much of it very recently, and some of this work will also be mentioned at appropriate places in the developmental narrative.

The third and final section of this chapter deals with the development of social cognition, particularly as this development is manifested in the infant's changing behavior towards other human beings. Just as the infant's growing understanding of his physical world presumably mediates and is mediated by his sensory and motor responses to physical, nonhuman objects, so also ought his burgeoning understanding of self and others be similarly related to his social behavior, for example, to the amount and kind of emotional attachment he displays to others. Moreover, we should be able to predict and find revealing connections and correlations between the baby's cognitive advances in the physical domain and his cognitive advances in the social domain (it is the same nervous system, after all, that is involved in both developments). Thus, the final section should be at least partly integrative with the first and second.

SENSORY-MOTOR INTELLIGENCE

Infant Cognition as Sensory-Motor Intelligence

If the five month old infant can be said to "think" and "know" at all, he certainly does not appear to do so in the usual sense of these terms. In what sense, then? What *does* the infant have or do that permits us to talk meaningfully about the nature and development of "infant cognition"?

What he or she demonstrates, in an increasingly clear and unambiguous manner as he grows older, is the capacity for organized, "intelligent-looking" sensory and motor *actions*. That is, he exhibits a wholly practical, perceiving-and-doing, action-bound kind of intellectual functioning; he does not exhibit the more contemplative, reflective, symbol-manipulating kind we usually think of in connection with cognition. The infant "knows" in the sense of recognizing or anticipating familiar, recurring objects and happenings, and "thinks" in the sense of behaving towards them with mouth, hand, eye, and other sensory-motor instruments in predictable, organized, and often adaptive ways. His is an entirely unconscious and self-unaware, nonsymbolic and nonsymbolizable (by the infant), knowledge-in-action or know-how type of cognition. It is the kind of noncontemplative intelligence that your dog relies on to make its way in the world. It is also the kind that you yourself exhibit when performing many actions which are characteristically nonsymbolic and unthinking by virtue of being so overlearned and automatized—e.g., brushing your teeth, starting the car, mowing the lawn, visually monitoring the grass in front of you for obstacles while doing so, etc. It is, to repeat, intelligence as inherent and manifest in organized patterns of sensory and motor action, and hence Piaget's description of infant cognition as presymbolic, prerepresentational, and prereflective "sensory-motor intelligence."

Sensory-Motor Schemes

In the previous chapter, I spoke of the child assimilating external data to _____ and accommodating _____ to external data, with the blank variously filled in with "mental framework," "favored ways of thinking about things," "cognitive structure," "conception," "concept," and similar expressions. All of these terms refer to some sort of enduring cognitive organization or knowledge structure within a child's head that does the assimilating and accommodating. When talking specifically about infantile, sensory-motor assimilating and accommodating, as contrasted with developmentally more advanced, symbolic-representational forms, Piaget fills in the blank with the word *scheme*.[1]

The meaning of *scheme* is easier to convey by example than by formal definition. A scheme generally has to do with a specific, readily labelable class of sensory-motor action sequences that the infant repeatedly and habitually carries out, normally in response to particular classes of objects or situations. The scheme itself is generally thought of as referring to the inner, mental-structural basis for these overt action sequences; it is, in other words, the cognitive capacity that underlies and makes possible such organized behavior patterns. Thus, the young infant that automatically sucks anything that finds its way into his mouth would be said to possess a "sucking scheme," that is, he possesses an enduring ability and disposition to carry out a specific class of action sequences (organized sucking movements) in response to a particular class of happenings (the insertion of suckable objects). Similarly, one can talk about sensory-motor schemes of looking, listening, grasping, hitting, pushing, kicking, and so on. A scheme is a kind of sensory-motor level counterpart of a symbolic-representational level concept. An older person *represents* (thinks of, verbally characterizes) a given object as an instance of the class, "nipple"; analogously, the baby *acts* or *behaves* towards the same object as though it belonged to the (functional) class, "something to suck."

A very important property of schemes is that they may be combined or coordinated to form larger wholes or units of sensory-motor intelligence. For instance, once he has achieved a certain level of cognitive development, the infant is capable of pushing aside ("pushing" being one motor scheme) an obstacle in order to seize (another motor scheme) a desired object. We see a similar integration of sucking and manual prehension schemes once the infant acquires the systematic tendency to bring to his mouth anything his hand chances to grasp. As elementary schemes gradually become generalized, differentiated, and above all, intercoordinated and integrated with one another in diverse and complex ways, the infant's behavior begins to look more and more unambiguously "intelligent" and "cognitive."

Adapted Intelligence, Imitation, and Play

We can now say that the infant's cognitive activity consists of *assimilating* external data to internal cognitive-structural units called

---

[1] In many secondary sources, the very same concept goes by the name *schema* (occasional plural: *schemata*). *Schema* is a mistranslation of the Piagetian French original, *schème*, perpetrated by writers (the present writer prominently among them) insufficiently versed in French, Piaget, or both.

sensory-motor *schemes*, and of simultaneously *accommodating* these schemes to the structure of the external data. For instance, the baby assimilates a rattle to his grasping scheme; he "interprets" it, behaviorally speaking, as something that can be grasped. In the course of doing so, he simultaneously accommodates his grasping scheme to the specific physical properties of that object. That is, he adjusts his hand actions to the particular size and shape of the rattle, thereby grasping it quite differently than he would a sugar cube, for example. In most such interactions between sensory-motor schemes and external data, assimilation and accommodation contribute about equally, with neither aspect seeming to be more salient or important than the other. Piaget uses the term *adapted intelligence* to refer to this, the prototypical situation where assimilation and accommodation are roughly in balance.

They need not be in balance, however; one or the other may dominate. If the emphasis should be on accommodation rather than on assimilation, the cognitive behavior will take the form of imitation (modeling, copying). If I imitate or copy your behavior as precisely and faithfully as I can, I am obviously putting all my cognitive effort into adapting or accommodating my behavior to you and your idea, rather than freely reconstructing or assimilating your behavior in accord with my own ideas. If, in contrast, the accent is heavily assimilative rather than accommodative, the outcome will be play or other self-expressive, less literal and "realistic" cognitive activities (fantasy, creative thinking, or even autistic or delusional thinking). If instead of slavishly parroting your behavior, I decide to execute a modern dance routine that expresses and symbolizes how your behavior makes me feel, the balance has obviously shifted towards a predominance of assimilatory activity. A photograph of a landscape is heavily accommodative; a Salvador Dali landscape is heavily assimilative.

Let us return now to the sensory-motor infant. If he explored the properties of a stick to find out what he could do with it (trying to "understand" the stick, in the sensory-motor meaning of the term), assimilation and accommodation would be in approximate balance and the infant's exploration would constitute an act of adapted intelligence. If he tried to mimic the appearance or behavior of the stick with his own body (e.g., banging first stick, then finger on the table), the accent would be on painstaking accommodation and we would label his behavior as imitation. Finally, if he pretended the stick were his doll, blithely ignoring blatant physical differences between stick and doll in order to do so, the accent would be on free assimilation (i.e., of the stick to his doll scheme or "concept"), and we would say he was playing. All three forms of cognitive functioning—adapted intelligence, imitation, and play—will be included in the description of sensory-motor development given below.

Cognitive Motivation

Up to this point I have described a cognitive system that is sensory-
motor rather than symbolic-representational in type, and one that functions and gradually transforms itself developmentally by simultaneously
assimilating data to schemes and accommodating schemes to data. The
nature or qualitative character of this scheme-data interaction was also
said to vary from play through adapted intelligence to imitation, depending upon the relative preponderance of assimilation versus accommodation. I have said nothing, however, about why the sensory-motor or
any subsequent cognitive system should ever operate in the first place,
nor about the circumstances under which it would be most likely to
operate with maximum intensity and persistence. What needs to be added
is an account of cognitive motivation, that is, of the factors and forces
that activate or intensify human cognitive processing. Once we have
some idea about the mind's power source and favored fuels, we will
finally be ready to describe its developmental itinerary during infancy.

Human beings obviously exercise their knowledge and cognitive
skills for a wide variety of reasons, in order to attain a wide variety of
goals. Some of these reasons and goals are basically noncognitive in character; they are *extrinsic* rather than *intrinsic* to the cognitive system
itself. The infant who grasps and sucks his bottle simply to satisfy his
hunger rather than to learn about the graspable and suckable potentialities of bottles is clearly activating his sensory-motor skills in the service
of an extrinsic, noncognitive need or goal. The same is true of the three
year old who makes intelligent use of a pair of footstools to obtain an
out of reach cooky, and of the high school student who studies hard
solely for parental approval.

More interesting, however, is the fact that a very great deal of
human mentation, at all developmental levels, is intrinsically rather than
extrinsically motivated. That is, the cognitive system is often turned on
and kept running by purely cognitive factors, rather than by bodily
needs or other motivational sources. The following behavioral episode,
brief though it is, illustrates most of the factors of this sort that psychologists have identified:

> Standing by the side of a low table the 12 month-old girl bangs on a peg-
> board with a block she has been holding; at the far end of the table the lid
> of an improperly closed coffee pot produces a loud rattle. The little girl
> freezes; her eyes explore the table top. She hits the pegboard again, and
> the small movements of the lid attract her attention. She moves over, picks
> up the lid, and rattles it against the pot; then back to her pegboard and
> block. She bangs: the lid rattles. The little girl gurgles, a wide smile ap-

pears on her face. A glance at her mother—still with that enormous smile—and on with her banging and the pot's rattling, to an accompaniment of gurgles, babblings, and small bounces of delight (Bronson, 1971, p. 269).

Why does the little girl bang on the pegboard in the first place? While it may sound like circular reasoning to say this, the best answer is that banging things to see, hear, and feel the results represents a common, probably universally acquired sensory-motor scheme, and it is simply in the nature of schemes to exercise themselves repeatedly, especially when first acquired. To ask why the child bangs when provided with a banging scheme and a compliant object to bang with is, for Piaget and many other psychologists, much like asking why she breathes when provided with lungs and air. There exists, in Hunt's words (1969, p. 37), "a system of motivation *inherent in* information processing and action" (italics mine). Consistent with this idea is research evidence proving that babies can be operantly conditioned using interesting sights and sounds as the only rewards. That is, babies will "work" (make repeated motor responses) for the sole privilege of viewing pictures, listening to voices, etc., just as they would "work" for traditional reinforcers such as food. The idea that cognitive activity is often intrinsically motivated does not mean that the disposition to engage in it could not be heightened or diminished by environmental factors. There is every reason to believe, for example, that sustained exposure to intellectually barren life circumstances can indeed substantially reduce this disposition. What it does mean is that there is a "natural bent," so to speak, to make use of the cognitive instruments that the species' evolution and individual's development have provided, and that the various noncognitive factors modulate this bent rather than actually create it *ex nihilo*.

When the coffee pot lid makes a loud rattle, the little girl freezes, visually explores the table top, and hits the pegboard again. This illustrates the fact that certain classes of inputs to the cognitive system tend to turn its operating volume way up. When these kinds of inputs are received, ongoing activities get temporarily suspended, the child becomes somewhat tense and aroused, and a variety of attentional, curiosity, exploratory, and other information-seeking behaviors are likely to ensue. The inputs that have this remarkable property may vary somewhat with the child's age, but at least from early-middle infancy on they will surely include: (1) stimulus events that are novel or not recently encountered; (2) events that are, considered in relation to the child's cognitive level, relatively complex rather than simple in structure; (2) events that are unanticipated and surprising, i.e., those that conspicuously violate his or her expectations as to what should happen in the present situation; (4) events that are puzzling and confusing, that lead to conflict or uncertainty in the child's mind. Notice that all of these events have the capacity to elicit the child's cognitive interest and activity only by virtue of their *relation* to his cognitive system. An input is never "puzzling," "surprising," etc., in and of itself; it is so described only if it proves surprising or puzzling *to* someone. Precisely because of differences in the make up of the infants' cognitive systems, the very same stimulus event may have the capacity to elicit surprise and its cognitive *sequelae* in an older infant but not in a younger one, or vice versa.

In early infancy, before the child has built up through experience many expectancies about how things should be, certain absolute, inherent-in-the-physical-stimulus types of input properties are the dominant elicitors of cognitive interest and action. In particular:

> The infant is predisposed to attend to events that possess a high rate of change in their physical characteristics. Stimuli that move or possess light-dark contrast are most likely to attract and hold a newborn's attention (Kagan, 1970, p. 298).

Such absolute properties do not lose their eliciting power in the months and years following early infancy (a moving object is likely to attract anyone's attention), but the more relative, child-times-stimulus ones like surprise and uncertainty become much more significant in these later periods.

There is a more specific hypothesis concerning these relative properties that a number of psychologists have put forward in one form or another. According to this hypothesis, the child is particularly intrigued by inputs that are somewhat or *moderately discrepant* from his current knowledge and expectations; that is, by events that are partly but not fully assimilable to his existing cognitive schemes. For an infant who has recently acquired a set of implicit expectations as to what human faces look like, for example, the hypothesis asserts that a picture of a distorted face (one eye placed in the chin region, etc.) should elicit a lot of cognitive interest and exploration. Such a stimulus is a seductive blend of the familiar and unfamiliar, of the expected and unexpected, and therefore should provoke a great deal of assimilative and accommodative effort. In contrast, a normal face should be less interesting to such an infant because it is wholly familiar (thus representing low versus moderate discrepancy), and a picture of a space craft should also be less interesting because it is wholly unfamilar and incomprehensible (high versus moderate discrepancy). A variation on this same hypothesis has it that *moderately complex* (again, relative to the child's cognitive level) stimuli are more likely to elicit interest than either very complex or very simple ones.

This hypothesis has a lot of surface plausibility and one feels that there simply has to be some truth in it. Nonetheless, efforts to verify it experimentally have so far met with mixed success. It has been difficult, for example, to determine just how "discrepant" a particular stimulus is for a specific, individual child, inasmuch as such a determination must depend upon a very accurate diagnosis of that specific child's cognitive level in relation to that particular kind of stimulus. Moreover, the particular kind or dimension of discrepancy involved may make a difference. Another problem, I suspect, is that at certain times and in certain psychological states, infants and older people alike may actually prefer to process comfortingly familiar, readily assimilable, low-discrepancy objects instead of tackling the more challenging and problematic, moderate-discrepancy ones. Our little girl's *initial* bang on the pegboard and her tacit anticipation of the kind of noise it would make might be a case in point (her *subsequent* bangings are something else again). As we are about to see, cognitive activity may also be recruited in enterprises that entail little if any uncertainty, surprise, unexpectedness, borderline incomprehensibility, moderate discrepancy from existing schemes, or the like.

The remaining highlights of the vignette also illustrate some important points about cognitive motivation. The little girl explores and experiments until she discovers the cause of the unexpected rattling noise, shows signs of extreme pleasure and satisfaction when she does discover it, and then repeats her banging again and again with great gusto. As indicated earlier, the states of cognitive uncertainty, surprise, puzzlement, interest, and so on, engendered by the occurrence of novel, unexpected, or otherwise not readily assimilable events, usually lead to cognitive activities designed to rectify the situation. Depending upon his level of cognitive development, the child may thereupon search and explore systematically or unsystematically, grope blindly or experiment intelligently. If he succeeds in mastering the problem, in finally comprehending that which initially was incomprehensible, a characteristic outcome is the sort of tension release and sense of pleasure shown by the little girl. Comprehension and understanding, especially following sustained cognitive effort, are likely to constitute a very positively reinforcing state of affairs for human beings of all ages. There is some research evidence, for example, that infants as young as 3–4 months of age may be capable of cognitive as well as social smiles and vocalizations. That is, in addition to smiling and gurgling at people, they also seem to smile and gurgle when they succeed in recognizing (assimilating, "comprehending") nonsocial stimuli.

Implicit in what has just been said is the notion that part of the motivation intrinsic to cognitive functioning is the motivation to master problematic situations, to be effective with respect to one's environment, to be competent. It is widely believed that this aspiration toward mastery,

effectiveness, and competence is an important part of the cognitive)
system's power source. The little girl joyfully repeats her rattle-producing
activity at least partly to savor and exercise her new found competence
to cause such an interesting phenomenon. Indeed, the whole behavior
episode was the preamble to a paper whose title began, "The growth
of competence. . . ." There is reason to think that infants, and perhaps
older children and adults as well, are particularly motivated to reproduce
actions of their own that they perceive as causes or instigators of interesting environmental events. Our 12-month-old would no doubt be cognitively titillated by the bang-rattle sequence even if someone else did the
banging. It could still puzzle and surprise, still give sensory pleasure, and
so on. But the fact that *she* produced the rattle, and also *knew* that she
produced it, added enormously to its interest. Any seasoned baby watcher
would predict that, had someone else first executed the sequence, the
child would have immediately hastened to try it herself. There is even
a hint in the research literature that babies may become emotionally
attached to objects whose behavior is often contingent in this way on
their own behavior. Such a process might even conceivably contribute
to the baby's attachment to its mother and other "responsive" human
beings (Yarrow and Pederson, 1972).

The foregoing has been a rather long story about the intrinsic aspects of cognitive motivation, and it would be nice if there were some
kind of memory aid or mnemonic device for remembering it. The ideal
mnemonic device would virtually prevent people from forgetting the
item to be retained even if they tried. My favorite is a mnemonic I heard
once for remembering the (approximate) height of Japan's Mount Fuji-
yama. Just recall that there are 12 months and 365 days in the year and
you automatically get your answer, 12,365 feet. It happens that there
does exist a fairly good mnemonic for reconstructing much of what has
been said in this section (those who do not *want* to remember what has
been said for the rest of their lives should read no further). Simply ask
yourself what a human cognitive system ought reasonably to be endowed
with if it is to have a good chance of learning the enormous number
and variety of things that members of our species do, in fact, routinely
learn. If you, as evolution's architect, wanted to build an efficient,
human-type knowledge-acquisition device, what sort of design would you
adopt?

It would seem sensible, first of all, to design it so that it did a lot
of spontaneous, noninstrumental, intrinsically rather than extrinsically
motivated cognitive functioning. The system should be disposed to notice
and do and remember things even when no noncognitive needs (e.g., for
food) are served thereby; it should exercise its schemes for the heck of
it as well as for practical ends, for fun as well as for profit. There is so

very much to learn that the system should not be permitted to lie around idle except when some tangible gain is in view.

The cognitive system should also be biased to attend to those situations or features of situations that present it with the most information, and especially, information that is new and therefore worth learning. Thus, its attention ought to be captured more by the contours of objects (contours are effectively zones of light-dark contrast) than by their interiors, and more by moving objects than by still ones. Moving objects are obviously apt to be important ones to pay attention to (human beings being prime examples), and contour, of course, provides information about an object's shape and hence its identity. Even more adaptive in this respect, perhaps, is the system's marked responsiveness to those relative, child-times-stimulus type properties mentioned earlier. Novel, surprising, puzzling, discrepant, uncertainty- and curiosity-provoking, or put most generally, not-readily-assimilable happenings—these are precisely the ones a learning, developing organism *ought* to be designed to notice, explore, and seek to understand, for they constitute the essential nutriments for its cognitive progress.

Needless to say, the cognitive system should be amply rewarded for its successful efforts at understanding such happenings, i.e., for the bit of learning and cognitive development it has achieved, and so we provide it with a purely cognitive kind of pleasure and sense of satisfaction whenever understanding dawns. We shall also want to make the system take pleasure in rehearsing its newly developed competence again and again, by itself and on its own. Such rehearsal for mastery's sake will tend to solidify and stabilize this competence through the overlearning it provides.

In sum, we have designed an organism that idly learns when there is no practical need to do so, that tries to learn what it most needs to learn, and that finds it rewarding both to learn these things initially and also to solidify and perfect its learning through subsequent practice. The human child appears to be just such an organism.

PIAGET'S SIX STAGES
OF SENSORY-MOTOR DEVELOPMENT

The age range designated below for each of Piaget's six stages is meant to be only a very rough average. Individual infants might therefore pass through any of the stages more rapidly or more slowly than these crude age norms would suggest. The *sequence* of stages, however, is believed to be absolutely constant or invariant for children the world over. Thus, Piaget claims that no earlier stage is ever skipped en route to any later one and no stages are ever navigated in a developmental order other than the one given. Finally, the accomplishments of each stage are said to cumulate: that is, skills achieved in earlier stages are not lost with the advent of later stages.

As you know, most research studies in psychology make use of dozens or even hundreds of subjects. The developmental sequence about to be described, on the contrary, was based solely upon Piaget's very detailed, day-by-day observations of his own three children, observations made some forty years ago. How seriously, then, should we take his story about sensory-motor development? A great deal of research on infant cognition has been done since that time, and especially during the past ten years (see Chap. 5). How does Piaget's account fare in the light of this recent evidence?

As I read this evidence, his original account holds up quite well overall. A number of investigators, using sizable samples of infants, have repeatedly observed the same basic sensory-motor behavior patterns Piaget reported, and observed them to occur in the same general sequence he described. A sample of three subjects is apparently not too small when someone of Piaget's genius is doing the looking.

However, some of the recent evidence does appear either to correct or to amplify the original story in certain details. As we shall see in the next section, this is particulary true in the case of object concept development. Furthermore, it may also be that Piaget's assertions about what an infant knows and can do at each stage often underestimate his actual capabilities. There are two reasons why this might be so. First, a great deal of evidence now suggests that the infant has more going for him cognitively than his initially poor and very slowly developing motor abilities would lead us to suspect. Neither Piaget nor anyone else could have known, even a dozen years ago, that the young infant would prove to be as readily conditionable as he seems to be, nor above all, as perceptually precocious as the evidence now indicates he is (Chap. 5). His obvious motoric helplessness—his inability to manipulate his environment with his hands, to explore it by moving himself through space, etc.—tends to give the mistaken impression that little cognitive learning and development could be taking place. But if he can, in fact, connect actions to reinforcements (be conditioned) and can perceptually process and retain environmental events at this tender age, he may well know more than even a Piaget could discern by naturalistic observation or impromptu experimentation. Charlesworth makes a similar point about the infant's perceptual versus motor precocity:

> . . . early organizations of information in the form of knowledge of the environment may take place before trial-and-error motor involvement

even occurs. When motor activity does take place, it is assimilated to pre-existing structures laid down by perceptual learning processes. In other words, the infant's visual system [and auditory system too, I would add] provides the initial matrix upon which later acquisition based on tactual contact and kinesthetic, proprioceptive feedbacks are mainly built (Charlesworth, 1968, p. 40).

Piaget may have also underestimated the infant on occasion because something he thought required considerable practice and experience for its development may really be innate or early-maturing, and thus be present in the child's cognitive repertoire earlier than Piaget assumed. For example, Piaget has described the development of the ability to coordinate eye and hand in grasping objects as a gradual, step-by-step process requiring much practice and experience. Others, however, have suggested that such coordination has strong innate components which can be demonstrated under proper experimental conditions (e.g., Bruner and Koslowski, 1972). As of this writing, the whole question of innate versus acquired aspects of eye-hand coordination and other sensory-motor achievements is very much unsettled (Chap. 5). Some studies point one way, some the other. My own reaction to the innatist position is rather similar to that expressed above concerning the moderate-discrepancy hypothesis. That is, I am currently taken with the idea that there must be a good deal of innately-given or early-maturing substructure for many of the infant's behavioral accomplishments, and that less practice and experience may be required for the genesis of these accomplishments than Piaget and others of us once believed. However, the actual research evidence so far presented in support of the idea has not seemed wholly unequivocal and convincing. In developmental psychology as in other scientific fields, one sometimes sees poor data adduced for good ideas, as well as (worse yet, in my opinion) good data adduced for bad ideas.

Stage 1 (Roughly 0–1 Months)

The infant comes into the world equipped with a variety of reflexes. Some of them are of no cognitive-developmental interest because they are destined either to remain unchanged with age and never become cognitively relevant (e.g., the sneeze) or to actually disappear entirely (e.g., the Moro response, a specifically infantile type of startle pattern). Others, like sucking, eye movements, and movements of the hand and arm, are destined to undergo significant developmental changes as a function of constant exercise and repeated application to external objects and events. Piaget attributed a great deal of importance to these latter reflexes because he regarded them as the initial, innately-provided building blocks of human cognitive growth. He conceived of them, in other words, as the infant's first sensory-motor schemes.

During the initial month of postnatal life, Piaget observed what appeared to be very small but possibly significant alterations in his children's sucking behavior. Although cautious on this point, he felt that these alterations might reflect minimal, beginning changes (consolidation, stabilization, generalization, and differentiation) in the structure of the infant's sucking scheme. Moreover, he believed the changes to be at least partly due to repeated practice and experience with "suckables" of different types, for instance, a soft and milk-producing nipple versus a harder and more arid thumb. Such experience-based changes in the sucking scheme would certainly comprise a humble but genuine instance of that gradual, "leg over leg" type of Piagetian developmental process described in Chap. 1 (pp. 10–11). Subsequent research by others has amply verified the occurrence of very early developmental changes in the sucking response:

> With lips tightly closed, the newborn's initial sucking pattern consists of an indissociable, almost unitary mass movement for creating negative pressure in the whole buccal cavity. A first successful execution sets the whole action going, but from there on there is change. . . . What is striking by the fourth week is that these earlier, undifferentiated patterns have been differentiated into a series of integrated components (Bruner, 1967, pp. 7–8).

It need only be added that the behavior and development ascribed to Stage 1 is largely of the "adapted intelligence" variety. That is, nothing clearly identifiable as either "play" or "imitation" occurs this early.

Stage 2 (Roughly 1–4 Months)

This stage is marked first, by the continued evolution of individual sensory-motor schemes, and second, by the gradual coordination or integration of one scheme with another. On the first point, individual schemes associated with such processes as sucking, looking, listening, vocalizing, and prehension (grasping objects) receive an enormous amount of spontaneous daily practice—recall our earlier discussion of intrinsic cognitive motivation. As a consequence, each of these schemes undergoes considerable developmental elaboration and refinement during these months. To continue with the Stage 1 example, sucking continues to be perfected as a motor skill. Toward the end of Stage 2 it may even occur anticipatively in response to associated visual or kinesthetic cues—in response, for instance, to the mere sight of the approaching nipple or the mere sensation of being held in the accustomed feeding position.

More interesting than this perfecting of individual, isolated schemes is the gradual coordination or coming-into-relation of one scheme with another. For example, vision and audition begin to become functionally related. Hearing a sound leads the infant to turn his head and eyes in the direction of the sound source (McGurk and Lewis, 1974). The activation of his listening-hearing schemes with their auditory assimilation-accommodation processes induces a corresponding activation of his looking-seeing schemes with their visual assimilation-accommodation processes.

Two other important scheme-scheme coordinations that get well established in Stage 2 are those of sucking-prehension and vision-prehension. In the case of sucking-prehension, the infant develops the ability (and very strong inclination) to bring to his mouth, and suck, his hand and anything the hand may have grasped, and also to grasp whatever may have found its way into his mouth. The coordination of vision with prehension permits the infant to locate and grasp objects under visual guidance, and reciprocally, to bring before his eyes for visual inspection anything an out-of-sight hand may have touched and grasped. The evolution of vision-prehension coordination is the more noteworthy development of the two. In the first place, an ability to coordinate hand and eye will obviously prove to be an extraordinarily important means or instrument for exploring and learning about the child's environment. In addition, Piaget's detailed account of its gradual, step-by-step evolution is very interesting. He described five such steps in all, of which the fourth is both the most intriguing and, currently, the most controversial. During this step, Piaget claimed, the infant is able to locate and grasp an object with his hand *only if both object and hand are simultaneously in view*. This alleged limitation is then removed in the fifth and final step: just as an adult would, the infant will now reach out and grasp a seen object even if the hand that does the reaching and grasping had initially not been simultaneously in view (e.g., had been under a blanket when the object was first sighted). However, there is presently some dispute among students of infancy whether this curious fourth step in the development of eye-hand coordination does actually occur, that is, whether Piaget rightly interpreted what he saw (e.g., Aronson and Tronick, 1971).

Piaget also reports some initial, quasiimitative or preimitative behavior during Stage 2. The infant may be a bit more likely to repeat one of his own habitual responses if someone else mimics that response immediately after he has made it. In other words, he may "imitate" (?) someone's imitation of his own action. Other researchers have also thought they have seen imitative-like behaviors in babies this young. A Stage 2 infant may also show what could be the dim beginnings of play behavior. For instance, he may "playfully" (?) repeat and repeat an already well-mastered, highly overlearned response routine—out of sheer assimilatory pleasure, in Piaget's opinion. It may be unwise, however, to try to read too much into these rather ambiguous, would-be forerunners of imitation and play.

Stage 3 (Roughly 4–8 Months)

The Stage 2 acquisition of visually guided manual activity helps make possible a new behavior pattern that constitutes the major achievement of Stage 3. The pattern begins when the infant chances to carry out some motor action, often a manual one, that happens to produce some unanticipated but perceptually interesting outcome in the environment. The pattern ends with the child delightedly repeating the action again and again, apparently for the sheer pleasure of reproducing and re-experiencing the environmental outcome. The child might grasp and shake a new toy, for instance, and that new toy might unexpectedly respond with a rattling sound. Whereupon, the child of this stage is likely to pause in wonderment, hesitatingly shake it again, hear the sound once again, more quickly and confidently shake it a third time, and then continue to repeat the action again and again for a considerable period of time.

There are several things to be said about this behavior pattern. First, students of learning will quickly recognize it as a variety of operant conditioning: a response occurs more or less spontaneously (shaking the toy), is immediately followed by positive reinforcement (the interesting sound), and the response thereby becomes more likely to recur. There is now definite evidence (not available to Piaget when he made his infant observations) that babies younger than 4–8 months can be operantly conditioned using sensory reinforcers of this sort. Consequently, it is a fair bet that some version of Piaget's prototypical Stage 3 behavior pattern may actually appear spontaneously prior to this stage.

Second, the behavior pattern is reminiscent of our 12-month-old girl's banging-and-lid-rattling sequence (pp. 19–20). In contrast to the one-year-old, however, the infant of 4–8 months is still too immature to have even an implicit, sensory-motor level sense of cause-effect relations, and will accordingly show none of the older child's efforts to explore the cause of the enjoyable perceptual experience. There is reason to doubt if the younger infant even distinguishes clearly between his motor action and its environmental result, whereas it is certain that the older infant makes this basic distinction.

Third, for the very reason that the action and its environmental result are likely not clearly separated in the Stage 3 infant's experience, Piaget is loath to credit him or her with a clear and unambiguous capacity for intentional, deliberate, goal-directed action. It just does not quite seem justified to say of him, as it will of the Stage 4 infant, that he kept shaking the toy *in order to* produce the sound, that is, as an intentional, deliberately-selected means to a clearly separate, anticipated end.

Finally, despite these limitations, the Stage 3 pattern represents genuine cognitive progress because it possesses one crucial feature. The infant of the two previous stages has been, in a manner of speaking, more preoccupied with his own actions than with the environmental effects these actions might produce. There is a kind of empty, "object-less" quality about the way the younger infant exercises his sensory-motor schemes. He seems to suck for the sake of sucking and grasp for the sake of grasping, evincing relatively little interest in the specific physical and functional properties of the objects sucked and grasped. From Stage 3 on, however, the baby shows an increasing interest in the effects of his actions on objects and events in the outside world, and in learning about the real properties of these objects and events by care-fully attending to those effects. The baby thus becomes more cognitively as well as more socially "extroverted" in the course of sensory-motor de-velopment. He gradually becomes an object explorer rather than a mere scheme exerciser, and the first small signs of this change are manifest in Stage 3.

The beginnings of genuine imitation are unmistakably present in Stage 3. However, the infant of this age is usually capable of imitating only: (1) those behaviors of the model (person imitated) that he himself already produces spontaneously (thus, he is unlikely to imitate novel responses); and (2) those behaviors of the model that he can see or hear himself produce (thus, he can imitate vocalizations and manual gestures but not, say, facial expressions). The distinction between serious and playful exercise of schemes likewise becomes a bit easier to make in this stage than in Stage 2, but clear and unequivocal instances of play are still hard to diagnose.

Stage 4 (Roughly 8–12 Months)

The major novelty of this stage is the appearance of unmistakably intentional, means-ends behavior. The child's actions are now unques-tionably purposeful and goal directed, and for this reason look more "intelligent," more "cognitive," than those of previous stages. As in Stage 2, individual sensory-motor schemes become coordinated and in-tegrated. However, the schemes in question are now primarily those outer-directed, environmental-effect-oriented, Stage 3 ones just mentioned, and their integration is more clearly an integration into a means-end action pattern. In Stage 4, the child intentionally exercises one scheme, as means, in order to make possible the exercise of another scheme, as end or goal. He may push your hand (means) in order to get you to continue to produce some interesting sensory effect (end) you had been producing for his benefit. Similarly, he may push aside (one motor scheme) an object in order to grasp (second motor scheme) another object; this particular means-end sequence plays a vital role in the evolution of the object concept, as we shall see.

There is also a parallel between Stage 2 and Stage 4 regarding the use of signs to anticipate events. It was said of the Stage 2 infant that he sometimes could respond anticipatively to a sign of an impending stimulus rather than having to wait until the stimulation actually occurred; he might occasionally commence sucking movements at the mere sight of the looming nipple, for instance. The Stage 4 infant also does the same thing, of course, and does it much better. In addition, however, the older child can read signs of impending events that are not directly connected, in stimulus-response fashion, with his own behavior. His mother starts to turn towards the door and the Stage 4 child may cry in anticipation of her departure. We might say that the younger infant anticipates the incipient exercise of one of his schemes whereas the older infant anticipates the occurrence of some event in the outside world. This change in how signs are read, in what they are taken to be signs *of*, is obviously in keeping with the aforementioned developmental trend towards cognitive extroversion, towards a heightened concern with the outside world in contrast to one's own purely egocentric, "objectless" actions.

The two limitations on imitative skill noted in connection with Stage 3 are now largely overcome. First, the infant now shows the ability to imitate behaviors which are in some degree different from those he customarily performs. This is an enormously significant developmental advance, because it means that he or she can henceforth *learn* by imitation, or more generally, through observation of the behavior of others. As Bandura and numerous other psychologists have stressed (Stevenson, 1972, Chap. 20), this sort of observational learning can be a very potent source of cognitive-developmental advance at all ages. Second, the infant can now imitate actions that he cannot actually see or hear himself perform, such as opening and closing his eyes after watching someone else do it. That is a remarkable cognitive feat, when you think about it, and how the infant does it is presently a total mystery. Sometimes his imitation of such actions is analogous rather than exact: he might, for instance, open and close his mouth instead of his eyes when the model does the latter. A recent report (Gardner and Gardner, 1970) suggests that this type of imitation may sometimes be observed considerably earlier than Stage 4.

Play becomes much more clearly playful at this age. For instance, after "seriously" practicing a new means-end integration for a while (an instance of adapted intelligence), he may ignore the end and pleasurefully exercise the means (play). As a case in point, one of Piaget's children began by practicing the feat of pushing an obstacle aside to obtain a toy and ended up by ignoring the toy in favor of pushing the obstacle aside again and again for fun. Play, like imitation, is beginning to become differentiated from adapted intelligence to become a distinctive instrument of cognitive growth. For whatever other functions play might serve in the child's life (and there are probably quite a few), no one has ever doubted that it is a major vehicle for learning and mental development.

Stage 5 (Roughly 12–18 Months)

Since symbolic-representational as distinguished from sensory-motor ways of knowing begin to manifest themselves during Stage 6, Stage 5 could be regarded as the last "pure" sensory-motor stage. Its essence is a very active, purposeful, trial and error exploration of the real properties and potentialities of objects, largely through the relentless search for new and different ways to act upon them. Infantile cognitive extroversion is now at its height; the child has a resolutely experimental, exploration-and-discovery oriented approach to the outside world. Present him with a novel object and he will actively try to lay bare its structural and functional properties by trying this, and that, and yet another action pattern on it, often making up new variations on old action patterns in the course of doing so. Similarly, while the Stage 4 infant would be apt to carry out a means-end behavior sequence in a more or less fixed, sterotyped way, the Stage 5 child would be likely to vary the means scheme in a deliberate, let's-see-what-would-happen-if sort of attitude; he might, to refer back to a Stage 4 example, remove the offending obstacle this way, then that way, then still another way.

With his strongly accommodative, exploratory bent, the Stage 5 child often discovers wholly new means to familiar ends. For instance, Piaget describes his discovering that an out-of-reach object can be secured by pulling a string attached to it, or a small rug on which it rests. These particular examples are intriguing because they might be early precursors of tool use, a type of intelligent behavior which is currently of great interest to primatologists and other students of hominid evolution as well as to developmental psychologists. Preliminary studies by Dr. William Charlesworth at the University of Minnesota suggest that the ability to use a variety of simple tools may undergo considerable development between 18 and 24 months of age, that is, just after the completion of Stage 5.

Given his active attempts at accommodation to the fine details of his environment, it is not surprising that the Stage 5 child proves to be a more painstaking and accurate imitator than his Stage 4 counterpart. His superiority is especially noticeable, predictably, when a successful imitation requires some trial and error experimentation on his part. The distinction between serious cognitive adaptation and lighthearted play becomes yet easier to see in Stage 5. For example, the child will sometimes elaborately complicate and ritualize some simple response, not because doing so teaches him anything useful or accomplishes any practical purpose, but for the sheer fun of it.

Stage 6 (Roughly 18–24 Months)

"Roughly 18 months on" would be just as accurate a dating for this stage, because its most important achievement remains an essential attribute of cognitive functioning for the rest of the individual's life. That achievement is the ability to represent the objects of one's cognition by means of symbols, and to act intelligently with respect to this inner, symbolized reality rather than simply, in sensory-motor fashion, with respect to the outer, unsymbolized reality. The Stage 6 child shows a beginning capacity to produce and comprehend one thing (e.g., a word) as standing for or symbolically representing some other thing (e.g., a class of objects). Moreover, the child becomes capable of mentally differentiating between the symbol and its referent, i.e., the thing the symbol stands for. As an example of this differentiation, the symbol could be physically quite different from its referent object and still be treated as a representation of that object. Similarly, the child might spontaneously produce the symbol and think about it even when the referent is not physically present. For the child to name a present object that he *sees* is quite possibly a symbolic act; for the child to name an absent object that he has just *thought of* is unquestionably a symbolic act. Responding to internal, self-generated objects of cognition is decidedly *not* a sensory-motor activity. Piaget refers to this newly developed, Stage 6 capacity for representation as the *semiotic* (or *symbolic*) function. The emergence of this supremely important function is worth a few pages of discussion. Let us begin with Piaget's account of adapted intelligence, imitation, and play à la Stage 6, in order to maintain continuity with our stage-by-stage narrative of the sensory-motor period, and then I shall make some additional comments about the semiotic function and related matters.

The Stage 5 child discovers new means to attain his behavioral objectives by overt, trial and error experimentation; he studiously varies his external behavior and, by doing so, may hit upon an effective procedure for achieving his goal. In contrast, the Stage 6, symbolic child may try out alternative means internally, by imagining them or representing them to himself instead of actualizing them in overt behavior. If an effective procedure is found in this fashion, by taking thought rather than by taking overt action, we might think of it more as invention or insight than as trial and error discovery. Accordingly, Piaget refers to this aspect of Stage 5 adapted intelligence as "the discovery of new means through active experimentation," whereas its Stage 6 counterpart is called "the invention of new means through mental combinations."

A celebrated example of the latter among Piaget readers was conveniently provided by his daughter Lucienne at the tender age of sixteen months. She wanted to extract a small chain from one of those old fashioned, sliding-drawer type matchboxes, but the drawer opening was too small for her to reach in and get it. After some unsuccessful, Stage 5 type fumblings she paused, studied the box, slowly opened and closed her mouth a few times, then quickly widened the drawer opening and triumphantly retrieved the chain. It seems reasonable to interpret her mouth movements as a primitive nonverbal, symbolic representation of a possible but as yet untried behavioral means to the desired end. To be sure, her representational response was very similar to its referent physically, and was also produced in the same immediate situation. Nonetheless, it would take unusually tough-minded and skeptical observers, I think, to find nothing of the genuinely symbolic in this behavior. We could at least assure them that they would never, never see anything remotely like it in the cognitive behavior of the six-month-old.

Stage 6 imitation and play also bear the clear imprint of a developing semiotic function. The child is now capable of *deferred imitation,* in which actions witnessed but not imitated on a given occasion are spontaneously reproduced in full detail at a later time. One of Piaget's children, for example, watched in mute fascination while another child threw a three-star temper tantrum. She then produced an excellent imitation of it the next day. As with Lucienne's mouth movements, the symbol (imitation of tantrum) physically resembled the referent (original tantrum). Unlike the mouth movements, however, the symbol was produced at considerable temporal remove from the referent, and therein lies the clearly symbolic character of deferred versus immediate imitation. The child presumably evoked or produced some sort of internal representation (possibly a visual image) of the tantrum as a guide or model for her imitative action; it was not a simple, more clearly sensory-motor case of precisely accommodating to an external, physically present, immediately perceptible model.

Pretense or *symbolic play* makes its first appearance in Stage 6 and continues to develop during the preschool years. At eighteen months, Piaget's daughter Jacqueline said "soap" while pretending to wash her hands by rubbing them together; at twenty months, she pretended to eat bits of paper and other inedibles, saying "Very nice." The representational, purely symbolic quality of this kind of play is obvious.

It may be wise to take stock of what has been said so far in this section before delving further into the nature and development of the semiotic or symbolic function. In my experience, Piaget's six stage account of general sensory-motor development tends to be difficult for most people to learn, and especially, to retain or remember. It tends to be hard for students, and it also tends to be hard for card-carrying developmental psychologists (myself included). There probably is no really good mnemonic for keeping it all straight, but Fig. 2-1 may be of some help. It is easier to remember any sequence of items if each item bears some logical or otherwise meaningful relationship to its predecessor and successor. Would that one's telephone number were 123-4567, for instance. Figure 2-1 tries to play up whatever relationships of that kind can be found in Piaget's sequence, in hopes that it will seem more rational, and thereby prove more memorable.

More on the Semiotic Function

It may be worthwhile to recommence by pointing up the momentous differences between symbolic-representational thought and sensory-motor intelligence. Sensory-motor actions must proceed slowly, step by step, one action at a time. Symbolic-representational thought can be much faster and more freely mobile in its operation; it can range over a whole series of past, present, and future events in one quick sweep of the mind. The former is by its very nature more oriented towards actions and concrete, practical results, whereas the latter can be more preoccupied with knowledge per se; the one focuses more on acts and outcomes, the other more on information and truth. The former is ineluctably concrete and earthbound. The latter is potentially abstract and free to soar, and, in fact, becomes increasingly so as the child matures. Indeed, it can eventually even take itself as its own cognitive object; that is, a relatively mature mind can think about its own thoughts. Finally, the former is necessarily private, idiosyncratic, and uncommunicable to

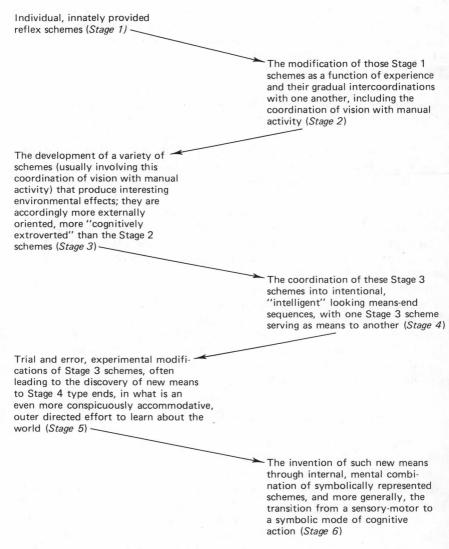

Individual, innately provided
reflex schemes (*Stage 1*)

The modification of those Stage 1
schemes as a function of experience
and their gradual intercoordinations
with one another, including the
coordination of vision with manual
activity (*Stage 2*)

The development of a variety of
schemes (usually involving this
coordination of vision with manual
activity) that produce interesting
environmental effects; they are
accordingly more externally
oriented, more "cognitively
extroverted" than the Stage 2
schemes (*Stage 3*)

The coordination of these Stage 3
schemes into intentional,
"intelligent" looking means-end
sequences, with one Stage 3 scheme
serving as means to another (*Stage 4*)

Trial and error, experimental modifications of Stage 3 schemes, often
leading to the discovery of new means
to Stage 4 type ends, in what is an
even more conspicuously accommodative,
outer directed effort to learn about the
world (*Stage 5*)

The invention of such new means
through internal, mental combination of symbolically represented
schemes, and more generally, the
transition from a sensory-motor to
a symbolic mode of cognitive
action (*Stage 6*)

Figure 2-1. A mnemonic for recalling the highlights of Piaget's sensory-motor stages regarding adapted intelligence (developmental changes in imitation and play are not included). Each earlier stage can be construed as a reasonable foundation or prerequisite for the one immediately following, and each later stage can be thought of as a plausible next developmental step, once its immediate predecessor is achieved.

others; each baby is imprisoned in his own separate cognitive world. The latter comes to make fluent use of a socially-shared symbolic system (natural language), and can thereby communicate with, and gradually become socialized by, other human beings.

We have already seen that the semiotic function can make use of a variety of symbolic media; it is not synonymous with the ability to speak and understand language, for instance. Piaget cites several expressions of the semiotic function that first appear in late infancy or early childhood: deferred imitation, symbolic play, drawing, mental images and, of course, language itself. The development of imitative ability is thought to play a very important role in the genesis of all of these processes. As indicated earlier, the infant gradually becomes quite good at imitating objects and actions that are immediately present. From this base, he develops the ability to generate symbolic surrogates, and overt and covert copies of absent, purely remembered objects and actions. Symbolic play uses both surrogates (e.g., bits of paper in place of food) and overt copies (pretending to eat the paper) of absent referents; deferred imitation obviously generates an overt copy of the original event; and a mental image of something can be regarded as a kind of covert, internal imitation or copy of that thing.

It is language, however, that eventually assumes preeminence among these various expressions of man's semiotic function. Piaget has long held some interesting ideas about the relation of language to thought, and these ideas currently appear to be gaining ground in the field (e.g., Furth, 1970; Macnamara, 1972; Nelson, 1973). Some scholars have viewed the language-thought relation as essentially one of "*LANGUAGE* (thought)": that is, thought is regarded as either virtually identical to language or else as utterly dependent on it for its functioning. Correlatively, the development of cognition is seen as either synonymous with the acquisition of language capability or else as completely parasitic on, and derivative of, that acquisition. In marked contrast, Piaget takes what might be depicted as a "*THOUGHT* (Language, mental image, drawing, etc.)" position. In the first place, he points out that thought, in the form of sensory-motor intelligence, begins its development well before language does. In addition, post-infancy thinking skills can mature to a surprising degree without benefit of language skills: deaf children who have not yet acquired much if any ordinary language or sign language skills can unquestionably think. Moreover, just as with normal children, their thinking skills also improve as they grow older (Furth, 1971). At the same time, Piaget willingly concedes that language does become by far the most important of man's symbolic vehicles. Furthermore, it does undoubtedly serve thinking and knowledge in varous direct and indirect ways from early childhood on, and it may even be indispensable for certain higher forms of cognitive endeavor. Unlike mental images and other symbolic media, therefore, it is depicted above as *"Language"* rather than "language."

According to this line of thinking, not only does intelligence begin its development before language does, but it also provides the cognitive wherewithal that makes the very development and use of language possible. It is the development of the semiotic function (i.e., of a general, cognitive capacity for symbol use) that makes it possible for the child to use words symbolically in the first place, just as it makes it possible for him to evoke covert mental images and overt deferred imitations as representations of nonpresent realities. Moreover, there is reason to think that linguistic development is, in good part, a matter of learning how *what you already know* is expressed in your native language (Macnamara, 1972). For example, 12–24 month olds can intelligently group (categorize) and order objects manually on the basis of various functional and physical relationships that hold among the objects, even though they may not yet be able to name most of these categories and relationships (Nelson, 1973; Ricciuti, 1965). The young child's months of sensory-motor activity have provided him with a great deal of this kind of uncoded knowledge about how objects can be related to one another, and it now remains to map all this knowledge into a linguistic system, so that he can tell himself and others what he knows implicitly. Piaget and a number of other psychologists take the position, then, that language development largely follows on the heels of general cognitive development, not the other way around. Macnamara puts it this way:

> I have continually insisted on the child's possessing nonlinguistic cognitive processes before he learns their linguistic signal. By this I do not intend to endow the infant at birth with a complete ready-made set of cognitive structures. I accept Piaget's thesis that children gradually develop many of the cognitive structures, which they employ in association with language. Neither do I suggest that the child has a complete set of cognitive structures at the moment when he begins to learn language. All that is needed for my position is that the development of those basic cognitive structures to which I referred should precede the development of the corresponding linguistic structures. Since the acquisition of linguistic structures is spread over a long period, there is no reason that the acquisition of the corresponding nonlinguistic ones should not also extend well into the period of language learning (Macnamara, 1972, p. 11).

Werner and Kaplan's account of early symbolic development. Even the briefest summary of the genesis of symbolic thinking would be remiss if it did not include something of Werner and Kaplan's (1963) penetrating analysis of the topic. As with Piagetian theory, it is unavoidable that I shall oversimplify Werner and Kaplan's ideas in the following synopsis.

In their analysis, the major entities in any symbolic act are the *symbol* itself, the *person* producing or comprehending it, and the symbol's *referent*. Initially, these three entities are largely fused together, or psychologically undifferentiated from one another, and a very important aspect of the development of symbolization is their mutual breaking apart, differentiation, or "distancing." The present summary deals only with the progressive distancing of first, person from referent, and second, symbol from referent.

Early in the sensory-motor period, the person's actions and the environmental objects these actions bear upon (the referents of his future symbols) are not clearly distinguished or dissociated from one another. As will be explained more fully in the next section on the object concept, objects are not yet seen as separate entities located "out there" in space, wholly distinct and independent of the self and the self's actions towards them. Therefore, a subsequent developmental process of differentiation or distancing of person from referent must exist. Werner and Kaplan aptly refer to this process as a movement from a psychological world populated only with "ego-bound things-of-action" to one containing "ego-distant objects-of-contemplation." Schaffer, Greenwood, and Parry (1972) have reported a developmental change that might reflect this movement towards a more objective, detached, and contemplative view of external objects. Infants of 6–8 months immediately grasp and manipulate both familiar and unfamiliar objects placed within their reach, whereas older infants are more apt to hesitate and visually inspect (ponder? "contemplate?") an unfamiliar object before touching it. Werner and Kaplan also cite a study that obtained rather similar results (1963, pp. 69–70). Until externals attain the conceptual status of independent entities "out there," to be pondered and contemplated rather than automatically assimilated to ("devoured by" one almost wants to say) some customary scheme of action, they cannot become true objects of symbolic reference.

Werner and Kaplan make some plausible suggestions about the early development of referential behavior. They suppose, for example, that the act of symbolic reference that we call manual *pointing* might have, as its sensory-motor precursors, actions such as turning to look at an object, reaching towards it, or touching it. The conscious and deliberate act of calling someone's attention to something by pointing at it is a symbolic act that, to the best of my knowledge, only human beings do. It is a fair guess that a being capable of this sort of behavior has acquired a reasonably clear self-object differentiation; that is, a clear idea that he is one object "over here" and that the thing he is pointing to is another, wholly separate and independent object "over there." Similarly, Werner and Kaplan argue, those strainful, "call sound" vocalizations that usually accompany the baby's motor strivings to see or touch an object may be the developmental forerunners of demonstrative *naming*. Thus, once the child has attained the necessary contemplative conception of objects and a basic capacity for symbolization, there are —lying around in his repertoire, so to speak—these various reaching and calling behaviors, all ready to be converted into symbolic acts of manual and verbal reference. In short, Werner and Kaplan have identified, within the sensory-motor period, some rather interesting analogues and potential ancestors of the symbolic-referential act of pointing with finger or voice.

There is a developing differentiation between symbol and referent as well as between person and referent. This particular differentiation is already somewhat familiar to us from Piaget's account of early symbolic development. Werner and Kaplan again distinguish between motor-gestural and vocal symbols while showing parallels in their developments. In both cases, the age trend toward symbol-referent differentiation or distancing takes two forms.

First, symbol and referent become more physically different from one another. In the motor-gestural case, the imitation (symbol) may become less literally and precisely a duplication of what is imitated (referent). Werner and Kaplan cite, for example, a three year old who represented the water stirred up by a passing boat by simply trembling her hands; the referent is not the action of another human being, and the imitation of it is suggestive rather than exact. In the same way, early vocal symbols sometimes resemble what they represent (e.g., a child imitating thunder by making a rumbling noise) but eventually become wholly unlike their referents (e.g., the spoken word "dog" bears no physical similarity to that "Faithful Friend to Man" it stands for).

Also, in both instances the child becomes increasingly capable of distancing symbol from referent in time and space—a point that Piaget also emphasized, you remember. In the case of motor-gestural symbolization, deferred imitation is a stellar example of how the model (referent) and the imitation of the model (symbol) can occur at different times and in different settings. In the same manner, vocal names first may be meaningful to the child only in the immediate presence of the objects they denote, and only subsequently be produced and comprehended in the absence of their referents.

THE OBJECT CONCEPT

Piaget's *object concept,* or *concept of object permanence,* refers to a set of implicit, common-sensical beliefs we all share about the basic nature and behavior of objects, including ourselves. We tacitly believe, first of all, that we and all other objects coexist as physically distinct and independent entities within a common, all-enveloping space. I am an object in that space, so are you, and so is this book; we are all more or less equal-status "co-objects" together, each of us with our own individual quantum of space-filling bulk and our own individual potential for movement or displacement within our common spatial habitat.

We also implicitly understand that the existence of our fellow objects, animate and inanimate alike, is fundamentally independent of our own interaction or noninteraction with these other objects. When an object disappears from our sight, for example, we do not assume that it has thereby gone out of existence. In other words, we do not confuse our own actions towards another object—our seeing it, hearing, touching it, etc.—with the physical existence of that object, and hence we do not think it automatically becomes annihilated once we lose behavioral contact with it. It *might* lose its integrity as an object (e.g., burn up) during its absence from us, of course, but it normally will not; above all, it will not become nonexistent merely *because* it is not currently being perceived or manipulated by us. "Out of sight" may mean "out of mind," but it certainly does not imply "out of existence" for someone who possesses the Piagetian object concept.

Finally, we believe that the object's behavior is also independent of our psychological contact with it, just as its existence is. We know that once gone from our sight, for instance, the object could perfectly well move or be moved from one location to another. It may or may not continue to await us at the place where we last saw it; we may or may not have to look elsewhere for it. In summary, we all possess an implicit, unarticulated conception of objects which asserts that other physical objects and ourselves are equally real and "objective," volume-occupying inhabitants of a common spatial world, and that the existence and behavior of other objects is fundamentally independent of our perceptual and motor contact with them.

Piaget made three rather startling claims about the object concept, again based upon observations of his own three infants' sensory-motor development. First, he claimed that this utterly basic, "obvious" conception of objects is not inborn but needs to be acquired through experience. Second, its acquisition is a surprisingly protracted one, spanning the entire sensory-motor period of infancy. Finally, this process consists of a universal, fixed sequence of developmental stages or subacquisitions, the infant picking up different aspects or components of the full concept at different stages. Thus, there is a sense in which it could be said that a one year old has "more of," or a "different level of" this concept than a six month old, for instance, although the one year old has not yet achieved the final, complete version of it.

It is almost inconceivable that anyone writing a textbook on cognitive development nowadays would fail to include something on the evolution of the Piagetian object concept. In the first place, the concept itself is so utterly basic and fundamental. If any concept could be regarded as indispensable to a coherent and rational mental life, this one certainly would be. Imagine what your life would be like if you did not believe that objects continued to exist when they left your field of vision. Worse yet, imagine how things would be if *nobody* believed it. It also happens that the developmental story here is just plain interesting to most people; it is simply one of the very best tales in the developmentalist's anthology. Moreover, a number of researchers are currently trying to clarify our understanding of just how this development proceeds, because there still remains a number of intriguing questions and puzzles concerning it (Bower, 1974; Bower and Paterson, 1972; Gratch, 1975). It is not merely an interesting story, therefore, but one that changes somewhat with each new telling.

Piaget assumes that the development of the object concept is intimately linked to sensory-motor development as a whole, and he therefore uses the same six-stage framework in describing it. It might be helpful to preface this stage-by-stage account of object concept development by recalling two earlier points having to do with objects. First, as he develops, the Piagetian infant becomes progressively more cognitively extroverted or external-world-oriented; that is, he becomes more concerned with exploring and discovering the real, objective properties of external things. Second, Werner and Kaplan (1963) postulated a progressive differentiation or distancing of person from referent, such that "ego-distant objects-of-contemplation" are eventually constructed by the developing mind as replacements for intial "ego-bound things-of-action." It is important to recognize that both of these developmental trends are essentially paraphrases of Piagetian object concept formation: namely, of the gradual mental differentiation of objects from ego's actions upon these objects, such that these objects, and also ego itself, eventually come to be conceived of as autonomous, independent, "objective" entities inhabiting a common space.

As with general sensory-motor development, most of what Piaget said about his children's object concept growth has been verified by subsequent investigators using much larger samples of subjects (e.g., Miller, Cohen, and Hill, 1970). There have been some interesting amendments and amplifications, however, and the more noteworthy of them will be mentioned below.

Stages 1 and 2 (Roughly 0–4 Months)

During this early period, the infant characteristically will try to follow a moving object with his or her eyes until it disappears from view, for instance, until it goes behind a screen of some kind. Whereupon, he will immediately lose interest and turn away or, at most, continue to stare for a short time at the place where it was last seen. There is as yet no behavior that could be interpreted as visual or manual search for the vanished object, and more generally, no positive evidence to suggest that the infant has any mental representation whatever of its continuing existence, once visual contact with it is lost.

Stage 3 (Roughly 4–8 Months)

The infant shows some progress during this stage in differentiating object-as-independent-entity from self's-action-toward-object, but it will become apparent that the differentiation process still has a long way to go. There are several positive accomplishments. By the end of Stage 2, the infant has become quite accomplished at tracking objects with his eyes, visually pursuing them when they move and visually fixating them when they stop moving (Bower and Paterson, 1972). During Stage 3, he begins to anticipate their future positions by extrapolating from their present direction of movement. If an object falls from his crib to the floor, for instance, he is now apt to lean over to look for it rather than simply staring motionlessly at the spot where it was before it disappeared from sight (he will, to be sure, lose interest and give up searching if he does not locate it right away). Similarly, after some experience in watching a toy train repeatedly enter and leave a tunnel on a circular track, babies in this age range begin to anticipate visually the train's reemergence from the tunnel rather than only looking toward the exit when the train actually appears (Nelson, 1971). The Stage 3 child may also recognize and reach toward a familiar object even if only a part of it is visible, something he could not do earlier. For instance, he might recognize and grasp at his bottle even when all but the nipple end of it is covered by a washcloth or some other opaque screen.

If this very same bottle should slowly and perceptibly disappear once again behind the opaque screen, however, it is an astonishing fact that he will *not* manually search for it (push the screen aside, etc.), even though he is physically competent to do so. The reaching hand can often be seen to drop in midflight once the desired object wholly disappears from view. Herein lies the essential limitation of Stage 3: the baby will exhibit brief and limited *visual* search for objects that have disappeared from sight, but he will show no *manual* search whatever. If the object is placed under a transparent cover, the Stage 3 child will try to retrieve it, but not if it is placed under an opaque cover (Bower, 1974, pp. 204–205; Cordes, 1970). Incredibly, he will not retrieve the object *even when he has already grasped it,* if you quickly cover both object and grasping hand with a washcloth (Gratch, 1972; Gratch and Landers, 1971). Instead, he is likely either to continue to hold onto the object and idly look around as if unaware that he has anything in his hand, or else to let go of it, remove his empty hand, and show no further search behavior. If a transparent cover rather than an opaque one is placed over hand and object under these conditions, he will, of course, continue to retrieve it in the normal way. Finally, the Stage 3 child is unlikely to look or act surprised if an experimenter covers an object placed on a high-chair tray, mischievously spirits the object away while under the cover (by means of a little trap door in the tray), and then removes the cover once again; needless to say, an older infant is apt to show considerable perplexity and searching behavior when the object inexplicably fails to reappear after the cover is removed (Charlesworth, 1966). These facts seem to suggest that in Stage 3 the object is not yet credited with an enduring life of its own, apart from and independent of the subject's perceptual contact with it.

Stage 4 (Roughly 8–12 Months)

The child will now manually search for and retrieve an object that he sees someone hide under a cloth or some other cover. The younger, debutant member of Stage 4 will do so only if the object is covered up while he is already engaged in the act of reaching for it, whereas the older, full-fledged Stage 4 child will retrieve it even if it is hidden before he can begin his reaching response (Gratch, 1972). Moreover, the child now will show surprise in the trick high-chair situation when the object is nowhere to be seen after the cover is removed (Charlesworth, 1966).

There is, however, a most peculiar limitation on this newly developed ability to find hidden objects. The child watches you hide object X under cover A and he gleefully pulls off the cover and grabs it. You repeat the hiding a few times; he repeats the finding each time. Then you very slowly and conspicuously hide X under cover B, located to one side of cover A, making sure that the child watches you do it. The Stage 4 child will immediately search under A once again, and then abandon the search when he fails to find anything there. Why on earth would he do such an odd thing? What level of object-concept development might this bizarre-looking behavior reflect?

We cannot say for sure from present evidence (Gratch, 1975), but there is reason to think that the Stage 4 child may not yet have a clear and conscious mental image of X quietly abiding beneath a cover. He may instead have evolved in this situation a little sensory-motor habit or behavioral "rule" that says, in effect, "Search over there, under that, and you'll have an interesting visual-tactile-manipulative experience." The object of the interesting sensory-motor experience (i.e., X) is psychologically embedded in the experience itself and remains secondary to it. According to this interpretation, the differentiation between self's action and object is not yet complete; X is not yet the genuinely action-independent "object-of-contemplation" it will eventually become.

The findings of several recent studies seem consistent with this interpretation. Infants of this age who are given initially a lot of experience reaching and finding object X in a specific location (under cover A) develop a stronger tendency to make the characteristic Stage 4 error of searching only at A when X is subsequently hidden elsewhere (under cover B) than do infants who are only given a little searching experience in the initial location. Moreover, the first-mentioned infants also develop a stronger tendency to make the Stage 4 error than do infants who have been given just as much experience in *watching* X get hidden there, but no experience in actually *searching* there (Landers, 1971). As suggested earlier, it may be a motor habit of mindlessly searching-in-a-particular-place that develops in Stage 4 infants, and the perceptual evidence as to where the object is located appears to get overridden or swamped by this motor habit. In fact, babies of this age sometimes appear to attend only briefly to B after seeing X hidden there (Gratch and Landers, 1971). They may even show the characteristic Stage 4 error (searching only at A) when some *new* object Y, rather than X, subsequently gets hidden at B (Evans and Gratch, 1972). Even though object Y has never been associated with location A, the child continues in robot fashion to search at A. What is he searching *for* in this case? My guess is that he is not searching specifically for either X or Y, as object-out-there, but is rather trying to reinstate a pleasureful sensory-motor action pattern.

Another finding indicates the degree to which the motor habit of finding-and-grasping could be overshadowing any budding mental image of X-out-there that an infant this young might conceivably possess. If X is hidden under A and then surreptitiously replaced by a different object Y, the Stage 4 baby looks a bit puzzled or confused, but then usually proceeds to examine or play with Y; in contrast, older infants tend to look even more puzzled, and also tend to search for X and the cause of its disappearance, even as you or I might (LeCompte and Gratch, 1972). The first behavior pattern is suggestive of a violation of a sensory-motor anticipation or expectancy, although some rudimentary mental representation might also be involved. The second strongly indicates the presence of an enduring, bona fide mental representation of an absent object—and a representation of it *as* a true object, in the object-concept, object-of-contemplation sense.

Stage 5 (Roughly 12–18 Months)

As Stage 4 draws to a close, the balance begins to shift from previous motoric success to present perceptual evidence, and the Stage 5 child gradually learns to search at whatever place the object was most recently seen to disappear. In the *AB* setup described previously, this, of course, means going directly to *B* when *X* is hidden at *B*, even though *X* had previously been hidden and found at *A*. Transitional responses between Stages 4 and 5 may include paying more visual attention to *B* than formerly, being in conflict as to which of the two places to search, and searching at *B* only after initially failing to find *X* at *A* (Gratch and Landers, 1971; Webb, Massar, and Nadolny, 1972).

The Stage 5 child seems to have progressed further than the Stage 4 child in the crucial matter of differentiating the object per se from his actions towards it. The older infant can read the visual evidence of *X*'s present location more or less objectively (no pun intended); he is no longer locked into a rigid dependence on previous patterns of successful action-toward-object. There is, however, one final limitation to be overcome: the Stage 5 infant cannot imagine or represent any further changes of location the object might have undergone after it disappeared from his view. Let's suppose you put a small object in a felt-lined cup, turn the cup upside down, slide it under a large cloth, silently deposit the object underneath the cloth, and withdraw the empty cup (Miller, Cohen, and Hill, 1970). The prototypical Stage 5 child is incapable of searching for the object anywhere but in the cup, because the cup rather than the cloth was the place where he saw it disappear. As yet, he cannot represent any unseen but readily (to us) inferable movement of the object when inside the cup. In Piaget's words, the child can cope with *visible displacements* but not yet with *invisible displacements*. More precisely, he can infer *X*'s present location from its most recent visible displacement (as the Stage 4 child could not do, you recall, when under the baleful influence of previous visible displacements), but cannot infer *X*'s invisible displacement on the basis of the visible displacements of its container. It is possible to construct very complex and difficult visible displacement problems, some of them even harder than the simpler forms of the invisible displacement task (Miller, Cohen, and Hill, 1970). A rather odd example of a difference in task difficulty level is the following: an infant who is in Stage 5 when only manual search is involved may still be in Stage 4 if he has to *crawl* to the hidden object (Heinowski, in Bower and Paterson, 1972). I mention this latter finding only as a bit of curiosa; all noncompulsive readers should promptly forget it.

Stage 6 (Roughly 18–24 Months)

The above-mentioned limitation is gradually overcome in this stage, with the child gradually acquiring the knack of using the visual evidence as a basis for imagining or representing X's unseen itineraries and hiding places. The really accomplished Stage 6-er can be very, very good at it. You put X inside your closed fist and move your fist first under cloth A, then under B, then under C, and then open it up, *sans* object (you have actually left it under cloth A). Many a two year old will grin with anticipation, and then systematically search each possible hiding place, sometimes in the reverse order from your hiding, i.e., first under C, then under B, and finally under A. He may also spontaneously try the same game on you, with him doing the hiding and you doing the finding (and it would be a cold-hearted experimenter indeed who wouldn't let him do it). The full-fledged object concept is so clearly "there" in such a child that you feel you can virtually mind-read it. You are *sure* that he is somehow mentally representing that object during its invisible perambulations, and *sure* that he implicitly regards it as an external entity that exists and may move about in complete independence of his own perceptual or motor contact with it. But, of course, he is now in sensory-motor Stage 6, and the essential accomplishment of that stage is precisely that of being able to evoke internal symbolic representations of absent objects and events (recall deferred imitation and symbolic play).

Is man the only animal that develops any semblance of a Piagetian object concept? Definitely not, according to recent research. Cats clearly show a rather humanlike, step-by-step development up through Stage 4, but do not seem to progress further (Gruber, Girgus, and Banuazizi, 1971). Rhesus monkeys pass through the same sequence, but they also go on to develop what looks like genuine Stage 6 competence (Wise, Wise, and Zimmerman, 1974); the same has been claimed for squirrel monkeys (Vaughter, Smotherman, and Ordy, 1972).

The Object Concept as an Example of Invariant Formation

The acquisition of the object concept fits into a larger developmental context that merits brief mention. The growth of the human mind partly consists of the successive attainment or formation of cognitive *invariants*. As its name suggests, an invariant is something that remains the same while other things in the situation change or undergo various transformations. The identification of constant features or invariants in the midst of flux and change is an absolutely indispensable cognitive activity for an adaptive organism, and it is particularly characteristic of human rationality.

First of all, there are some early-appearing perceptual invariants that undoubtedly have a strong innate component. For example, young babies seem to have at least fairly good *size constancy*. As you probably know, a smaller object situated closer to you can actually produce a visual image on your retina equal in size to a larger object presented farther away, and yet you effortlessly and correctly perceive the one object as smaller and closer and the other as larger and farther away. Therefore, the perceived size of an object remains roughly invariant or constant (hence, "size constancy") despite continual changes or transformations in the size of its retinal image as you or it move in relation to one another. Additionally, the shape of the retinal image of the object constantly alters with changes in the object's spatial orientation with respect to you, and yet you ordinarily have little trouble in perceiving the object's true shape. Young babies also appear to have some measure of *shape constancy,* as this ability to perceive the real versus apparent (retinal) shape of objects is called.

Such perceptual constancies are themselves early invariants, and together they help the infant achieve another invariant that might be termed *object constancy.* This refers to the ability to recognize an object as being the same one seen a moment ago, despite intervening changes in its orientation and distance with respect to the observer and all the modifications in retinal size and shape produced by these changes. The motto of this invariant would be something like, "Despite substantial changes in retinal impression, I know this is the same thing (or the same perceptual experience) as before." The Piagetian *object concept* is a later-developing invariant, and its verbal expression would be something like, "Despite a change from retinal image to no perceptual image at all (or more generally, from sensory-motor contact to no contact), the entity that produced that retinal image probably still exists out there in space, in the same or in a different place than where last seen." As we shall see, additional invariants-amid-transformations are identified or constituted during the postinfancy years. The child comes to see himself and significant others as retaining their identity as specific individuals, despite momentary or enduring changes in mood, behavior, physical appearance (e.g., aging, sickness). He also discovers certain quantitative invariants-amid-transformations that Piaget has made famous (the so-called "*conservations*"), for instance, that the amount of clay I have in my hand remains exactly the same when I mold the clay into different shapes, providing only that none gets lost in the process. As you can see, getting straight just what does and what does not stay the same under this versus that salient change is a ubiquitous and extremely important task for a developing mind.

SOCIAL COGNITION

Social cognition means cognition of human objects and their doings. It includes perception, thinking, and knowledge regarding the self, other people, social relations, social organizations and institutions—in general, our human, social world. It hardly needs to be said that social cognition represents an extremely important psychological process in the daily lives of most people, and its development in children is correspondingly interesting to study.

There is surprisingly little solid research evidence on infant social cognition, and a really detailed understanding of its step-by-step development is not yet available. As to general trends, the very plausible suggestion has often been made that much of infant social development entails the now-familiar process of psychological differentiation—in this case of self from nonself, of human objects from nonhuman objects, etc. As Loevinger (1966) succinctly put it:

> In the first stage of the ego [i.e., during infancy] the problem is to distinguish self from nonself. This stage can be divided into the presocial and the symbiotic stages. In the presocial or autistic stage animate and inanimate parts of the environment are not distinguished. In the symbiotic stage the child has a strong relation to his mother (or surrogate) and is able to distinguish mother from environment, but self is not clearly distinguished from mother. The ego can hardly be said to exist prior to the end of this stage (p. 198).

Thus, the child has as one of his major developmental tasks in this area the gradual evolution of a sense of himself as a distinct and separate entity, clearly differentiated from all the other entities, human and nonhuman, that populate his everyday world. He must acquire some conception of himself both as a physical object and as a psychological subject, that is, both as a thing among things and as a person among persons. This process of articulation and definition of self, and especially of self as person or psychological subject, has not progressed terribly far by the end of infancy. A definite beginning has been made, however.

The infant also makes a start at acquiring knowledge about other people. As Loevinger indicated, human objects gradually become distinguished from nonhuman ones. The suggestion has recently been made that the presence versus absence of affective arousal may help the infant make this differentiation, in that whereas "things are primarily interesting, people are both interesting and emotionally arousing" (Wenar, 1972, p. 259). People are perhaps also more likely than things are to provide a variety of stimulation and to be responsive to the infant's needs and behaviors (Yarrow and Pederson, 1972). There is, furthermore, reason to believe that children of two years of age or even younger have acquired some understanding of the fact that other people can perceive objects and experience certain emotions (Flavell, 1974). Young children may also credit some inanimate objects with such exclusively psychological capacities, however, a tendency Piaget long ago described as *animistic thinking*. Some grasp of the person-nonperson distinction is achieved by the end of infancy, therefore, but the distinction is still a somewhat blurred one. Needless to say, a more detailed and penetrating knowledge of the psychological characteristics of personhood (e.g., that people act out of inner motives, that they may not mean what they say, etc.) is still a thing of the distant future for a child of this age.

In addition to distinguishing persons from nonpersons, the infant comes to distinguish one person from another. Certain people, such as his mother, become familiar, easily recognizable, and above all, highly significant emotionally. He gradually becomes emotionally *attached* to such people, and they to him. The development of the capacity and disposition to form such affect-laden bonds to selected others is commonly referred to nowadays as the development of social *attachment*. There is more research evidence available on the developmnt of attachment during infancy than on the parallel and intimately related developments of the concept of self and of others as persons (Bowlby, 1969; Maccoby and Masters, 1970; Yarrow and Pederson, 1972.) Moreover, explicit attempts have been made to tie the growth of social attachment to the growth of cognitive skills, especially to the development of the Piagetian object concept. Let us look first at the developmental highlights of social attachment formation, and then examine its possible links to infant cognitive growth.

Development of Social Attachment

Social attachment is always a reciprocal process of social interaction, necessarily involving the feelings and behaviors of both parties in the interaction. I shall concentrate mainly on the infant's half of the interaction, however, intentionally slighting the mother's own obviously very important attachment feelings and behaviors toward him. Infant social attachment is here taken to refer both to an underlying disposition and to various overt behaviors that implement or express that disposition. The underlying disposition is a strong affection and yearning for one or more specific people, especially the mother or mother substitute. Many of the overt behaviors which reflect this emotional bond have to do with the maintenance of a suitable (from the child's point of view) degree of proximity or physical nearness to the attachment figure. Depending on his age, the infant does some things which bring or keep him satisfactorily close to her (clinging, sucking, crawling after), and other things which tend to bring or keep her near to him (smiling, crying, calling). Again depending on his age, the infant may show signs of acute fear or unhappiness if this desired level of proximity is not achieved or maintained, for instance, if the mother puts him down or leaves him alone in his room. Other indices of attachment may include lack of positive social response or outright fear in the presence of people other than the current object or objects of his attachment (e.g., a strange person), and the use of the attachment object as a source of comfort and security (e.g., retreating to her when frightened or ill, being more venturesome with strange people or objects when she is nearby).

Now to the actual development of social attachment. It should be borne in mind that there is substantial variation from infant to infant, throughout the course of this development, as to what behaviors are exhibited and when. It is *not* a really neat and tidy developmental progression, although general trends can be indicated.

During the first few weeks of life at least, the infant appears to show a complete lack of differentiation between human and nonhuman stimulus inputs. For instance, he or she seems to have no inborn preference for looking at people's faces as contrasted with nonsocial stimuli which possess comparable visual properties (similar amounts of contour, contrast, movement, etc.).

People as a class do appear to become especially interesting objects of perception during the next several months, but there is little or no apparent differentiation within this class. A two month old, for instance, may be capable of a genuinely social smile, but he is likely to be disconcertingly promiscuous in his use of it: he will smile just as winningly at a total stranger as at his mother, although perhaps more broadly at both than at most inaminate objects. Such a child is no longer quite presocial, but his lack of ability or disposition to discriminate one person from another still makes him "preattached."

During or around the age period 3–6 months, the baby may begin to smile a bit more brightly and gurgle a bit more happily at one or more familiar people than at the rest of mankind. However, he may still exhibit no fear or poker-faced "sobering" in the presence of strangers, and may show no more tendency to protest when mother leaves him than when anyone else does. Genuine social attachment to specific, individualized persons seems imminent, but perhaps not quite there yet.

Most babies show unmistakable signs of having begun to form specific social attachments sometimes during the third quarter of their first year. For example, they may show pronounced negative reactions to the approach of a stranger, especially if in an unfamiliar setting or if mother is not close by. Stranger anxiety is sufficiently regular in its occurrence to have won the label of "eight months anxiety," but, in fact, not all babies exhibit it, and among those who do, it does not necessarily first occur or reach its peak at that age. They are also likely to show decidedly negative reactions to separation from one or more specific individuals, rather than either showing no such reaction at all or showing it to almost anybody's departure. Moreover, the child's functional definition of "proximity" versus "separation" changes with age from this period onward. Younger children may require actual physical contact to feel content (negative reaction to being put down), older ones only perceptual contact (negative reaction to seeing mother leave the room), and still older ones only potential or symbolic contact (negative reaction only if mother is known not to be somewhere in the house, or known not to return soon, etc.—otherwise, the child acts as though no *psychological* separation has occurred). "Social attachment" in the somewhat negative, emotionally-dependent sense of the term gradually wanes in most children during the preschool and school years; in the more positive sense of love and affection felt for significant others, however, it may of course endure for the rest of one's life.

Attachment Development as Social-Cognitive Development

There is undoubtedly some sort of mutually-facilitative, reciprocally-mediative developmental relationship between cognitive processes and social behavior. This is true during infancy, and it is also true at later periods of development. On the one hand, the infant's social interactions and emotional relations with his caretakers must constitute a nearly indispensable crucible for the formation and development of cognitive processes. It is difficult to conceive how there could be any significant cognitive development at all if the amount and quality of the infant's social relations with other human beings fell below some unknown minimum. Human beings are intrinsically social beings, and human cognitive development requires human social relations.

A little thought will indicate that something like the reverse also has to be true. Social behavior is always partly managed and mediated by cognitive processes, and the developmental level or quality of social behavior that an individual is capable of showing must be at least partly dependent on the developmental level or quality of his mental abilities. The latter is conceived as a necessary but definitely not sufficient condition for the former. That is, having achieved a certain general level of cognitive development does not *ensure* the occurrence of a particular kind of social behavior, or a particular kind of social cognition either, for that matter; it only makes it *possible*. For example, I cannot cooperate with another person in some common endeavor (social behavior) unless I have the wherewithal upstairs (cognitive processes) to integrate and coordinate my responses with his in such a way as to merit the term "cooperative behavior." At the same time, the mere possession of the necessary penthouse equipment obviously does not *oblige* me to be cooperative. For want of sufficient cognitive skill, babies *cannot* cooperate; for want of sufficient motivation rather than sufficient cognitive skill, misanthropes *can* cooperate but *will not*.

How might the course of infant attachment development reflect or be partly mediated by the course of infant cognitive development, in the necessary-but-not-sufficient-condition sense just described? One very plausible cognitive prerequisite for the formation of specific and focused social attachment is the developing infant's increasing ability to make fine visual discriminations (Yarrow and Pederson, 1972). Until he is perceptually capable of discriminating one looming face from another (no mean achievement, when you think about it), he obviously cannot recognize or identify particular faces as special, recurrent, and familiar ones; and until he can do the latter, he can hardly form social-emotional bonds to particular individuals.

The same argument can, of course, be made with regard to the development of auditory (Horowitz, 1975) and probably other sensory discriminations. The mother constitutes a complex bundle of sights, sounds, feelings, and smells, and this bundle has to become quickly and easily distinguishable from other, quite similar bundles before the infant can become differentially attached to it.

The following statements reiterate the general point about the dependence of the social on the cognitive and also suggest some additional cognitive-developmental prerequisites for various levels of social attachment:

> The nature of cognitive structure, in the sense of the total system of an individual's information processing strategies, differs with age and thus sets limits on the kinds of social behavior that one can expect at various stages of development: the extent of memory span, for instance, will have implications for the infant's ability to differentiate one person from another, and in the absence of object conservation [he means the Piagetian object concept] infants can hardly be expected to show any orientation towards the mother in her absence (Schaffer, 1971, p. 247).

The basic tenet is that any behavior of a child is a function of the level of cognitive development he has achieved. An illustrative derivation of this principal applied to attachment is that: a child cannot develop a specific attachment until he can both discriminate and recognize an individual person. Even after an infant can do these things, however, he still may not know that the person continues to exist when out of sight. The development of object constancy [again, the Piagetian object concept is meant] should introduce a new phase of attachment behavior, for example, signaling [e.g., crying for, calling] when the attachment figure is not in view. When time concepts begin to be mastered, this should mean both that the child will begin to respond to signs of the mother's impending departure (showing anticipatory protest), and that he will be able to anticipate her return during an absence and derive some comfort thereby. Reactions to death of an attachment figure should vary greatly with the age of the child, depending on the level of understanding of the permanence of death (Maccoby and Masters, 1970, p. 91).

It is worth noticing that both of these excerpts cite the object concept as a candidate prerequisite. As a matter of fact, it is probably the most frequently proposed candidate to be found in the literature, and a few researchers have even tried to check the merits of its candidacy empirically (see Bell, 1970; Cook, 1972). The logic seems straightforward enough. If an infant were too cognitively immature to differentiate external objects from his own actions and to conceive of them as independent entities that continue to exist when perceptually absent, he could scarcely either yearn for or search for an absent mother, since she is, of course, also an external object. So long as "out of sight, out of mind" applies to his mother as well as other objects, one could hardly say that a baby's "social attachment" to her had progressed very far. Conversely, once the object concept is established, he can bridge her physical absences by symbolic-representational means and thereby sustain an enduring affective link to her that we can comfortably refer to as genuine social attachment. Moreover, Piaget and others have suggested that the mothering figure might well become the very *first* of the infant's permanent objects, a most plausible idea in view of her general emotional and attentional salience for him, and in view of the frequency with which he must see her disappear and reappear every day. Constituting the mother as a permanent Piagetian object could be regarded as one of the most important accomplishments of infant social-cognitive development.

However, you just do not know the field of psychology unless you know how often perfectly reasonable ideas prove to be either wrong or inordinately hard to demonstrate experimentally. The latter currently seems to be the fate of the hypothesized dependence of attachment development on object-concept development. In two very careful studies, Cook (1972) was unable to find any meaningful pattern of correlations among measures of these two developments. Moreover, she argues persuasively that previous research by other investigators has also not provided convincing evidence for this hypothesized dependence. It seems appropriate to end the chapter on this rather dissonant note, because it shows how the area of cognitive development actually appears to those who study it full time: that is, as a morass of difficult problems rather than as a tidy collection of established facts.

The problem may be partly methodological and partly conceptual. First, it is very difficult to define precisely and measure adequately different "degrees" or "developmental levels" of social attachment. The same is also true of the object concept, but perhaps to a lesser extent. Second, as Cook (1972) points out, it remains unclear exactly which newly attained levels or stages of object-concept development should logically constitute the cognitive supports or underpinnings for exactly which new steps in attachment development, even assuming one could adequately identify and measure these steps. For example, should Stage 4 of object-concept development be regarded as a crucial, "breakthrough" type cognitive support for the formation of genuine specific attachments? The first manual search for an absent object does, after all, occur during this stage. While this idea seems reasonable enough, Cook (1972) was unable to obtain any positive research evidence to support it. Perhaps, instead, genuine attachment presupposes a Stage-6 ability to generate, spontaneously and without external supports, a mental representation of an absent object. This seems even more reasonable until one realizes that unambiguous specific-attachment behavior occurs well in advance of Stage 6. But maybe this only means that "mother permanence" is indeed acquired earlier—perhaps even a good deal earlier—than ordinary, inanimate-object permanence. We simply cannot decide among these alternatives on present evidence, however.

It may be, as Cook (1972) suggests, that the simple ability to *recognize* mother (during Stage 3 or thereabouts) when she is *present,* rather than the ability to actively *recall* her when she is *absent* (spontaneously produce a Stage-6 type representation of her), suffices for at least the beginning period of genuine specific attachment. This sequence seems about right chronologically but not quite so right logically, since it would seem that even early specific attachment ought to require some persisting cognitive orientation towards the currently absent attachment figure. It might be, however, that the capacity for such continuing orientation develops somewhat earlier than we have been led to think, again perhaps because object permanence for attached-to human objects may develop precociously. Schaffer (1971) reports an amusing observation that is at least consistent with this idea. It also illustrates the basic plausibility of some sort of connection between object permanence and early social relations, the sort of plausibility that makes us all so loath to give up on this connection merely because of a lack of substantiating research evidence. His six- and twelve-month-old subjects seemed a bit uneasy when serving in a visual perception experiment, so he requested their mothers to sit behind them during the testing. After watching what happened, he quickly found himself recording the number of times the infant turned away from the visual stimulus set before him in favor of looking at the mother:

> The results are clear-cut. The younger infants hardly ever turned—they tended to behave in a "stimulus-bound" fashion and acted towards the mother in an "out of sight out of mind" manner. The older infants, on the other hand, frequently turned in the course of the experimental session from one stimulus to the other, apparently well able to keep in mind the perceptually absent object, integrating it with other activities, and so showing a much more flexible type of behaviour (pp. 257–258).

SUMMARY

The human cognitive system undergoes truly momentous changes during the period from birth to the end of infancy. The cognition of the infant is *sensory-motor* rather than *symbolic-representational* in nature. His is an entirely unreflective, practical, perceiving-and-doing sort of intelligence. It is not the conceptual, self-aware, symbol-using kind that words like "cognition," "thought," and "intelligence" usually connote.

According to Piaget's theory, much of infant cognitive development consists of the elaboration and intercoordination of cognitive units or structures called *schemes*. Schemes refer to classes or categories of organized, repeatedly exercised action patterns. Examples include sucking, listening, looking, striking, grasping, dropping, and pushing aside. External data (objects and events) are *assimilated* to sensory-motor schemes, and schemes simultaneously *accommodate* to these data. If assimilation and accommodation are roughly in balance and of roughly equal importance in a given scheme-data encounter, the child's cognitive act is said to be one of *adapted intelligence*. In contrast, the act is referred to as *play* if assimilation outweighs or dominates accommodation, and as *imitation* if the reverse happens.

A kind of mnemonic device or memory aid was proposed to help you remember essential points concerning *cognitive motivation:* ask yourself what propensities or dispositions a human cognitive system ought to have built into it if it is to have a reasonable chance at learning the enormous number of things human beings do typically learn. First and foremost, the system should be disposed from the outset to do a lot of spontaneous information processing, even when there is no tangible objective to be gained by it (e.g., securing food). There is so very, very much to learn that the system cannot be allowed to remain unplugged except in moments of urgent organismic need. It should therefore be outfitted with its own, built in, *intrinsic* motivation to function repeatedly and frequently, and thereby to learn and develop with reasonable speed. It should also be disposed to focus its attention on those external data that are likely to be most informative to it, given what it already knows. Accordingly, we shall preset it to notice and further investigate movement and contour, and especially inputs that are novel, surprising, puzzling, curious, or otherwise discrepant from and not immediately assimilable to existing cognitive structures (during infancy, this means to existing sensory-motor schemes). Finally, we cleverly endow the system with a pleasureful sense of personal competence in achieving and repeatedly reasserting its mastery over the previously unassimilated situation, thus giving the resulting cognitive progress a chance to solidify.

Piaget's six stages of general sensory-motor development provide a good, overall picture of how the human mind changes from birth to age two or so. Most of what was said about this sequence of stages is summarized in Fig. 2-1 and need not be repeated here. However, two facts should be borne in mind. Figure 2-1 deals only with the development of adapted intelligence, omitting that of imitation and play, and it seriously underrepresents the text on the Stage 6 development of symbolic representation (Piaget's *semiotic function*).

The two most important generalizations about the evolution of imitation and play during infancy are probably these: (1) each becomes more and more clearly differentiated and easily distinguishable from adapted intelligence as the infant progresses from stage to stage; (2) the development of the capacity for symbolic representation in Stage 6 makes possible interesting new forms of each, namely, deferred imitation and symbolic play.

Symbolic-representational thought is vastly more rapid, mobile and far-ranging, abstract, truth- and knowledge-oriented, self-reflective, and communicable than sensory-motor intelligence. The semiotic function makes use of a variety of symbolic media, of which natural language ultimately becomes the most important. General intelligence begins its development well before language does, however, and many now believe that it also remains the more fundamental process of the two, with language development and language use being more derivative or dependent on it than the other way around. Werner and Kaplan describe the development of symbolic ability as a gradual differentiation or "distancing" of person from referent, and of symbol from referent. In the former case, there is a progression during infancy from a reality consisting of "ego-bound things-of-action" to one populated by "ego-distant objects-of-contemplation"; this progression is virtually synonymous with the development of the Piagetian object concept. In the latter case the developmental trend is for symbol and referent to become more physically dissimilar (e.g., the printed symbol "dog" versus the animal it refers to) and more spatially and temporally separated (e.g., imitating something that is no longer physically present).

The Piagetian object concept is the implicit, common-sensical belief everyone has that we are all physical objects in a common space, and that our fellow objects continue to exist and may move about in this space even when we have lost perceptual contact with them, for instance, after an object has disappeared from sight behind a screen. Surprisingly, so fundamental and "obvious" a conception of objects seems to require the whole first two years of a person's life to become fully established.

The highlights of its gradual establishment are described below using Piaget's sensory-motor stages as framework. As in all developmental chronologies, the ages given are *very* rough estimates, subject to considerable variation from child to child and also heavily dependent on the particulars of the testing situation. Whenever you cannot remember both, be sure always to concentrate on the sequence of any set of developmental events rather than the rough age norms associated with that sequence.

Stages 1 and 2 (roughly 0–4 months). The baby tracks a moving object until it disappears, then immediately loses interest or stares briefly at the point of disappearance.

Stage 3 (roughly 4–8 months). He can now extrapolate from the moving object's itinerary and extend his visual tracking beyond the point of its disappearance (e.g., leaning over to look for a fallen object). He can also recognize an object on the basis of seeing only a part of it sticking out from behind a screen or cover. If he sees it completely disappear behind the screen, however, he does not retrieve it with his hands even though physically capable of doing so.

Stage 4 (roughly 8–12 months). He now manually retrieves a covered-up object. After a few trials at finding it under a given cover, however, he will continue to search under that same cover even though he has just watched you place it under a different one.

Stage 5 (roughly 12–18 months). He searches for the object only in the place where it was most recently *seen* to disappear, e.g., under the second cover in the above example. Thus, if the object is first inserted into a small container, then conveyed to the cover inside the container, and finally released from the container underneath the cover so that the container comes out empty, the child will look inside the container for the object but not under the cover, since it was last *seen* disappearing inside the container.

Stage 6 (roughly 18–24 months). The child can now use his newly developed symbolic skills to represent to himself possible *invisible displacements* of the hidden object instead of only being able (as in Stage 5) to operate in terms of its seen or *visible displacements.* He can eventually solve a wide variety of container-inside-cover problems.

Of course, this is only a summary *description* of what new behavior patterns emerge at each stage. The *interpretation* of each new pattern as reflecting progress in the establishment of the Piagetian object concept is given in the text. The text also suggests that the object concept is but one of a number of cognitive *invariants* that get formed in the course of human development. Perceptual *object constancy* is an earlier invariant; the various *conservations* (of mass, length, weight, etc.) are later-developing examples.

Despite its obvious importance, relatively little is known about infant *social-cognitive* development, that is, the development of cognitions concerning the human, social world. In very general terms, this development may be described as a gradual process of differentiating self from nonself (the latter including both other objects and other people), persons from nonpersons, and one person from another; in the course of this process of differentiation, tacit conceptions of self and others are slowly developed and elaborated. The best-researched aspect of infant social development at present is the growth of social *attachment,* which involves this differentiation of person from nonpersons, and especially, of one person from another.

On the infant's side of the social interaction, attachment refers to the formation of a strong emotional bond to one or more specific people, and to the constellation of behaviors and feelings that testify to the existence of that bond. For instance, the baby engages in certain behaviors (crying, crawling, etc.) which tend to maintain a desired level of physical proximity to the object of his attachment—his mother, say— and exhibits certain feelings (pleasure, fear, etc.) when that level of proximity is achieved or lost. The development of social attachment during infancy normally proceeds something like this: at first, no differentiation between human and nonhuman stimuli; then, particular attention and interest given to people as a class but no significant discrimination among people; next, the recognition of certain people as familiar and especially pleasureful objects; finally, unmistakable and intense emotional attachment to one or a select few clearly differentiated and identified people, complete with strong protest when separated from such people and, frequently, when other people approach too closely ("stranger anxiety").

Social behavior mediates cognitive growth and vice-versa. The "vice-versa" is of much current interest in the particular case of infant social attachment: what aspects of infant cognitive growth might provide necessary (but not sufficient) preconditions for the genesis of social attachment? Several possibilities were mentioned, most prominent among them was object-concept development. It is virtually impossible on logical grounds to imagine how these two developments, object concept and social attachment, could proceed in mutual isolation, neither having any effect on the other. At the same time, it has so far been surprisingly difficult to demonstrate empirically any object-concept basis for the formation of social attachments; in fact, we are not even quite sure precisely what sort of link between the two developments we ought to expect on theoretical grounds. The issue rests where most issues in cognitive development tend to rest—stubbornly encamped in midair.

3

early and
middle childhood

The first two-thirds of this chapter contains an overview of cognitive development during early childhood and middle childhood (2–11 years, approximately). An effort is made to describe the most general and most significant intellectual achievements of each of these broad periods, and also to highlight the most noteworthy differences between an early-childhood and a middle-childhood mind. The narrative becomes more concrete and specific in the remaining third of the chapter, which offers a close-up of developmental change in one particular cognitive area (number skills and concepts). Some important aspects of the intellectual growth of children from 2–11 years of age are deferred for space and expositional reasons to Chap. 4, notably social-cognitive development.

COGNITIVE DEVELOPMENT DURING
EARLY AND MIDDLE CHILDHOOD: AN OVERVIEW

Early Childhood (Roughly 2–6 Years)

The six year old is an incomparably more mature-looking thinker and knower than the two year old. His cognitive functioning clearly exhibits a wide variety of positive (i.e., developmentally progressive) attributes when contrasted with that of the younger child. There is also a negative side, however. The six year old, and even more obviously the four and five year old, shows some striking cognitive immaturities when compared with the eight or ten or twelve year old child. These immaturities have played an important role in Piaget's and other theorists' account of cognitive growth, with the unfortunate if unintended result that the mind of the preschool child is often described in primarily negative terms. In Piaget's theory, for example, the one year old is "sensory-motor," the ten year old "concrete-operational," and the fifteen year old "formal-operational"—all good, positive-sounding designations. The poor three year old, on the other hand, gets labeled *"preoperational"* (even at times *"pre*conceptual"), and our description of his thinking is all too often little more than a dreary litany of his wrong answers to concrete-operational tests.

A more balanced characterization is obviously called for, one that stresses the positive intellectual accomplishments of this period as well as those cognitive features which are destined for developmental renovation or replacement. In keeping with this spirit, the positive side of early childhood mental growth is presented in this section. Its residual immaturities or negative features will be described in the next section, where they will help to highlight the positive intellectual accomplishments of the middle childhood period.

Communicability: Information and Control

One of the most striking differences between the six year old and the two year old is the six year old's vastly superior ability to communicate with others, especially by means of spoken language. A truly extraordinary amount of language development gets accomplished during the early childhood period—in fact, we have only recently begun to appreciate just *how* much. The older child is therefore much more accomplished than the younger one both in sending messages and in receiving them, that is, both in verbally expressing his own thoughts and in comprehending the verbalized thoughts of others (see Chap. 5). Likewise, his capacity for sending and receiving various types of nonverbal communications is greatly superior to that of the younger child, a point that will be seen as important in subsequent discussion. This marked increase in communicative prowess is associated with some equally pronounced changes in his overall cognitive life. A distinction between two types of communication will help clarify the nature of this close association between communicative development and intellectual growth during early childhood.

Some communications are primarily *informative* in character; their content consists largely of facts and ideas of one sort or another. As the child's communicative skills improve, he becomes increasingly able to receive, transmit, and otherwise manipulate information about the world around him. First and probably foremost, he acquires the crucial ability to learn by absorbing information conveyed to him by others through language or other communicative media. Conversely, he becomes able to transmit information to others, a vital means of getting corrective feedback from others as to the adequacy of his facts and ideas. Finally, he develops the ability to "communicate" to himself, for instance, to symbolize, store or retain, and think about the products of his own daily experiences. All of these abilities make for profound changes in the child's cognitive life. Much more than was true of the infant, the young child becomes an "open system" with respect to information flow. Information of all sorts flows into, out of, and inside of the system at a rate and in a manner impossible for any purely sensory-motor, pre-symbolic organism.

Other communications have a primarily *controlling* rather than *informative* intent. Their main aim is not so much to impart ideas and facts as to control the actions of the recipient. Their function and objective is to impel, inhibit, direct, guide, shape, or otherwise influence the recipient's behavior. The young child's growing communicative competence helps to make him an increasingly active trader in behavioral control as well as in information. Moreover, the patterns of flow are much the same as in the informative-communication case, i.e., other-to-self, self-to-other, and self-to-self.

First, a six year old is intellectually much more able than a two year old to comply with another's request, demand, instruction, behavioral demonstration (which serves as a model for the child to imitate), or any other control-oriented communication. Such communicative inputs are capable of producing increasingly detailed and fine-grained effects as the child grows older. Instructions to carry out complex behavior sequences may elicit precisely those sequences in a willing six year old, for example, whereas the most acquiescent of two year olds may simply lack the cognitive equipment to comply with such instructions.

Control-oriented communications from child to others also exhibit marked age changes during early childhood. Quite obviously, two year olds can and do "control" the behavior of those around them in myriad ways. Again, however, they show nothing like the six year old's ability to elicit desired behaviors in compliant others through purposeful and sometimes fairly elaborate verbal instructions, gestures, physical demonstrations, and the like.

Finally, the growing child becomes increasingly capable of exercising control over his own behavior. He develops at least some ability: (1) to initiate a behavioral intention, plan, or set and then sustain it over a period of time; (2) to deliberately inhibit tempting but forbidden or otherwise situation-inappropriate behaviors; (3) to wait and suspend action; (4) to postpone and delay gratification; (5) and a variety of other types of self-management. Thus, early childhood is the period in which numerous forms of *self control* begin to develop. The word "begin" needs emphasizing, since even the first grader's capacity for self-regulation is of course far from absolute (as is the adult's, for that matter); his self control is sometimes absent, often precarious and short-lived, and usually quite variable in quality from situation to situation. Nonetheless, the emergence of some capacity for voluntary self control is clearly one of the really central and significant cognitive-developmental hallmarks of the early childhood period. Its critical emergence, together with the child's greater susceptibility to communicative control by others, has been the subject of a highly influential theory by the Russian psychologist A. R. Luria and his colleagues (Luria, 1959, 1961; see also Wozniak, 1972).

Luria's theory of the development of verbal self regulation. By now, you should be able to anticipate what it is my bounden duty to say next: What follows is the usual brief and highly selective summary of what is in actuality a rather extensive and complex theoretical system. More detailed and sophisticated presentations of the work of Luria and other Soviet psychologists are readily available, however (e.g., Wozniak, 1972; Cole and Maltzman, 1969).

Luria postulates two parallel and interrelated developments with respect to the verbal regulation of behavior. The first development concerns the *origin* and the *nature* of the speech that does the regulating. Initially, only the overt speech of others (adults or older children) can regulate and guide the child's actions. For instance, another person may be able to direct the young child's attention to various objects and events by verbal means. Similarly, the child may be able to comply with simple commands or requests verbally conveyed to him by the other person, although some important initial limitations on this ability to follow instructions will shortly be mentioned. In the beginning, then, the only speech that can influence the child's behavior is *other-external:* It emanates from another person *(other)* rather than from the child himself, and since the child must hear it in order to be influenced by it, it is, of course, overt *(external)* rather than covert.

Subsequently, the *nature* of the controlling speech remains the same but there is a crucial change in *where* it can originate. As before, the speech remains overt rather than covert. Now, however, in addition to being able to respond to the control-oriented communications of others, the child acquires some capacity to produce *and be governed by* his own overt speech. Whereas before the adult could give the child a simple command and the child would follow it, the adult now may be able to induce the child to generate the same command himself at the appropriate moment, and then to follow his own command. As Luria's famous teacher L. S. Vygotsky long ago pointed out, cognitive development consists partly of the gradual transfer of control from others to the self; a function that was initially divided between two people eventually comes to reside in one of them, namely, the developing individual himself. Thus, this second step in the developmental process can be called *self-external*.

Once the controlling message becomes self-to-self rather than other-to-self, there is no longer any essential communicative reason why it must continue to be overt rather the covert. You obviously cannot regulate the behavior of others with covert speech (this is no place to debate the scientific status of ESP, thought control, and other possible counter examples). On the other hand, it is quite plausible that you could learn to regulate your own behavior by means of internal, inaudible, and perhaps even quite fragmentary speech, e.g., just a "key word" here and there. Luria (after Vygotsky) argues that verbal self-regulation does, in fact, become increasing internal and abbreviated toward the end of early childhood. In the third and final stage of the developmental process under consideration, therefore, the possible origin of the controlling speech remains the same (self), but its nature changes (from overt to covert). We shall, of course, label this final stage *self-internal*.

The second, parallel development concerns the *type of control* exercised by regulative speech. At first, the control is said to be primarily *impulsive* rather than *semantic*. During this initial period, speech often is responded to as just another physical stimulus, rather than as the carrier of a specific, symbolic meaning. Thus, a spoken word or phrase is frequently responded to by the young child as if it were simply a meaningless noise, rather than a genuinely semantic, meaning-laden message. It is a fact that noises are capable of exerting crude, gross kinds of control over people's behavior. A sudden noise may have an inhibitory effect, for example, causing you momentarily to stop whatever you had been doing or thinking. Under other circumstances, the same noise may impel (or disinhibit) a response one is all set to perform; the starter's gun at a track meet is a familiar example. When Luria talks of the *impulsive* side of speech, he has in mind this physical-stimulus type capacity of the word-as-noise to inhibit and disinhibit responses. In

Luria's research, much emphasis is given to the word's releasing-disinhibiting function in the case of young children, and hence the appropriateness of his term "impulsive" for this function.

As development proceeds, verbal control becomes more frequently and more generally semantic rather than impulsive. The child's behavior becomes increasingly controllable by *what* is said to him (semantic aspect) rather than by the purely physical-stimulus effect of saying *something (anything)* to him at that particular moment (impulsive aspect). Here is an example of the distinction between the semantic and the impulsive aspect of verbal control. Luria (1959) reports a Russian study in which a young child clearly demonstrates a basic comprehension of the verbal expressions, "Put on the ring," and "Take off the ring." That is, given a stick and some rings that can be put on it and taken off it, he shows that in many circumstances he can correctly follow either command. However, if he has just been putting on a whole series of rings and has another in hand, all ready to add to the pile, "the instruction *'Take off the ring'* loses its directive meaning and begins to function non-specifically, merely accelerating the activity of *putting on* the ring . . ." (Luria, 1959, p. 343). While this example nicely illustrates the impulsive effects of speech (with speech "merely accelerating the activity"), it also points up the fact that even young children do not always and only respond in this words-as-noise fashion. Indeed, Luria's example would have had no force at all if the child had not shown some genuine comprehension of, and ability to comply with, those two simple instructions. What we are dealing with, in other words, is an hypothesized age *trend,* a trend from more to less susceptibility to impulsive-type verbal effects, and from less to more ability to respond in terms of the verbal meaning alone.

How do these two major developmental progressions interlock with one another? Table 3-1 provides a somewhat oversimplified representation of Luria's answer. As always, the age ranges cited for each

**TABLE 3-1 Major Stages in Luria's Account
of the Development of Verbal Self Regulation**

Dominant Type of Verbal Control	Origin and Nature of the Regulating Speech		
	Other-External	Self-External	Self-Internal
Impulsive	Stage 1 (1½–3 yrs.)	Stage 2 (3–4½ yrs.)	
Semantic			Stage 3 (4½ yrs. and older)

stage are to be regarded as extremely rough guidelines only, subject to considerable variation from child to child and task to task.

In Stage 1, some measure of control over the child's actions can be achieved by the overt verbalizations of other people. The control is often of the impulsive rather than semantic type, however, and cannot yet be initiated by the child's own verbal productions. The rings-on-stick child cited earlier was obviously in Stage 1.

In Stage 2, the child gradually becomes capable of influencing his own behavior by his own speech, but the speech must still be overt and its influence frequently remains impulsive rather than semantic in character. There are some related developments during these first two stages that are not represented in Table 3–1. For example, as his linguistic and other cognitive abilities mature during this three year period, there is naturally a considerable increase in the complexity of the tasks and task instructions he can manage *at all,* i.e., even unsuccessfully.

As Table 3–1 shows, the advent of Stage 3 is marked by two new developments rather than one. First, the child's verbal self control becomes increasingly semantic rather than impulsive. Second, the verbalizations which do the controlling begin to go "underground," with the result that the child's self management is increasingly carried out by inner speech or verbal thought. Luria usually speaks of these two developments as occurring simultaneously, although there is the occasional suggestion (Luria, 1961, p. 61) that the latter (internalization of speech) might lag a bit behind the former (semantic control).

Luria cites a wide variety of research findings in support of his developmental model, but the following experimental set up illustrates its major points particularly well. Lights of two different colors flash on in random sequence. The child is instructed to squeeze a rubber bulb once whenever the light of one color comes on (positive stimulus), and not to squeeze the bulb whenever the light of the other color comes on (negative stimulus).

According to Luria, the Stage 1 child does poorly in this task situation generally and does even worse if required to produce an appropriate, potentially self-regulative verbalization as one or both lights appear (e.g., to say "Squeeze" when the positive light comes on). As would be expected at Stage 1, however, continuous verbal prompts from the experimenter are of some help.

During Stage 2, some behavior regulation can be achieved by means of the child's own speech. For instance, if the child is induced to say "Squeeze" out loud each time the positive light comes on, he is more apt to respond correctly. That is, he is more likely to squeeze the bulb rather than to fail to squeeze it; also he is more likely to squeeze just once rather than to produce a burst of uncontrolled, perseverative squeezes. Saying "Squeeze" (or "Press," or "Go," etc.) thus helps him to avoid both errors of omission and of commission. The child's verbal control of his own behavior remains impulsive rather than semantic in this situation, however, as attested by the fact that getting him to say "Don't squeeze" when the negative light appears actually produces *more* squeezing to that light (errors of commission) than if he says nothing at all. "Don't squeeze" and "Squeeze" both function primarily as physical stimuli—words-as-noise—at this stage, and therefore are equally likely to trigger or impel squeezing responses.

With the advent of Stage 3, however, the regulative function of the child's speech in this task situation becomes more exclusively semantic, and consequently *both* saying "Squeeze" to the positive light and "Don't squeeze" to the negative one may be helpful in producing the correct, appropriate reaction to each light. On the other hand, saying anything aloud soon becomes unnecessary during this stage, since the child becomes increasingly more capable of regulating his behavior by means of his own internal, covert speech.

Critique of Luria's theory and some opinions about the development of communicability. Luria's is just the sort of developmental theory that most developmental psychologists (this writer included) both want to believe and find it easy to believe. We *want* to believe it for several reasons: specific theories about early-childhood cognitive growth are just not all that plentiful; Luria's theory obviously deals with a very important but largely neglected developmental phenomenon, i.e., the genesis of self control; the theory tells a developmental story that is at once dramatic and easy to grasp (it makes an interesting and readily communicable class lecture or textbook section, for example). The beliefs of scientists are more influenced by such considerations than either the public or the scientists often recognize. We find it *easy* to believe this theory both because it seems inherently plausible on its face and because Luria's presentation of it is studded with references to supporting experimental data.

These credentials notwithstanding, I personally believe Luria's theory has a dubious future, at least as presently formulated (for a more sympathetic and optimistic appraisal, however, see Wozniak, 1972). In the first place, some of the more crucial of his reported age changes in task performance have proven very difficult to replicate in other laboratories. For example, Miller, Shelton, and Flavell (1970) tested young children of four different age groups (mean ages in years and months: 3-2, 3-7, 4-1, and 4-11) in the Lurian bulb-squeezing task situation described above. At each of these four age levels, one-fourth of the children were instructed to say both "Squeeze" to the positive light (and then to squeeze the bulb just once) and "Don't squeeze" to the negative light (and then to refrain from squeezing), one-fourth to say "Squeeze" to the positive light and nothing to the negative, one-fourth "Don't squeeze" to the negative light and nothing to the positive, and one-fourth nothing to either light.

None of the specific effects predicted by Luria's theory were found in this study. Saying "Squeeze" did not help the child respond correctly to the positive light at one age level and hinder correct responding to it at another age level, as the theory would predict; the same was true of saying "Don't squeeze" with respect to the negative light. There was, in fact, little evidence that overt self-instructions had any appreciable effect on behavior in this task—impulsive *or* semantic—in any of the age groups tested. The only really strong and unequivocal positive finding in the study was that the older children were considerably more adept at all variations of this simple two-choice task than the younger ones were. Thus, our study found what all attempted replications of Luria's work have found: a strong increase with age across early childhood in *some* sort of general ability to guide and regulate one's own behavior by internal means.

What might be wrong with Luria's theory? One possibility, of course, is that there really *is* nothing wrong with it, and that future experiments, perhaps guided by a better understanding of the theory than those done to date, might well provide satisfactory empirical support for Luria's views (Wozniak, 1972). My own suspicion, however, is that while the theory is unquestionably on the track of an extremely important cognitive process, it may be interpreting that process incorrectly. The process is that of self control, and developmental psychology is much indebted to Luria for calling attention to its very substantial growth during childhood. My suggestion is that the error lies in interpreting the source and vehicle of human self control as exclusively or even primarily *verbal*. It is, of course, true that other people often do control the child's behavior by means of verbal inputs, but they also frequently exert control nonverbally (through gestures, through manipulation of the physical environment, etc.). Moreover, even verbal inputs from another person must be interpreted, stored, and subsequently acted upon by cognitive processes in the child, and there is no reason to believe that these cognitive processes are themselves exclusively verbal in nature.

This last point may become clearer when one considers behavioral control that originates in the child himself rather than in another person. Instead of asking whether saying "Squeeze" can or cannot control a given child's bulb-squeezing behavior, perhaps we ought to ask instead what it is in the child that "controls" the act of saying "Squeeze" each time the positive light appears. It is scarcely credible that the child covertly says something like, "Say 'squeeze'," to himself each and every time that light appears. Even if he did, we would then have the "control" of *that* verbalization to explain, and so on into an infinite regress of one verbal imperative eliciting another, which in turn elicits another, and so on. It seems more plausible to suppose that the child tries to adopt and continuously maintain some sort of mental set or intention (of what composition or "stuff" we surely cannot specify at present) *both* to say "Squeeze" *and* to squeeze the bulb each time the correct light appears. In the Miller, Shelton, and Flavell (1970) study, young children fairly often failed to squeeze the bulb when the positive light appeared. Even more often, however, they failed to produce the would-be controlling verbalization itself, i.e., they did not say "Squeeze" or "Don't squeeze" when they were supposed to. It seemed to us that those subjects who both had to verbalize appropriately and to squeeze selectively indeed did have a self-regulation problem. But the problem was that of somehow regulating *both* verbal *and* manual behavior, and there is no reason to suppose that this "somehow" has to refer to a *verbal*-regulative process. The reader may note that this emphasis on the priority of general (nonverbal) cognitive processes over purely linguistic ones is consistent with the THOUGHT (*Language* . . .) position outlined in Chap. 2 (pp. 37–38).

Perhaps we would do better to think of this area of early childhood cognitive development in the broader terms used at the beginning of the chapter section. As the child develops during this age period, he makes enormous strides in his ability to "communicate" to self and others, broadly speaking, and to assimiliate and use communications from others. This is true both of informative and controlling types of communications, and within each type, of those that involve language and those that do not. In the case of self control in particular, a verbalized self instruction, plan of action, or the like, may, of course, be produced and may, of course, help to guide and regulate an individual's behavior. On the other hand private verbalizations, whether overt or covert, are probably neither necessary nor sufficient ingredients of at least a good deal of human self governance; in fact, one could even imagine them impeding the self-regulative enterprise in some instances.

Table 3-2 summarizes the major types of communication patterns that seem to evolve during early childhood. Notice that it explicitly allows for the possibility of verbal self control (in the sequence Child-Verbal-Self, reading the table from left to right); such control is accorded no privileged status, however. Moreover, Table 3-2 implicitly allows for *nonverbal* self regulation of *verbal* behavior, since self's action

TABLE 3-2   **Patterns of Information and Control Flow**
That Develop During Early Childhood

Source of Information or Control	Medium of Information or Control	Destination of Information or Control
Child	Nonverbal	Self
		Other
	Verbal	Self
		Other
Other	Nonverbal	Child
	Verbal	

in the sequence Child-Nonverbal-Self could be linguistic as well as non-linguistic.

It is hard to overemphasize just how radical a transformation the advent of these new abilities creates in the life of the child and of those who interact with him. He becomes increasingly *teachable,* increasingly *trainable,* and (as every developmental psychologist well knows) increasingly *testable.* He develops a measure of purposefulness in his daily activities, at home and at school. He can sometimes inhibit a forbidden unwanted response, even though the response is prepotent and the temptation to let it go is very strong. He becomes a comprehending and comprehensible, governable and self-governing, internally-guided and truly "voluntary" organism—and all that adds up to a radical transformation by anyone's standards.

An interesting test of self regulation that comes from the child's world rather than the psychologist's is the game of *Simon Says.* In case you have forgotten the game, simple commands (e.g., "Raise your hands") from the leader are to be executed by the follower if and only if these commands are prefaced with the words "Simon says." Needless to say, there is nothing intrinsically verbal about this homemade self-regulation test: response inhibition also could be effected if the omitted preface to the command were a flash of light or a sonar beep rather than the words "Simon says," and the command itself could also be conveyed by gestures (e.g., the leader actually raising his hands) or other means rather than by words. It is clear from all the foregoing discussion that older children ought to be much more able than younger children to cope with the rather rigorous set-maintenance and response-inhibition demands of this game, and this is precisely what Strommen (1973) discovered when she had children of different ages play it in the laboratory.

The most interesting published observations that I have read of really lifelike, flesh-and-blood type self-control efforts by young children appear in a paper that, curiously, makes no mention of the Lurian research literature at all (Mischel, Ebbesen, and Zeiss, 1972). In this study, preschool children (circa 4½ years old) had the choice of obtaining a less desirable reward immediately or else waiting for an unspecified period of time for a more desirable, delayed reward. I leave it to you to judge whether children of this age have any capacity for self control, and also whether that capacity should be thought of as being exclusively or fundamentally verbal in nature:

> When the distress of waiting seemed to become especially acute, children tended to reach for the termination signal, but in many cases seemed to stop themselves from signaling by abruptly creating external and internal distractions for themselves. They made up quiet songs ("Oh this is your land in Redwood City"), hid their heads in their arms, pounded the floor with their feet, fiddled playfully and teasingly with the signal bell, verbalized the contingency ("If I stop now I get _____, but if I wait I get _____),," prayed to the ceiling, and so on. In one dramatically effective self-distraction technique, after obviously experiencing much agitation, a little girl rested her head, sat limply, relaxed herself, and proceeded to fall sound asleep (Mischel et al., 1972, p. 215).

Identities and Functions

It was pointed out in Chap. 2 (pp. 47–48) that the conceptual formation or attainment of *invariants* amid flux and change is a very general and exceedingly important function of the developing mind. Perceptual object constancy and conceptual object permanence were cited as sensory-motor examples of invariant formation. The well known conservations of the middle-childhood, concrete-operational period are regarded by Piaget as quantitative invariants, and therefore represent much later-developing examples. Piaget and his co-workers have recently suggested that still other cognitive invariants are acquired during the intervening, early-childhood or preoperational period (Piaget, 1968, 1970*b*; Piaget, Grize, Szeminska, and Vinh Bang, 1968; Piaget, Sinclair, and Vinh Bang, 1968).

The Piagetians currently believe that preoperational thinking does possess a kind of logic. It is, however, a partial logic or semilogic when compared with that of middle-childhood, concrete-operational thinking, because it lacks the latter's crucial property of operational reversibility. The meaning of this difference will be made clearer in the later section on middle childhood (those who have read a fair amount of Piaget will already have some idea of what is meant by it). For the present, however, there are three things worth noting. First, the attribution of even a semilogic to early-childhood thought does represent a positive characterization of that developmental period's cognitive achievements, and thus accords with the leitmotif of this chapter section. Second, the application of preoperational semilogic to the child's everyday world produces a very broad and significant body of knowledge subsumable under the headings of *identities* and *functions*. Finally, functions, and even more clearly, identities, represent additional examples of invariant formation. Like the sensory-motor object concept but unlike the concrete-operational conservations, identities and functions are fundamentally qualitative rather than quantitative in nature; that is, they entail no sense of quantitative precision or measurement, as do the conservations and other concrete-operational achievements. A feeling for measurement and quantification is primarily a middle-childhood accomplishment. However, some feeling for qualitatively describable constancies, consistencies, recurrent environmental regularities, predictable covariations among actions, objects, and events, and the like, does develop during early childhood and that is what Piaget's identities and functions are all about.

Identities. A qualitative identity refers to the child's cognitive isolation or differentiation of a permanent quality of an object, namely, its identity or "same-thingness," from such potentially alterable and variable properties as the object's form, size, and general appearance. To illustrate, suppose that we administer Piaget's classic conservation-of-liquid-quantity task to a five year old: (1) the child first agrees that two identical glasses contain identical amounts of water; (2) the water from one glass is poured into a third, taller and thinner glass, with the child watching; (3) the child is then asked if the two amounts of water are still identical, or whether one glass now contains more water than the other. As you know, a child of this age is likely to deny that the quantities are still the same. As a result, he would be diagnosed at least tentatively as a nonconserver of liquid quantity; that is, we would tentatively conclude that he has not yet acquired this particular conservation or quantitative invariant.

What questions in this task situation could he answer correctly? He could, of course, readily say that the glasses and their contents would still exist if they were hidden from his sight, since that particular invariant (object permanence) had been acquired several years ago. He would also probably agree, moreover, that the water that was poured is still the *same water* it was before, despite the act of pouring and the consequent changes in the water's shape (it has, of course, now conformed to the shape of the taller and thinner container into which it was poured). The water is still believed to be the "same entity" as before, in some nonmetric, purely qualitative sense of "sameness" (preservation of basic identity), despite the fact that the amount or quantity of that entity is no longer regarded as equal to that of its mate in the other glass (nonconservation of quantity). For this particular physical transformation, then, Piaget would say that our child possesses a type of qualitative invariant called *identity* but has not yet acquired a markedly different, quantitative invariant called *conservation of amount*. As such, his behavior reflects preoperational rather than concrete-operational logic.

Piaget and his colleagues have studied the developmental establishment of a number of other identities. In one task, for example, a straight iron wire is bent into an arc and then unbent, and the child is asked if it remains the "same wire" in the course of these physical transformations (Piaget, Sinclair, and Vinh Bang, 1968, pp. 5–20). The experimenters were able to identify four developmental levels of performance on this task. Most of the three year olds blandly asserted identity for any and all modifications of the wire, seemingly paying little detailed attention to the physical changes witnessed. The majority of the four year olds, in contrast, would frequently deny continued identity, justifying their denial by calling attention to these same physical changes. (Sometimes the reward for a child's growing information-processing skills is a temporary conceptual mistake, a mistake he was previously too cognitively immature to make and one he will subsequently correct when he matures still further. The behavior of these four year olds seems to be an interesting example of such a "growth error.") Most of the five and six year olds readily accepted the fact that it was always the same wire (qualitative identity) but, in typical preoperational fashion, they did not believe that its length remained the same during the various bendings and straightenings (nonconservation of length, another quantitative invariant). As one five year old put it:

> Yes, it's the same wire but it isn't always the same thing; there's one that's longer and one that's shorter. It's always the same, but you keep making it bigger (*ibid.*, p. 14, my translation).

Finally, the majority of the seven and eight year olds believed in both qualitative identity and quantitative conservation of length.

What about irreversible physical changes, as in the growth of an organism? Piaget, Sinclair, and Vinh Bang (1968, pp. 21–31) tested a small sample of 4–8 year olds and found that most of even the youngest subjects seemed to believe in the continued existence of the "same me" over chronological age (the different-aged selves were represented by drawings). A highly original study by DeVries (1969) entailed both a living organism as the object and reversible physical changes as the transformation. As Fig. 3-1 shows, the organism was an extraordinarily

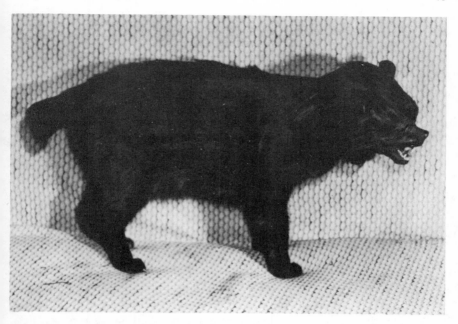

Figure 3-1. Maynard the cat wearing a dog's mask. (From R. DeVries, "Constancy of generic identity in the years three to six," *Society for Research in Child Development Monographs*, 1969, *34*, No. 3 [Serial No. 127], p. 8. By permission.)

forbearing cat (Maynard by name) who would docilely allow the experimenter to put over its head an extremely lifelike mask of a fierce-looking little dog, complete with hair and bared fangs. In one task condition, individually tested 3–6 year olds were first confronted with Maynard as Maynard. After each had identified him verbally as a cat and petted him, the experimenter said: "Now this animal is going to look different. You keep an eye on his tail end, and in a minute I'll show you." While carefully screening the front end of the cat from the child's view, she put the dog mask on and then, turning Maynard around again, said, "Look, now it has a face like a dog. What is this animal now?" A wide variety of questions and procedures ensued, both while Maynard remained masked and after subsequent unmasking and remasking in full view of the child. All of these questions and procedures were designed to clarify the child's actual beliefs about the possibility-impossibility of genus changes, i.e., concerning the particular qualitative invariant DeVries called "generic identity."

Belief in the constancy of generic identity showed a very marked developmental increase from three to six years of age. Many of DeVries' younger children really did seem to believe that Maynard had somehow become a dog, even though his hind end had been clearly visible throughout the masking period. They would show apprehension and refuse to pet him, and would also assert under questioning that he was indeed a real dog, could bark, had a dog's rather than a cat's bones and stomach, and the like. In contrast, the older children were more likely to think that some kind of trick had to be involved, and also to believe that a cat could never turn into a dog, not even "by magic." DeVries found similar age trends in the same sample with respect to the child's analogous belief in the constancy of sex-role identity: The younger subjects were more likely than the older ones to believe that a girl could become a boy if she wanted to, if she did boyish things, if she wore boy's clothes, etc. The author concluded with Piaget that "appreciation for the constancy of qualitative invariants does appear to constitute a pre-operational level of development which occurs before the concrete-operational development that leads to the ability to conserve quantitative invariants" (DeVries, 1969, p. 58).

Functions. In mathematics, x is said to be a function of y, i.e., $x = f(y)$, if the value of x depends upon and covaries with the value of y. This is essentially the meaning Piaget has in mind when he asserts that the preoperational child acquires some cognitive grasp of functions as well as of identities. The child of this age is able to note simple functional relationships and recurrent covariations among observable events. He is able to say that this happens when that happens, that changes in one thing tend to be associated with changes in another. In keeping with the general preoperational character of his thinking, however, the early childhood subject has no precise, quantitative conception of the functional relationship involved. His functions, like his identities, are thus purely qualitative in nature.

Figure 3-2 shows an experimental setup Piaget and his colleagues used to study the young child's ability to detect functional relationships (Piaget, Grize, Szeminska, and Vinh Bang, 1968, p. 62). A spring X is attached to a string or wire of constant length $(Y + Y')$ that runs over a pulley. Both the pulley and the right-hand end of the spring are fixed in place. Different weights (Z) can be attached to the bottom end of the string. The addition of a weight causes the spring to stretch, which in turn leads to a reduction in the length of the Y segment of the string and, of course, an exactly equivalent lengthening of the Y' segment. Segment Y is set against a green background and Y' against a red background, thus permitting the experimenter to speak, for instance, of the "green string" whenever he wants to refer to the Y segment, whatever its length happens to be at that moment. The arrows and scale markers $(Fa$ and $Fb)$ permit precise comparisons of the movements of the spring

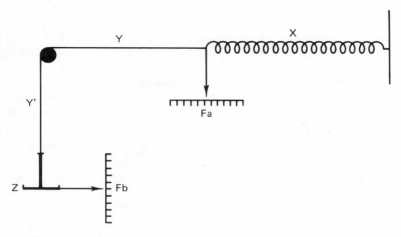

Figure 3-2. An experimental setup for studying children's ability to detect functional relationships. (From J. Piaget, J. B. Grize, A. Szeminska, and Vinh-Bang, *Epistémologie et psychologie de la fonction*, Paris: Presses Universitaires de France, 1968 [Vol. 23 of the *Études d'Épistémologie Génétique* series], p. 62. By permission.)

and the string. Children of different ages were asked to predict what would happen to the various elements of this physical system if weights were attached to the string, and then to describe and explain the various changes witnessed when weights were, in fact, added.

The average 4–6 year old subject in this study was indeed able to describe some of the functional relationships involved, particularly after seeing a weight added. He could, for example, usually recognize that the addition of weights made the spring longer; we might represent this state of affairs by the expression $X = f(Z)$ or $\Delta X = f(\Delta Z)$. Similarly, he might note that Y shortens as Y' lengthens, and also that when one arrow moves the other one does too. (Parenthetically, he also understands the string maintains its basic identity throughout the proceedings.) Predictably, however, his representation of these functional dependencies is qualitative rather than quantitative. He is likely not to believe that the distance $X + Y$ and the total string length $Y + Y'$ remain quantitatively invariant during weight addition. Similarly, the arrow deflection along Fa is not generally seen as necessarily equal in magnitude to the simultaneous arrow deflection along Fb, nor is any decrease in the length of Y ordinarily understood to be compensated for by an absolutely identical increase in the length of Y'.

As Piaget would put it, the child of this age lacks the system of reversible mental operations necessary to infer such rigorous compensations and to appreciate their significance with respect to total length, namely, that the total length $Y + Y'$ must be conserved because all increases in Y' are exactly compensated for by equal decreases in Y. The older subjects in the sample could usually quantify all the various functional relationships in this fashion.

Other experiments have yielded comparable findings. One little study is characteristically Piagetian in the extreme leanness of its supplies and equipment budget: the task materials consisted of three different-sized toy fish (5, 10, and 15 cm) and 50 beads representing their diet of meatballs (Piaget, Grize, Szeminska, and Vinh Bang, 1968, pp. 50–57). The subjects were told simply that they should give the middle-sized and largest fish twice and three times as much food, respectively, as the smallest one. Five year olds proved quite capable of understanding that the amount of food given ought to be some positive function of the size of its recipient. They seemed to have a genuine feel for the (qualitative) dependency of the one upon the other. Thus, they would give more (*some* amount more) beads to the biggest than to the middle-sized one, and also more (*some* amount more) to the middle-sized one than to the smallest one. It was once again the older children who sought to make the function a fixed and precise quantitative one, e.g., scrupulously giving no more and no fewer than 4 beads to the middle-sized fish and 6 to the largest one if the smallest had initially received 2.

Why should a developing sensitivity to identities and functions be regarded as an important achievement of the early childhood period? Because it seems to express or reflect the young child's growing awareness of consistencies, invariants, regularities, and other "predictables" in his everyday world. That world just becomes a more predictable, orderly, and coherent place when one knows that X will continue to retain its X-hood over time and transformations (identities), and that Y will continue to happen every time X happens (functions). Needless to say, an attunement to environmental predictables is not the exclusive prerogative of this age group. However, early childhood is the period when regularities first become objects of representational rather than sensory-motor knowledge, and the fact that the child's initial representation of them is qualitative rather than quantitative in character hardly detracts from its significance as a cognitive-developmental milestone.

Like his increasing communicability, the young child's increasing ability to detect and mentally represent continuity, order, and regularity in everyday phenomena is so pervasive and commonplace a developmental change that it is likely to be overlooked in descriptions of human intellectual growth. It is an instance of what someone has aptly called " 'mundane cognition,' or the cognitive behavior of everyday life" (Social Science Research Council, 1973, p. 25), but of course that is precisely the sort of cognition which is of greatest personal significance for most human beings the world around. Neimark nicely characterizes part of this genre of cognitive attainment in the following passage:

> . . . formulation of contingencies and functional relations has to do with detecting recurrent regularities in ordering and correlation or covariation among events (such as a response and its environmental consequences) . . . formulations of contingencies and relations are stored in the form of norms, rules, and empirical principles. It is, in effect, a process of "learning the rules of the game" where "the game" may refer to cultural conventions (e.g., for constructing a grammatical utterance, or being a good child), explanations for natural phenomena (notions of causality), heuristic strategies (for discrimination, concept attainment, and problem solving tasks), and environmental regularities of individual experience (Grandpa always buys me candy; the cat usually hides under the raspberry bushes; etc.) (Neimark, 1970, p. 356).

Although communicability, identities, and functions cover a lot of cognitive ground, of course they do not encompass everything that gets developed during early childhood. Additional acquisitions will be mentioned in the course of describing middle-childhood achievements.

Middle Childhood (Roughly 7–11 Years)

Perhaps the best way to highlight what is distinctive about cognition in middle childhood is to contrast it with that of early childhood. The dimensions of contrast described below are derived in a large part from Piaget's developmental account (Flavell, 1963, pp. 156–163).

Contrasts Between Early-Childhood and Middle-Childhood Cognition

Perceived appearances versus inferred reality. Piaget's test for conservation of liquid quantity (see p. 73) can be used to illustrate the meaning of this and the other contrasts. The typical preschool nonconserver is apt to conclude, after the liquid has been poured, that the taller and thinner glass now has more water in it than the other glass. Why? Usually for the sole and simple reason that it *looks* like it has more to him, and he is more given than the older child is to make judgments on the basis of the immediate, perceived *appearances* of things. More than his or her school-age counterpart, the preschool-age child is prone to accept things as they seem to be, in terms of their outer, perceptual, phenomenal, "on-the-surface" characteristics. (As we shall see in Chap. 4, the young child's knowledge and reasoning about human objects—

i.e., his social cognition—also tends to be "superficial" in much the same sense.)

The middle-childhood conserver, on the other hand, may also think that the tall glass *looks* like it contains more water because the liquid column is higher, but he goes beyond mere appearances to *infer* from the available evidence that the two quantities *are really* still the same. That is, he makes an inference about underlying reality rather than merely translating perceived appearances into a quantity judgment. More generally, the older child seems to be more sensitive to the basic distinction between what seems to be and what really is, i.e., between the phenomenal or apparent and the real or true. Of course, this is not to suggest that young children never make inferences about unperceived states of affairs or that older children never base conclusions on superficial appearances. Stark and unqualified age contrasts of this sort are virtually never justified in developmental psychology. It is to suggest, however, that there does exist a definite age trend in this respect across this broad segment of childhood.

Several studies have provided more or less direct evidence for such a trend (e.g., Braine and Shanks, 1965a, 1965b; Daehler, 1970). There are ways to create the illusion that one object is bigger (darker, etc.) than another when in fact the opposite is the case; the true state of affairs can then often be ascertained by some measurement procedure (e.g., superimposing one object on the other to establish their real comparative sizes). Children have been tested by such procedures for their sensitivity to the distinction between, for example, the concept "*looks* bigger" and the concept "*really, really* bigger." The basic capacity to make such distinctions does seem to be generally present by the end of early childhood; the various qualitative identities described earlier may actually implicate or presuppose some such basic capacity, in fact. However, the preschool child is certainly not as likely as his elders to make such distinctions spontaneously, without some training or instruction, nor is he as likely to know how to verify (e.g., by superimposition) that what may "*look* bigger" is not necessarily "*really, really* bigger." Braine and Shanks (1965a) are hardly overestimating the scope and significance of this segment of cognitive development when they speak of "a broad conceptual distinction between real and phenomenal attributes—the distinction which probably provides the intellectual basis for the fundamental epistemological construct common to science, 'folk' philosophy, religion, and myth, of a real world 'underlying' and 'explaining' the phenomenal one" (pp. 241–42).

Centration versus decentration. The foregoing contrast emphasizes the younger child's heavy reliance on perceptual input when dealing with conceptual problems like Piaget's conservation-of-liquid-quantity task. But, of course, the older child also is carefully attending to the perceptual input throughout that task, even though he or she recognizes that the task ultimately calls for a conceptual rather than a perceptual judgment. Moreover, he is apt to be distributing that attention in a more flexible, balanced, and generally task-adaptive way than the younger child is. The preschooler is more prone to concentrate or *center* (hence, *centration*) his attention exclusively on some single feature or limited portion of the stimulus array that is particularly salient and interesting to him, thereby neglecting other task-relevant features. In the present example, the difference in the heights of the two liquid columns is what captures most of his attention (and "capture" often does seem the apposite word), with little note given to the compensatory difference in column widths.

In contrast, the older child is likelier to achieve a more balanced, "decentered" (hence, *decentration*) perceptual analysis of the entire display. While, of course, attending to the conspicuous height differences, just as the younger child does, he also carefully notes the correlative differences in container width. He therefore attains a broader and more inclusive purview of the stimulus field. That is, he is likelier to notice and take due account of *all* the relevant perceptual data—in this case, the lesser width as well as the greater height of the new liquid column. Piaget (e.g., 1970*b*, p. 52) believes that the younger child's centration tendency often takes the form of relying heavily on *order* or *ordinal* information in making quantitative judgments. If one of two identical pencils is slid ahead of the other, for example, it is apt to be judged as longer than the first (nonconservation of length). Ordinal relationships like "ahead of," "first," "out in front," "X has passed Y," etc., are very salient for the preoperational child and are often used inappropriately as the sole basis for quantitative comparison.

By using a special camera that records the child's eye movements during task solution, O'Bryan and Boersma (1971) have actually succeeded in measuring "live," ongoing patterns of visual centration and decentration in various conservation tasks. Their data lead them to conclude that:

> There seems little doubt that the nonconserver centrates on the dominant part of the visual display, and that the transitional *S* displays a type of dual centration on both parts, shifting infrequently between the two. By contrast, the conserver appears to have overcome the perceptual distortion presented by the transformed element in that she displays many shifts of fixation and seems completely decentered (O'Bryan and Boersma, 1971, pp. 167–68).

States versus transformations. The test of conservation of liquid quantity can be thought of as comprising two *states,* one initial and one final, plus a *transformation* or process of change that links these two states together. In the initial state, two identical glasses of water contain identical amounts of water. In the final state, two dissimilar glasses contain identical amounts of water (identical in "reality," if not in "appearance"). The transformation that links them together is, of course, the process of pouring water from one glass to another. The act of pouring is a dynamic event that changes, in the course of a brief time period, one static situation into another static situation; it is a transformational process that produces or creates a later state out of an earlier state.

Piaget has made the profound observation that younger children, to a greater degree than older ones, tend to focus their attention and conceptual energies on states rather than state-producing transformations, and also on present states more than on past or future ones. When solving problems of all sorts they are less likely to call to mind or keep in mind relevant previous states of the problem, or to anticipate pertinent future or potential ones. In particular, Piaget argues, they are both undisposed and relatively unable to represent the actual, detailed processes of transition or transformation from one state to another. Thus, they exhibit a kind of "temporal centration" analogous to the spatial one just discussed. That is, they center their attention on the present spatial field or stimulus state to the exclusion of other relevant states and state-linking transformations in the "temporal field," which consists of the recent past, the immediate present, and the near future. They do this just as, within the present spatial field itself, they center their attention on a single, privileged segment of that field. To put it more briefly and concretely, the preoperational subject tries to solve the conservation problem by attending only to the present stimulus field ("temporal centration") and, within it, only to selected, highly salient stimulus features ("spatial centration"). In contrast, the conserver is likely to make spontaneous reference to initial state and intervening transformation when asked to justify his conservation judgment. He might say that the two quantities had, after all, been identical at the outset (initial state), or that the experimenter had merely poured the water from one container to the other, and without spilling any or adding any (intervening transformation). The older child might even say that the continuing equality of amounts could be proved by pouring the liquid back into its original container (future or potential transformation, yielding new state equal to initial state). The conservation task is a conceptual problem rather than a perceptual one precisely *because* of the real or potential existence of such nonpresent states and transformations of states. The older child is more attuned to these background, not-now-perceptible factors and uses them in producing a conceptual solution to this and other, similar conceptual problems.

Irreversibility versus reversibility. A full explanation of the meaning and significance of this contrast within Piaget's theoretical system would require a detailed presentation of his logical-mathematical models of concrete-operational thought (i.e., his various grouping and group structures). The interested reader will have no trouble finding such presentations (e.g., Flavell, 1963, Chap. 5; Ginsburg and Opper, 1969, pp. 127–133), and it would be unduly space-consuming to include one here. According to Piaget the middle-childhood subject possesses *reversible* intellectual operations; his thought is said to exhibit the property of *reversibility*. Contrariwise, the preschool child's mental operations are *irreversible*, and his thought said to show *irreversibility*. In the particular conservation problem we have been using as an example, the older child can exhibit reversibility of thought or reversible mental operations in two distinct ways.

On the one hand, he may recognize that the effect of the initial pouring of the water into the tall thin glass can be exactly and completely undone or negated by the inverse action of pouring the water back into its original container. The older child readily senses the possible existence of such an inverse, wholly nullifying action that changes everything back to its original state, and he may cite this possibility as a justification for his conservation judgment. A middle-childhood mind is more sensitive than an early-childhood one to the fact that many mental and physical operations have opposites that exactly—in a rigorous, precise, quantitative way—negate them, and thereby reset the whole situation to zero, so to speak.

On the other hand, the older child similarly recognizes that something equivalent to situation zero can also be achieved by an action that compensates for or counterbalances the effects of another action, rather than one that literally undoes it in the manner of the inverse or opposite action just described. For example, the child might justify his belief in conservation by pointing out that the increase in height of the liquid column which results from the pouring transformation is exactly offset or compensated for by the accompanying decrease in column width. According to this kind of reversible thinking, the column loses in width what it gains in height, and hence the quantity must remain the same. The width decrease obviously does not literally wipe out or annul the height increase, as actual repouring would. It has the same effect and cognitive significance (i.e., it provides a rational justification for a conservation verdict), but it does so by virtue of constituting an indirect compensation rather than a direct, literal negation. As with direct negation, the older child is more attuned than the younger one to the potential existence of such indirectly countervailing, compensation-type factors, and he or she better understands their utility in making rigorous quantitative inferences.

Other examples of these two forms of reversible thinking abound in Piagetiana. Recall that conservation of length can be assessed by first placing two identical pencils (sticks, rods) side by side so that their ends exactly coincide and then, after the child agrees that they are equal in length, sliding one a bit to the right, so that its end leads or is ahead of the other's end on that side. The younger child focuses "irreversibly" on this "transformation"-produced, immediately-perceptible "state" of the sticks ("temporal centration") and, within that state, equally irreversibly "centers" his attention on the right-hand portions of the sticks ("spatial centration"); mistaking "appearances" for "reality," he then concludes that the rightmost stick is now longer than its companion. (Whereby is it demonstrated that all four of our early childhood—middle childhood contrasts can be insinuated into a single sentence, although the use of the semicolon does admittedly represent a bit of fudging on my part.) In the same situation, the older conserver may exhibit reversible thinking, either by appealing to the results of the inverse, directly-negating act of realignment of the pencils, or by suggesting that the length gained by the displaced stick at its right end is exactly compensated for by the length lost at its left end. These two types of concrete-operational reversibility are often referred to by Piagetians as *inversion* and *compensation,* respectively. For reasons we need not go into, the terms *reciprocal* and *reciprocity* also are frequently used in describing reversible operations of the latter, compensatory type (e.g., Piaget and Inhelder, 1969, pp. 98, 102).

Recent research strongly suggests that a real sensitivity to compensating factors in conservation or conservation-like task settings is, in fact, not often seen in the preschool period; indeed, it may still have some developing to do at the end of middle childhood. In one study (Gelman and Weinberg, 1972), for instance, children were presented with a standard beaker which already contained a certain quantity of water and a second, empty beaker which was either taller and narrower or shorter and wider than the standard. Each subject was given a pitcher of water and told to pour the same amount into the second beaker ("so that both of us have as much to drink in our glasses"). He was also questioned afterwards as to how he knew he had poured the same amount. Not until third grade did a majority of their subjects pour in even a roughly compensatory way, e.g., producing any lower-than-standard-beaker water level in the shorter and wider beaker, rather than simply matching the two water levels. Moreover, only a minority of their *sixth*-grade sample (mean age 11 years, 9 months, and the oldest subjects tested) provided clear and explicit compensation-type explanations for their equalization efforts. However liberally or conservatively diagnosed, this sort of flexible, reversible, quantitatively-oriented thinking does appear to be a relatively late-emerging developmental outcome.

A General Characteristic
of Middle-Childhood Cognition

There is a general characteristic of middle-childhood cognition that is implicit in what has been said already about the two periods of development. More than is true of the preschooler, the elementary-school child has what might be called a *quantitative attitude* toward many cognitive tasks and problems. He seems to understand better than the younger child that certain problems have precise, specific, potentially quantifiable solutions, and that these solutions may be attained by logical reasoning in conjunction with well-defined *measurement* operations. The younger child often lacks the cognitive equipment to do other than guess or make simple perceptual estimates. As pointed out earlier, the identities and functions he acquires are qualitative rather than quantitative affairs. In contrast, the older child has come to understand that wholes are potentially divisible into unit parts of arbitrary size, and that these parts can serve as units of measurement in making a quantitative judgment about the whole.

Once again, Piaget's conservation problems are useful in illustrating this difference between a qualitative, "guestimate"-minded approach and a quantitative, measurement-minded one. Six wooden matches are placed end-to-end but nonlinearly, so that they form a jagged, angular "road" on the table. An objectively shorter (e.g., only "five matches long") but perfectly straight stick representing a second road is placed directly above the first. Because it is straight, the crow's-flight distance between its end points is actually longer than the distance between the end points of the other, crooked road. Who makes the longest trip, the experimenter asks, the person who drives the entire length of the crooked road or the person who drives the entire length of the straight road? The second person, says the nursery school child, centering only on the end points. The first person, says the fourth grader, carefully attending to what lies *between* the end points. Unlike the younger subject, he recognizes that total lengths (distances, areas, volumes, etc.) are composed of, and are conceptually divisible into, subparts of any arbitrary desired magnitude. He understands that whole lengths are potentially fractionable into so-and-so many length segments of such-and-such size, or alternatively, into some different number of segments of any other, arbitrarily-selected size. If asked to prove that the crooked road was actually longer than the straight road, appearances notwithstanding, he might, of course, simply straighten it out, align the two and point to the difference. He might instead, however, use one of the matches as a convenient, pre-formed unit measure, and prove to you that the crooked road was "one match longer" than the straight one. Equivalently, he could use a ruler, or a meter stick, or a hairpin, or anything else that would allow him to arrive at a rigorous, exact, quantitative solution to the problem. Such a child we would say, has a metric, genuinely quantitative conception of length. He has what Bearison (1969) has termed a "quantitative set," and it allows him to envision exact solutions to a variety of quantitative problems (Bearison's article, be it noted, is entitled "Role of measurement operations in the acquisition of conservation.")

I suspect, however, that what the typical middle-childhood mind has achieved even goes beyond this important disposition and ability to deal quantitatively with quantifiable problems. I believe it has a better general understanding that certain inputs do and certain inputs do not constitute "problems," that problem-type inputs require reasoning, measurement, or other forms of intellectual activity, and also that the right sort of intellectual activity could produce a satisfactory, possibly unique solution to the problem. In other words, the older child has a much better sense of what a conceptual problem is, of what a problem solution is, and of the fact that it normally takes more than a quick perceptual judgment to get from the former to the latter.

NUMBER SKILLS AND CONCEPTS:
A SPECIFIC EXAMPLE OF COGNITIVE DEVELOPMENT
DURING EARLY AND MIDDLE CHILDHOOD

So far, this chapter's description of early- and middle-childhood thought has been quite general. Its aim has been to provide a broad overview of what appear to be the most important achievements and changes occurring during this extended period of childhood. It should also be made clear, however, that a large number of more specific cognitive skills and concepts also emerge and undergo development during these years (Flavell, 1970a). Some of them primarily have to do with the social world and these will be sampled in Chap. 4. Others concern the logical-mathematical and natural worlds. Prominent among these are the child's progressive understanding of classes, relations, number continuous quantity (e.g., our old friend, liquid quantity), weight volume, space, time, movement, velocity, and causality. A quick look at these developmental stories (Flavell, 1963, 1970*a*) will convince the reader that only the use of microfiche would allow me to deal with all of them in the chapter space remaining. There is certainly room to say something about one of them however, and that one had best be number development.

There are several reasons for selecting number development if obliged to choose only one conceptual area to detail. First of all, number seems to have a central position in all three "worlds." Numbers are basically logical-mathematical entities, of course, but we frequently exploit them in our attempts to think about natural and social phenomena. A closely related second reason is that developmental changes in this specific area nicely illustrate the more general cognitive-development trends already described. As examples, a concrete-operational level understanding of number entails or is accompanied by an understanding of reversibility (e.g., that subtracting 2 is the inverse of adding 2), a bent towards precise, frequently numerical measurement operations (e.g., this big rod is 4 little rods long), and a reliance on conceptual inference rather than perceptual appearance in making numerical estimates (e.g., counting a large array of objects to determine how many there are rather than just looking at them and guessing). Number development is a microcosm in which virtually all these general cognitive trends can be detected.

This conceptual area also exhibits an interesting blend of the informally learned and the formally taught (Brush, 1972). Of course, many mathematical concepts and operations are only taught and learned in school; less obviously perhaps, there are a number of elementary concepts that somehow get acquired prior to formal schooling. More than some of the other concepts mentioned, perhaps, the growth of number understanding is of interest to both developmental psychologists and educators. As a final reason, some rather exciting research has been done on number development recently, especially on these early, informally-acquired precursors of the more mature, middle-childhood level number concepts and operations.

Understanding of Number in Middle Childhood

The average child of the middle years is likely to have achieved a great deal of basic knowledge about the nature and uses of the number system. The present section presents a summary of that basic knowledge, pieced together from various writings on this topic (e.g., Brush, 1972; Gelman, 1972*a*, 1972*b*; Klahr and Wallace, 1973; Piaget, 1952—see also Flavell, 1963, pp. 309–316, and Flavell, 1970*a*, pp. 1001–1006; Potter and Levy, 1968; Schaeffer, Eggleston, and Scott, 1974; Wang,

Resnick, and Boozer, 1971; Wohlwill, 1960). Once we have a clearer idea of the elementary knowledge that is eventually acquired in this area, we will be in a better position to examine (next section) some of the possible developmental precursors of that knowledge.

Subitizing. For a long time, the middle-childhood subject has been able to look at small sets of objects (e.g., 1–3) and, at a glance, without counting them, accurately perceive how many there are. The act of perceiving the numerical value of small sets more or less directly, without recourse to counting, is called *subitizing.* The older child, like the adult, doubtless understands that the accuracy of such purely perceptual estimations diminishes as set size increases. He knows, in other words, that perceptual judgments are perfectly trustworthy when there are two objects in the array but not when there are twenty; when there are twenty, he knows he would be well advised to count.

Counting. Of course, the child of this age can count *in vacuo,* i.e., simply recite number words in correct sequence without actually enumerating any concrete objects in the process. He can probably also do fancier things of the same genre, such as count by twos or by tens as well as by ones, and count backwards as well as forward. Much more importantly, the child is able to enumerate sets of objects by counting. His counting is accurate and it also conforms to task specifications.

His counting is accurate in that each object in the set gets counted once (he does not skip any objects) and only once (he does not count any objects twice). The child tries to ensure the accuracy of his count by enumerating the objects in some systematic way, exploiting whatever spatial structure the set of objects affords in order to do so. If the objects happen to be aligned in two horizontal rows, for instance, he would doubtless take advantage of this fact and count them by rows rather than some other way.

The child's counting also conforms to task specifications. For example, he is quite capable of counting out only some predetermined number of objects from the entire set before him. If asked to remove ten objects from a set of fifteen, for instance, he counts out exactly ten of them and then remembers to stop counting; he does not continue to enumerate, robot fashion, just because there still remain some uncounted objects in front of him. He can, in fact, behave according to task specifications in either of two directions. Given the instruction to get "ten" objects, he readily counts out exactly ten of however many are there. Conversely, given a pile of ten objects and the instruction to find out how many there are in the pile, he immediately counts them out and says "ten."

Cardinal and ordinal aspects of number. When he counts his tenth object, our prototypical middle-childhood subject is implicitly aware of two related facts. First, he realizes that this object is the *tenth* (ordinal aspect) object counted in the ordered series of counting actions, "one, two, three . . . ten." Second, he simultaneously knows that the total number or quantity of counted objects, including that tenth object, is *ten* (cardinal aspect). Thus, he understands that "ten" can refer both to a particular position (tenth) in an enumeration sequence and also to the total number (ten) of objects thus enumerated to that point. If n objects have been counted one by one, the last object counted will be the nth one enumerated; conversely, if the nth one in the series has been enumerated, the cardinal-numerical or quantitative value of those enumerated objects must be n. Such a child knows that 8 is a "higher" number than 7 in the number series (ordinal aspect), and also a "bigger" number; i.e., it denotes a larger set (cardinal aspect).

Numerals. The child can read and write arabic numerals as well as comprehend and produce spoken numbers. Moreover, he understands and can do the same things with written numerals as with verbal numbers. For example, he can count out precisely ten objects whether the quantity requested is communicated orally or in print.

Correspondences. If the elementary-school child were given one set of objects and asked to constitute another set of the same quantity or cardinal-number value, he would be able to do it by simply counting the first set and then counting out a second set numerically equal to the first. But he might also be able to do this, without recourse to counting, simply by placing each object from the second group next to a different object in the first set. The child knows that two sets whose elements can be put in one-one correspondence in this fashion, with no "leftovers" in either set, must be numerically equal. Moreover, he is likely to have intuitions about how to use one-one or one-many correspondences to perform simple set multiplication and division operations. For instance, he recognizes that the above two equalized sets taken together constitute a set twice as large as either. He is also apt to understand that set B is twice as large as set A if the two sets had initially been constituted by repeatedly pairing two B elements with one A element. Similarly, he may know that one way to divide a set into two equal or near-equal subsets is, in effect, to put its elements in one-one correspondence with one another, e.g., taking out two at a time and putting them in separate piles.

Comparing set sizes. Given two sets, children in this age range typically have a correct, comparative-numerical understanding of "more than," "less than" and "equals." They know, for instance, that "more than" refers to a relation between quantities rather than to any single, absolute amount (as a matter of fact, they understand this relative-absolute distinction in a wide variety of concept areas). Moreover, they can generally determine the comparative sizes of two sets by subitizing them if the sets are small, by counting each set and comparing the numbers thus produced, or by attempting to put all elements from one set into one-one correspondence with those of the other and noting any leftover, unpairable elements.

Once the intial sizes of the two sets are determined, the child also understands the precise effects that adding or subtracting variable numbers of elements to one or both sets can have. If the set sizes were initially equal, for instance, he or she knows that the addition or subtraction of equal numbers of new elements to or from each set will preserve this equality relation, but that addition or subtraction of elements to or from only one set will make the two sets numerically unequal. Furthermore, if set *A* initially contained, say, five elements more than set *B*, he of course recognizes that the subsequent addition of two elements to *B* makes *B* itself have more elements than it did before (present *B* is "more than" past *B*, or there is "more of" *B* than previously), but he also clearly understands that *B* does not thereby now have "more than" *A* as well. As indicated above, quantitative terms like "more" have acquired very precise, differentiated meanings.

Relevant and irrelevant transformation. A set changes its numerical value if, and *only* if, elements are added to it or taken away from it. A row of objects does not become more numerous if you make it longer and less dense by spreading out the objects, or if you make it shorter and more dense by pushing them together. Addition and subtraction of elements are transformations that are relevant to number, whereas spatial rearrangements of set elements constitute number-irrelevant transformations. The acquisition of this particular fact is the most famous part of the number-development story, since it amounts to the acquisition of Piagetian number conservation.

You probably know how nonconservation-conservation of number is commonly assessed. Two parallel rows of *n* objects each are formed by one-one correspondence. Each object in row *A* is lined up directly above an object in row *B*, so that the rows are equal in length, density of elements, and, of course, number. After the child agrees that the rows are indeed numerically equal (e.g., "I have just as many candies to eat as you do"), the experimenter spreads out one of the rows and asks if they are still equal. Conservers say "yes" and nonconservers says "no," the latter usually maintaining that the longer row has more. Conservation of number is generally the first of the Piagetian conservations to be acquired (Inhelder and Sinclair, 1969); there is good evidence that it is regularly attained earlier than liquid quantity conservation, for example (e.g., Brainerd and Brainerd, 1972).

It hardly needs saying that addition and subtraction not only come to be seen as number-relevant operations, but also as number-relevant operations that stand in inverse relation to one another. The addition of n elements can always be completely negated by the subsequent subtraction of exactly n elements. The reversibility-minded elementary-school child is well aware of this relation, and it constitutes an important part of his basic understanding of number.

The nature and generation of the set of whole numbers. Children in the middle years also have some grasp of the basic principle by which the number series is generated and indefinitely extended. They are capable of recognizing the fact that a next higher number can always be generated by adding one to the number already attained. There is an at least tacit recognition that the set of whole numbers comprises an ordered, asymmetrical series that can be indefinitely extended upward by repeatedly adding an integer. Accordingly, older children come to understand that big numbers are basically the same sorts of creatures as small numbers; it is recognized that they are generated according to the same rules, are amenable to the same arithmetic operations, etc. Older subjects know that two sets built up by one-one correspondence (i.e., adding an element to one set whenever you add an element to the other) will always remain numerically equal, no matter how huge they might get (Flavell, 1970a, p. 1004). They also know that medium and large quantities are conserved under number-irrelevant transformations, just as small, subitizable quantities are.

Developmental Precursors of Number Understanding

In detailing all those items of middle-childhood number knowledge and ability, I have obviously given part of the game away as to what number development is all about. As you have doubtless guessed, there is reason to think that each of those items does, in fact, *need* acquiring; that is, each seems to be the outcome or product of a period of early childhood learning and development. It was worth the space to detail them, in other words, because they specify much of what is developing during early-middle childhood. In a more practical vein, parents and teachers might find them useful sources of hypotheses as to what their young children are and .are not understanding in their dealings with the number system.

A mnemonic for early number development. It is often possible, in fact, to make an educated guess as to what sorts of problems a young child might have in coping with tasks requiring these items. First of all, the very description of the item is often of considerable help. (Given that a subject did not succeed on a test of item X, what are the *logically possible* ways he could fail?) It is also often helpful to remember the nature of the information processing device that is doing the failing in these cases. (Given that an organism with a preoperational type mind did not succeed on such a test, what are the *likely* ways *he* would fail?).

Take, for example, the ability to "count to task specifications" (see the section on *Counting* above). Suppose that a young child were asked to count out exactly eight objects from a randomly arranged group of eleven. He could fail because his ability to recite number names in correct order is not yet well developed. He might, for example, skip a number or two, perhaps producing a counting sequence like this: "1, 2, 3, 4, 6, 8." He might also fail by counting the same object more than once. Potter and Levy (1968) have demonstrated that the ability merely to *touch* each member of a set of items once and only once, a likely precursor to *counting* each member once and only once, improves considerably over the $2\frac{1}{2}$–4 year age range. As a final example, the young child could err by failing to keep in mind the number of objects he had been asked to count out (eight), with the result that he keeps on counting until the last (eleventh) available object has been duly enumerated. This is, in fact, an error young counters are prone to make (Wang, Resnick, and Boozer, 1971). The last two errors, especially, have at least a hint of the preoperational about them. Here is a preoperational child absorbed in a counting routine, a temptingly countable object catches his eye, and so he proceeds to count it. His here-and-now, "perception-first" cognitive orientation may lead him to forget (or forget to remember) that this particular object had already been counted, or that counting it takes him over his target number. Thus, at least a weak mnemonic for comprehending and remembering certain aspects of early number development exists: Think of what the prototypical concrete-operational child can do in this or that test of number understanding, and imagine what someone with a preoperational mentality might do in the same test situation. You will often be right.

Possible developmental interactions between number skills and number knowledge. Let us turn once again to that large set of "items" the middle-childhood subject was said to have acquired. A useful if imperfect distinction can be made between two kinds of items in this cognitive domain (see Gelman, 1972a, for a similar breakdown). There are number *skills* (e.g., counting objects, reading numerals) and there is number *knowledge* or understanding (e.g., number conservation—knowing that mere spatial rearrangement of a set of objects cannot change the number of objects in the set). As Gelman (1972a) has shown, most of the early research on number development dealt with the acquisition of number skills, often referred to in the old literature as "number facts." Subsequently, as Piaget's work on number conservation and related topics became well known, research attention shifted to the childhood acquisition of number knowledge.

It is now becoming apparent, however, that we must pay close attention to both sorts of acquisitions if we are ever to achieve an integrated picture of number development. The reason is that, almost certainly, number-skill acquisitions developmentally facilitate (mediate, underpin, serve as building blocks for, etc.) number-knowledge acquisitions, and vice-versa. It seems very likely that number development will someday be seen as a complex mosaic of subdevelopments, each one assisting the genesis of its contemporaries and successors, and each similarly assisted by its contemporaries and predecessors. The same general kind of story will eventually be told about most areas of cognitive development, I strongly suspect (Flavell, 1972).

The following is an example of this sort of developmental interaction, loosely derived from Gelman (1972a), Klahr and Wallace (1973), and Schaeffer *et al.* (1974). It is at best a semihypothetical example, since the research support for it is scanty and indirect as yet, but I think you will agree that it has some plausibility. One fragment of number knowledge is the recognition that "two" designates the quantity of any two-item set of things, whatever the things happen to be and whatever their spatial arrangement is. Since a two-item set is so very small, the child can always verify that indeed "two" things are there just by looking (subitizing); that is, he can actually *see* that there are two, rather than one, or three, or some indefinitely larger, nonsubitizable quantity. Also because the set is so small, he can easily count it out, again ending up with that very same number word, "two." He thus has two different and independent procedures for assessing the quantity of this tiny set, subitizing and counting, and because its small size permits him to use these procedures without error, they always yield the same, consistent result. By using these convergent procedures again and again, he could eventually notice that the number of things in this tiny set does not change when spatially rearranged, but does change when things are added or taken away. He also could learn that the number word spoken when the last object is counted (ordinal aspect) is always the very same number word that designates the total quantity of objects in the set (cardinal aspect). And finally, he could eventually infer that counting would also give him the correct numerical value of larger sets—sets too big to "read" by subitizing.

Conversely, all this developing number knowledge should, in its turn, reinforce and motivate the further development of the very number skills that helped engender it. This should be particularly true of counting, in the present case. Accurate counting to ever-higher numbers becomes a more interesting pursuit once the young child recognizes that it amounts to more than just rote-learned verbal recitation, i.e., once he realizes that counting provides·him with quantitative information about the world. According to this hypothesis, then, skills such as counting help give the young child an initial toe hold on the meaning of number; reflexively, his burgeoning number knowledge lends an assist to the further development of these same skills. In all likelihood, reciprocal developmental influences of this sort occur more or less continuously as higher and higher levels of number skill and knowledge acquisition are gradually attained.

Additional highlights of early number development. A few more highlights of early number development are worth noting. First, in number development as in other domains, one is apt to encounter "growth errors" (see p. 74), that curious state of affairs wherein older (but still transitional) children make a certain type of error more frequently and consistently than younger ones. Children who do not conserve number often base their judgment on the length of the two rows of objects; consequently, when one of two initially equal rows is lengthened, the nonconserver is likely to say that there are more objects in that row than in the other. It appears that the older nonconserver is more likely than the younger nonconserver to make consistent use of length as an index of number in this way (Pufall and Shaw, 1972; Pufall, Shaw, and Syrdal-Lasky, 1973). The older nonconserver has presumably learned better than the younger one that longer rows do, in fact, usually contain more elements than shorter rows (the fiendish exception being Piaget's number conservation task), and hence the possible origin of his "growth error."

A recent study by Brush (1972) nicely illuminates the subtle difficulties a young child may have with quantitative thinking. Four, five, and six year old children were given a battery of number tasks, including the following. The subject and the experimenter begin with nine objects each. The subject understands that the two sets are numerically equal. Next he is given four more objects to add to his set and says, in response to nondirective questioning, that he now has more than the experimenter does. The experimenter then adds one object to his own set and again queries the child regarding the comparative magnitudes of the two sets (now 10 versus 13, in case you haven't been keeping track). The questions were always of the general form: Are there the same number of X's here and here? Does one place have more? Why is that?

Some of her subjects said that the experimenter's set had "more" after the one object had been added to it. It appeared from their answers to the "why" question that these subjects may, in characteristic preoperational fashion, have restricted their thinking to the immediate present and/or the currently most salient stimulus event. That is, they acted as though they had focused exclusively on the experimenter's set and what had just happened to it, neglecting to compare it with their own set and what had earlier happened to it. Therefore, the word "more" may have at least momentarily taken on th'e meaning of "more than before," the experimenter's set perhaps being viewed as having more than it had a moment ago. Notice that the earlier comparison could never have revealed any such subtle misunderstanding of "more." When four objects are added to the child's set, his set *both* has more than the experimenter's *and* has more than it did a moment ago. To further confound us, the very same child who misunderstands the intended meaning of "more" in this curious way when the problem is 9 + 1 versus 13 may interpret it absolutely correctly when the problem is 2 + 1 versus 15; the extreme difference in size between the two sets appears to help the child construe the experimenter's question in the conventional way.

A generalization about cognitive growth and illustrations from early number development. This last finding illustrates an important generalization about children's cognitive growth and its assessment, namely, that the maturity of the child's thought and behavior in response to a cognitive task is apt to depend a good deal on the specific structure and content of that task. Some tasks make it easier than others for a child to use a newly acquired and still fragilely held concept, such as "more than" in the above example.

There is another, very interesting illustration of this generalization in the area of number development. It was previewed in the earlier discussion of the possible developmental interplay between skill and knowledge, using the concept of "two" as an example. The illustration is that the child is initially more cognitively mature when dealing with very small, readily subitizable numbers than when dealing with larger ones. His number skill and number knowledge are apt to be far more advanced with respect to numbers like 1, 2, and 3 than they are in respect to 6, or 16, or 60. A task that happens to make use of larger numbers thus may fail to reveal knowledge and skills that the child actually does "possess," at least in the restricted sense of being able to exhibit them in response to an identical task that uses very small numbers. Piaget has referred to this gradual spread of the child's mastery from smaller to larger numbers as the "progressive arithmetization" of the number series (Piaget, 1960).

An ingenious study by Gelman (1972*b*) nicely illustrates this generalization and is also a good act to end the chapter on (it would in any case be a very hard act to follow). Her subjects ranged in age from 3–6½ years. The subject saw two plates, each with a row of mice on it. There were three mice in one row and two in the other. For some subjects at each age level, the lengths of the rows were identical, with the two-mouse row naturally being less dense than the three-mouse one (since the middle mouse was missing). For others, the densities or spaces between the mice were identical, with the three-mouse row consequently being longer than the two-mouse row. The child's initial task was simply to learn which plate was the "winner" (always the one containing three mice) and which the loser (always the two-mouse plate). Notice that the child could learn to identify winners and losers in this task without paying the slightest attention to number and number differences. In the first group, the winner row is denser as well as more numerous; in the second group, it is longer as well as more numerous. The child was reinforced for correctly identifying winner and loser plates but was never told why a given choice was correct. The experimenter never made any reference to number, length, or density, although she did on three randomly chosen trials ask the child why a given plate was winner or loser.

After a series of such trials, the experimenter surreptitiously made a change in the winner row before exposing the plates to the child. For some subjects in each group, she removed one mouse from the center or end of that row, thereby making the two rows numerically equal. For others, she shortened or lengthened the winner row. Surprise reactions were noted and the children were subsequently asked various questions about what happened.

Gelman's results are startling to anyone acquainted with the research literature on Piagetian number conservation. That literature indicates that young children are apt to respond in terms of row length (or, sometimes, row density) when asked questions about the comparative numerical value of two rows; indeed, the child arrives at his nonconservation response by attending to these irrelevant dimensions instead of number or quantity. Gelman found, however, that even her three and four year old subjects conceptualized the winner and loser rows in terms of number rather than length or density. For example, 29 out of 32 three year olds gave number descriptions of the rows at some point in the experimental proceedings, often using the terms "three" and "two"; in contrast, not one ever referred to differences in length or density. Reactions following the experimenter's surreptitious change in the winner row also clearly showed that number, not length or density, was what the children were attending to in this task situation. When length of row was changed (and number not changed), the children showed little surprise and continued to identify the three-mouse row as a winner, even when it had been made shorter than the two-mouse row. When a mouse was removed from the three-mouse row, on the other hand, they showed surprise, were uncertain as to which row was now the winner, asked where the missing mouse was or searched for it, and the like. It was also apparent that most of Gelman's subjects had some understanding of the fact that addition reversed the effect of subtraction in this situation, an obviously important component of mature number knowledge.

Why this striking discrepancy between Gelman's results and those of most number conservation studies? Gelman makes a good argument that successful management of the classical conservation task requires more in the way of cognitive processes and skills than the number knowledge it was designed to measure. Since, according to her argument, task solution here is the result of the integrated functioning of number knowledge X *plus* skill Y, concept Z, etc., a young child could, of course, possess X, lack Y, Z, etc., and hence give a nonconservation response. In support of her position, children of the same age as those who did so well on her mouse task were found to do poorly on a standard conservation task that made use of rows *containing only three items* (Gelman, 1972*b*).

Another reason for the child's precocity on Gelman's mouse task, however, may be the fact that the sets *were* so very, very small. Sets of two and three are easy to subitize and easy to count, even at age 3–4 years, and it is not unreasonable that the young child should first intuit some of the fundaments of the number system when perceiving and acting upon such minute collections. As Gelman points out (1972*b*, p. 89), however, we still have much to learn about how the child's understanding subsequently extends to larger sets and to more complex number properties and skills.

SUMMARY

The period of early childhood extends from late infancy to kindergarten or first grade age (about 2–6 years of age), while that of middle childhood roughly coincides with the elementary school years (about 7–11 years of age). These two periods also correspond, respectively, to Piaget's *preoperational* and *concrete-operational* stages of cognitive growth. Preoperational thinking is often described in purely negative terms, as though it were a cognitive malady from which the child gradually recovers with the advent of concrete operations. A number of positive intellectual accomplishments take place during early childhood, however, and the chapter begins by describing some of the major ones.

There is, first of all, enormous progress in all aspects of *communicability*. Some communications function primarily to *inform* their audience, others to *control* their audience's behavior. If the child is both the sender and the receiver of a verbal, control-type message, he can be said to be engaging in *verbal self-regulation*. The development of verbal self-regulation during early childhood has been the subject of an influential theory by the Russian psychologist A. R. Luria. This development is said to take place in three stages (see Table 3-1). In the first stage (1½–3 years), the controlling message has to be sent by another person, because the child cannot yet use his own speech to direct, control, or regulate his own actions. Moreover, the type of control exercised by this *other-external* speech is primarily *impulsive* rather than *semantic*. That is, the other person's communication functions more like a meaningless physical stimulus than like a meaningful message. As such, it can only inhibit or impel (hence, *impulsive*) ongoing or incipient responses. In the second stage (3–4½ years), the child himself becomes capable of producing overt, self-regulating verbalizations *(self-external)*, but the type of verbal control remains predominantly impulsive. In the final stage (4½ years and older), the child's controlling speech becomes largely internal and subvocal *(self-internal)*, and his behavior conforms to the semantic content of his self command. In sum, he now can do what he silently tells himself to do.

Luria has called attention to an extremely important and pervasive achievement of early childhood, namely, the development of voluntary self direction and control. Doubts can be raised, however, as to the exclusively, or even primarily *verbal* nature of this direction and control. A broader and perhaps more balanced picture of what develops in the area of communicability is shown in Table 3-2. Both informative and control-oriented communications can be nonverbal as well as verbal, and can flow from self to other, other to self, and self to self.

Recent research by the Piagetians has suggested two other major intellectual products of the early-childhood period: *identities* and *functions*. An *identity*, like a conservation, reflects an understanding that something has remained invariant while other things have changed. In the case of an identity, however, the something is a purely qualitative, nonquantifiable invariant. In the case of a conservation, on the other hand, the something is a measurable quantity of some kind. In a test for conservation of liquid quantity, for example, the preoperational child fails to understand that the amount of water stays the same after the pouring (absence of a quantitative conservation), but he does understand that the liquid poured is the "same water" as before (presence of a qualitative identity). Crucially significant identities achieved during early childhood include the belief that one's own unique identity as a particular person, and one's own sexual identity as a female or a male, remain constant over time, growth, and life circumstances.

Functions refer to the child's increasing recognition of simple functional relationships and regular co-occurrences or covariations among everyday objects and events. The preoperational child's functions, like his identities, are purely qualitative affairs. Together with his identities, however, their gradual acquisition makes the young child's world a much more orderly, predictable, coherent, and generally sensible place to live in.

Early-childhood and middle-childhood mentation contrast on a number of dimensions. The former is apt to rely on the immediately-given, *perceived appearance* of things when making judgments; the latter goes on to make *inferences* about the *reality* that underlies these appearances. The older child accordingly is clearer about the epistemologically fundamental distinction between the *phenomenal* or apparent and the *real* or true. The preoperational subject is wont to *center* (*centration*) his attention on a single, particularly salient portion of a stimulus display, whereas the concrete-operational subject *decenters* (*decentration*) his attention, achieving a more balanced analysis of all parts of the display. The latter also attends to the *transformations* that change one *state* of an object or situation to another state; in contrast, the former is more likely to limit his attention to the present state, thus exhibiting a kind of "temporal centration" analogous to the "spatial centration" just mentioned. Finally, early-childhood thought tends to be *irreversible,* while middle-childhood thought tends to be *reversible.* The reversibility of the elementary-school child's mental operations allows him to sense both how one action can literally annul or negate its opposite *(inversion),* and also how one action or factor can more indirectly undo or make up for the effects of another which is not its opposite *(compensation).* In general, the middle-childhood thinker tends to have a more *quantitative attitude* towards problems, and he is more oriented towards *measurement* as a cognitive tool. More general yet, he seems to have a better sense of what an intellectual problem is, what a problem solution would look like, and what sorts of intellectual efforts may be required to get from the problem to the solution.

Developmental changes in the area of number skills and concepts were used as one specific example of cognitive growth during early and middle childhood. (It should be borne in mind that a whole book's worth of other examples could easily be added to this one.) The typical child comes to know, and know how to do, a very great deal in the realm of number during these years. He can *subitize* (perceptually estimate, without counting) very small sets of objects with considerable accuracy. He learns to *count*, both accurately (no objects missed or counted twice) and to task specifications (e.g., count out exactly 10 objects from a set of 16). He knows the relation between the *ordinal* (n^{th}) and the *cardinal* (n) aspects of number. For instance, he knows that if he has just counted the *fifth* object in a series, then there are exactly *five* objects counted out so far. He can read printed *numerals* as well as comprehend spoken numbers. He knows that two sets formed by putting elements in one-one *correspondence* are numerically equal, and that correspondences can be used to divide and multiply sets. He can *compare set sizes*, correctly interpreting and using comparative terms ("more than," "less than," "equals"). He can distinguish set transformations that are *relevant* to number (addition or subtraction of elements) from those that are numerically *irrelevant* (e.g., spacing out the elements), and he knows that any addition of elements to a set can be reversed or annulled by an equivalent subtraction. Finally, he implicitly understands that the set of whole numbers constitutes an ordered, asymmetrical series that is *generated* by addition of integers and can be indefinitely extended in this fashion; he also recognizes that large numbers follow the same rules and are amenable to the same arithmetic operations as small numbers.

Several points were made about developmental precursors of the number knowledge detailed above. First, it is often possible to use one's knowledge of the preoperational mind and of the number system to guess at the behavior the former might produce when trying to operate upon the latter. Second, it is hypothesized that many of the various forms of number knowledge and skill develop in reciprocal, mutually-facilitative interaction with one another, e.g., with form X assisting in the development of form Y and vice-versa. Third, the tendency to use length of row as an index of number actually appears to *increase* for a time during early childhood (a "growth error"), and "more" sometimes takes on unexpected meanings in the young child's comparative judgments of set sizes. Finally, a concrete illustration from the number domain was given of the generalization that a child's ability to cope with a cognitive task depends upon the specific structure and content of that task, as well as upon his general cognitive-developmental level. The concrete illustration is that the young child is typically more advanced in his conceptual management of small numbers (e.g., 2) than of medium or large ones. A recent study by Gelman (1972*b*) was then cited to illustrate the illustration.

4

adolescence

This chapter begins with an account of general cognitive growth from preadolescence to young adulthood (i.e., to biological maturity), thereby concluding the developmental narrative begun in Chap. 2. Possible changes in intellectual functioning during the adult years will not be considered in this book, although some of them undoubtedly are very important. A long section on postinfancy social-cognitive development follows, and the chapter ends with a very brief section on some other aspects of intellectual growth.

ADOLESCENT AND ADULT THINKING

An experimenter and a subject face one another across a table strewn with poker chips of various solid colors (Osherson and Markman, in press). The experimenter explains that he is going to say things about the chips and that the subject is to indicate whether what the experimenter *says* (i.e., his *statements*) is true, false, or uncertain ("can't tell"). He then conceals a chip in his hand and says, "Either the chip in my hand is green or it is not green," or alternatively, "The chip in my hand is green and it is not green." On other trials, he holds up either a green chip or a red chip so that the subject can see it, and then makes exactly the same statements.

Middle-childhood subjects are very likely to try to assess the truth value of these two assertions solely on the basis of the visual evidence. That is, they focus on the concrete, empirical evidence concerning poker chips *themselves* rather than on the nonempirical, purely logical properties of the experimenter's *statements* about the poker chips. Consequently, they say they "can't tell" on the trials where the chip is hidden from view. When it is visible, both statements are judged to be true if the chip is green and false if it is red. In other words, if the color (green) mentioned in the statement matches the color of the visible chip, the statement is said to be true; if there is a mismatch, it is judged false; and if the chip cannot be seen, its truth status is uncertain. What they fail to appreciate is that such "either-or" statements are always true and such "and" statements always false, regardless of the empirical evidence. Logicians call the former a *tautology* and the latter a *contradiction,* and they are true and false, respectively, solely by virtue of their formal properties as propositions.

Adolescent and adult subjects, on the other hand, are likelier to focus on the verbal assertions themselves, and evaluate their internal validity as formal propositions. They appear to have a better intuition than the younger subjects do of the distinction between abstract, purely logical relations and empirical relations. These more mature thinkers recognize that one can sometimes reason about propositions as such, instead of always "seeing right through them" to the entities and states of affairs they refer to. Thus, Osherson and Markman's data hint at some of the important changes in the nature and quality of thought that tend to occur during the adolescent years. I shall now try to describe these changes more explicitly and systematically, drawing most heavily on the Piagetian account of the transition from concrete- to formal-operational thought (Inhelder and Piaget, 1958). Other useful sources on this transition include Flavell (1963, 1970a), Lunzer (1968), Neimark (1975a), and Piaget (1972).

CONTRASTS BETWEEN MIDDLE-CHILDHOOD AND ADOLESCENT-ADULT COGNITION

Real Versus Possible

Piaget has argued convincingly that adolescents and adults tend to differ from children in the way they conceive of the relation between the real and the possible. The elementary school child's characteristic approach to many conceptual problems is to burrow right into the problem data as quickly as possible, using his or her various concrete-operational skills to order and interrelate whatever properties or features of the situation he can detect. His is an earthbound, concrete, practical-minded sort of problem-solving approach, one that persistently fixates on the perceptible and inferable reality right there in front of him. His conceptual approach is definitely not unintelligent, much less non-symbolic, and it certainly generates solution attempts that are far more rational and task-relevant than anything the preoperational child ever produces. It does, however, hug the ground of detected empirical reality rather closely, and speculations about other possibilities, i.e., about other potential, as yet undetected realities, occur only with difficulty and as a last resort. A theorist the elementary-school child is not.

An adolescent or adult is likelier than an elementary-school child to approach problems quite the other way around, at least when operating at the top of his or her capacity. The child usually begins with reality and moves reluctantly, if at all, to possibility; in contrast, the adolescent or adult is more apt to begin with possibility and only subsequently proceed to reality. That is, he may examine the problem situation carefully to try to determine what all the *possible* solutions or states of affairs might be, and then systematically try to discover which of these is, in fact, the *real* one in the present case. For the concrete-operational thinker, the realm of abstract possibility is seen as an uncertain and only occasional extension of the safer and surer realm of palpable reality. For the formal-operational thinker, on the other hand, reality is seen as that particular portion of the much wider world of possibility which happens to exist or hold true in a given problem situation. Possibility is subordinated to reality in the former case, whereas reality is subordinated to possibility in the latter case. The significance of this developing reversal of the reality-possibility relation will become clearer as we examine other differences between the concrete-operational thinking of middle childhood and the formal-operational thinking of adolescence and adulthood.

Empirico-Inductive Versus Hypothetico-Deductive

This subordination of the real to the possible expresses itself in a characteristic method of solving problems. The formal-operational thinker inspects the problem data, *hypothesizes* that such and such a theory or explanation might be the correct one, *deduces* from it that so and so empirical phenomena ought logically to occur or not occur in reality, and then tests his theory by seeing if these predicted phenomena do in fact occur. More informally put, he makes up a plausible story about what might be going on, figures out what would logically have to happen out there in reality if his story were the right one, checks or does experiments out there to see what does, in fact, happen, and then accepts, rejects, or revises his story accordingly. If you think you have just heard a description of textbook scientific reasoning, you are absolutely right. Because of its heavy trade in hypotheses and logical deductions from hypotheses, it is also called *hypothetico-deductive* reasoning, and it contrasts sharply with the much more nontheoretical and nonspeculative *empirico-inductive* reasoning of concrete-operational thinkers.

Notice that this kind of thinking begins with the possible rather than the real in two senses. First, the subject's initial theory is only one of a number of possible ones that he might have concocted. It is itself a possibility rather than a reality, and it is also only one possibility among many. Second, the "empirical reality" predicted by or deduced from his initial theory is itself only a possibility, and also only one possibility among many. Actual, concrete reality only enters the scene when the subject tries to verify his theory by looking for the "reality" it has predicted. If it is not found, new theories and new theory-derived realities will be invented, and thus the sampling of possibilities continues. It is important to emphasize that these theories and theory-derived realities are purely conceptual entities, not physical ones. They are complex objects of thought constructed by a mature, abstract reasoner on the basis of a careful analysis of the problem situation; they are not mere representations of the perceived situation itself.

What would really good, vintage hypothetico-deductive thinking sound like if it were verbalized aloud? Here are two made up examples, "deduced" from those "hypotheses" about formal reasoning given above.

> "Well, what I have just seen gives me the idea that W and *only W might* have the power to cause or produce Z, that the presence of X *might* prevent W from causing Z, and that Y *might* prove to be wholly irrelevant to the occurrence of Z. Now if this idea is right, then Z should occur *only* when W is present and X is absent, whether or not Y is also present. Let's see if these are, in fact, the only conditions under which Z does occur. . . . Oh no, that idea is shot down, because I've just found that Z also occurs sometimes when neither W nor X is present. I wonder why. Hey, I have another idea. . . ."

> "I am a college student of extremely modest means. Some crazy psychologist interested in something called 'formal-operational thinking' has just promised to pay me $10 if I can make a coherent logical argument for the proposition that the federal government should under no circumstances ever give or loan money to impecunious college students. Now what could a nonperson who believed *that* possibly say by way of supporting argument? Well, I suppose he *could* offer this line of reasoning. . . ."

Intrapropositional Versus Interpropositional

The child of elementary school age can construct mental, symbolic representations of concrete reality and can also evaluate their empirical validity under many circumstances. He might, for example, quite explicitly formulate the proposition that there is still the same number of objects in the two rows after one has been spread out (number conservation test), and then he might prove it to you by counting the objects in each row. Although the term "propositional" is often applied to formal-operational reasoning to distinguish it from the concrete-operational type, middle-childhood subjects can indeed produce, comprehend, and verify propositons. There is, nonetheless, an important difference between the two in the way they deal with propositions. The child considers them singly, in isolation from one another, testing each in its turn against the relevant empirical data. Since what is confirmed or infirmed in each case is but a single claim about the external world, Piaget calls concrete-operational thinking *intrapropositional,* i.e., thinking within the confines of a single proposition. While a formal-operational thinker also naturally tests individual propositions against reality, he does something more that lends a very special quality to his reasoning. He reasons about the logical relations that hold *among* two or more propositions, a more subtle and abstract form of reasoning which Piaget terms *interpropositional.* The less mature mind looks only to the *factual* relation between one proposition and the empirical reality to which it refers; the more mature mind looks also or instead to the *logical* relation between one proposition and another.

The first of the two examples of hypothetico-deductive reasoning given in the previous section illustrates this distinction particularly well. The individual's initial theory asserts ("proposes") that the logical relation called *conjunction* holds between three propositions: W is the sole cause of Z *and* (conjunction relation) X neutralizes W's causal effect *and* (conjunction relation) Y is not causally related to Z at all. Conjunction is also used to interconnect a set of hypothetical propositions or predictions about external reality: the conjunction of W present and X absent produces ("conjoins with") the presence of Z, and none of the other logically possible conjunctions involving the presence or absence of W and X will yield Z; moreover, the conjunction of Y's presence or absence with the foregoing changes nothing. There are other logical relations which our imaginary subject might also apply to various combinations of these propositions, although he would not necessarily use the logician's terminology in describing them. For instance, he would understand that, within his theory, the presence of Z (one proposition) *implies* (logical relation) the presence of W (another proposition), whereas the reverse implication, W implies Z, does not hold due to the *incompatibility* (logical relation) between X and Z. Above all, the "if . . . then" phrasing in his second sentence shows that he knows that the entire complex of conjoined propositions which constitutes his theory logically *implies* the entire complex of conjoined propositions which constitutes his predicted reality. That is, he establishes a logical relation between two *sets* of propositions, the constituent propositions of each of which he has already knitted together by logical connectives. This is certainly "interpropositional" thinking in the fullest sense.

It should now be clear why this kind of reasoning is also called *formal*. To reason that one proposition "logically implies" ("contradicts," etc.) another is fundamentally to reason about the relation between a pair of *statements,* not about any *empirical phenomena* to which these statements might refer. The statements in question may not be factually correct assertions about the real objects and events to which they refer; they may not refer to real objects and events in the first place; or indeed they may not even refer to anything at all, real or imaginary. Consider the following bit of formal reasoning: if A is true in all cases where B is true, then B will be false in all cases where A is false (equivalently: if B implies A, then not A implies not B). This is logically valid reasoning, but its validity has to do with the way the statements are related, not with the referential meaning of A and B (they have been given none). It is now apparent why the Osherson and Markman (in press) questions described at the very beginning of this chapter might differentiate a formal reasoner from a concrete one. The formal reasoner knows that the experimenter is asking about the logical truth or falsity of pairs of statements as a joint function of what they state (affirmation, negation) and how they are logically linked (conjunction, disjunction); he knows that the experimenter is not really asking anything about the color of chips.

The second of the two hypothetical hypothetico-deductive reasoners described in the previous section illustrates a closely related insight, namely, that one does not have to believe something is either true or just in order to argue for it (although it sure helps). Formal-operational thinkers understand that logical arguments have a disembodied and passionless life of their own, at least in principle. Concrete-operational thinkers have enough trouble seeing what logically follows from credible premises, let alone from premises that actually contradict one's knowledge, beliefs, or values.

Finally, formal-operational reasoning is an abstract, derivative-type of mentation by virtue of its interpropositional nature, in that it entails thinking about propositions rather than about reality directly. As Piaget puts it, whereas concrete operations are "first degree" operations that deal with real objects and events, formal operations are "second degree" operations that deal with the propositions or statements produced by the first degree, concrete ones (Inhelder and Piaget, 1958, p. 254). Another way to conceptualize it is to say that formal operations constitute a kind of "metathinking," i.e., thinking about thinking itself rather than about objects of thinking. Children certainly are not wholly incapable of this and other forms of "metacognition," e.g., thinking about other psychological processes such as language, perception, and memory (Flavell and Wellman, 1976; Kreutzer, Leonard, and Flavell, 1975). They are not as able and disposed to engage in it as adolescents and adults, however, as we shall see later in this chapter when we look at social-cognitive development during the post-infancy years.

Combinations and Permutations

One difference between concrete-operational and formal-operational reasoners that Piaget makes much of is the latter's superior ability to make a systematic combinatorial analysis of a set of elements (variables, propositions, or whatever). That is, the mature thinker is likelier to be able to construct a systematic, efficient method for generating all the possible combinations (and also permutations) of a set of elements. Given the elements A, B, C, and D, for instance, he could systematically generate all the pairwise combinations by first doing all the ones involving A (AB, AC, AD), then doing all remaining ones involving B, etc.; the possible combinations of three elements (ABC, etc.) could also be produced in a similar, highly systematic way that would ensure that none are missed. His ability to be correspondingly planful and orderly about generating all possible permutations could be tested by seeing how he sets about trying to generate all the different license numbers that can be made up from rearrangements of the numbers 1, 2, 3, and 4 (Leskow and Smock, 1970; Martorano, 1974; Neimark, 1975b).

Piaget believes that the ability to generate all possible combinations, in particular, is especially important in solving scientific, control-of-variables type problems (e.g., Inhelder and Piaget, 1958, Chap. 7). The reason is that the solver has to determine exactly which combinations of the physical variables isolated produced exactly what results. Recall our imaginary thinker who sought to determine just what combinations of variables (W, X, Y, etc.) did and did not co-occur with Z. If he had no method of systematically generating all possible combinations, he might fail to think of some, and would therefore fail to test their effects.

Inversion and Compensation

Another adolescent-adult cognitive achievement emphasized by Piaget is the ability to integrate the two forms of reversible thinking described in Chap. 3, *inversion* and *compensation* (or *reciprocal,* as the latter is often called). Imagine a scale balance that just has had more weight added to one pan than to the other, thereby causing that pan to tip down and the other one to tip up. How could one reverse the effects of that added weight, so that the two pans would, say, be restored to perfect balance, with neither one higher than the other? The older subject is more likely than the younger to know that there are two basically different ways he could counteract the effect of the added weight. The most direct way (inversion) would of course be to remove the added weight, thus literally "reversing" the initial, weight-adding operation. A second and less literal kind of reverse operation here (compensation or reciprocal) would be to leave the added weight on the pan but move the pan itself closer to the fulcrum, so that this arm of the balance is shorter than the other. An alternative form of compensation would be to add weight to the other pan.

Piaget believes that the middle-childhood subject is largely limited to using the inversion form of reversibility in certain task situations and the compensation-reciprocal form in different ones. In contrast, the adolescent and adult can apply them both to the same problem, and more importantly, can also appreciate the dynamic structure or system that they and their two opposite (i.e., direct) operations jointly constitute. In the balance problem and in a number of others, there are two distinct ways to produce an effect and also two distinct ways to counteract it. Inversion and compensation-reciprocal operations figure very importantly in Piaget's mathematical-logical theoretical models of concrete-operational thought. The dynamic system which they and their opposites constitute, together with the earlier mentioned combinatorial system and some propositional logic, play a similarly crucial role in his theoretical model of formal-operational thought (e.g., Flavell, 1963, Chaps. 5 and 6). These models are far too space-consuming to describe in this book, however. Moreover, it seems increasingly likely that they will eventually be judged by the field as inadequate scientific models of middle-childhood and adolescent-adult thinking (Brainerd, 1975, 1976; Bynum, Thomas, and Weitz, 1972; Osherson, 1974; Wason and Johnson-Laird, 1972). Whether history will be any kinder to various neoPiagetian and alternative models recently proposed (e.g., Pascual-Leone's, see Case, 1974; Osherson's, 1974; Klahr and Wallace's, 1973; Schaeffer's, 1975) is of course difficult to predict.

Information Processing Strategies

This category of developmental changes has considerable overlap with the preceding ones and also is very difficult to characterize in a simple and precise way (Neimark, 1970, 1975a). When adolescents and adults attempt to deal with problems or tasks of a wide variety of types, they are generally apt to be more planful, strategic, and efficient than children in their organization and manipulation of the available information. This difference between older and younger individuals is not by any means absolute and would naturally vary with the problems and individuals considered. There is an important trend here, nevertheless. As Chaps. 5 and 6 will show, this trend is very apparent in the more flexible, task-adaptive way older subjects deploy their attention, organize the task data for easier learning and better subsequent recall, and otherwise deal effectively with the situation. With respect to "problem solving" in the narrower, more traditional sense, it is instructive to watch how individuals of different development levels attempt to solve "Twenty Questions" type problems when asked to do so as efficiently as possible, i.e., using the fewest possible questions (Bruner, Olver, and Greenfield, 1966; Eimas, 1970; Neimark and Lewis, 1967; Nelson and Earl, 1973). Adolescents and adults are likelier than children to adopt a systematic question-asking strategy that is very efficient, and also very "strategic" in its abstract, circumlocutious, clearly planful quality. Of course this strategy consists in asking a series of increasingly constraining categorical questions, with each subsequent question carefully selected on the basis of the yes or no answer given to its predecessor. For instance: "Is it alive?"— "Yes"—"Is it animal rather than vegetable?"—"No"—"Do people eat any part of it?" etc. It is easy to see the systematicity that this approach shares with a methodical generation of all possible combinations or permutations, with a dogged checking out of all variables that might have causal effects, and other formal-operational propensities mentioned earlier. The younger subject is likelier to adopt the more concrete-minded and considerably less efficient procedure of asking specific questions from the outset ("Is it a dog?," etc.). Notice just how concrete this approach is and just how unconcrete the other is. You told the subjects to find out what object you are thinking of and the younger ones do, in a sense, exactly what you told them to: they ask a question the answer to which could indeed identify that object. In contrast, the older ones ask a question the answer to which they know full well could not *possibly* specify that object. They are prepared to get to the object only at the end of a series of questions and answers. This is an "information processing strategy" by the most stringent definition. It is, moreover, one that the subject himself spontaneously imported into the situation; you never told him to solve the problem that way. This tendency to impose one's own structure on the task situation, rather than simply trying to decipher the structure that is already there, is, of course, consonant with what was said earlier about beginning with the possible rather than the real, and with being hypothetico-deductive rather than only or always empirico-inductive. As Lunzer puts it, formal reasoning entails a "systematic *reconstruction* of reality" (1968, p. 300, italics mine).

Consolidation and Solidification

It certainly seems reasonable to assume that the sensory-motor skills and knowledge acquired during infancy become further consolidated and solidified during the postinfancy years. It seems equally plausible that the same thing may happen to middle-childhood cognitive acquisitions. I refer here particularly to the various concrete-operational attainments described in Chap. 3, together with the numerous others that were alluded to (p. 86) but not described for want of space. What could the assumption mean that these attainments become "further consolidated and solidified" during adolescence and early adulthood? It might mean that they are progressively integrated into more and larger networks or structures of knowledge, thereby becoming related to an ever greater number of other concepts, beliefs, skills, etc. To illustrate, the notion of "adolescent-adult thinking" has, I hope, been acquiring just that sort of added conceptual wiring in your head as you continue to read this chapter. It might also mean that, should the adolescent or adult have occasion to think about something that had originally been acquired during middle childhood, he now would be capable of thinking about it in a formal-operational as well as a concrete-operational way. The outcome might be, for instance, new and deeper justifications for a belief that had earlier been more minimally justified, if ever explicitly rationalized at all.

These two interpretations of "further consolidated and solidified" are not really very different. Under both interpretations, a concrete-operational attainment is presumed to undergo some sort of change in its relation to the rest of the cognitive system. It does so because the rest of the cognitive system—its "internal environment," so to speak—has itself undergone developmental change as the individual approaches intellectual maturity. Furthermore, since concrete-operational attainments will continue to be useful and valid adaptations to reality in adulthood as in childhood, we may assume that the above-mentioned change in relation does indeed have a consolidating and solidifying effect on them. Additional maturation and experience should fix them more firmly in the subject's cognitive system and consequently should make them more resistant than they initially were to any attempt to alter or extinguish them.

There is much less evidence for consolidation and solidification than for the other developmental changes described in this chapter, but there is a little (see also Flavell, 1971a, pp. 431–435). The best available evidence concerns two concrete-operational achievements which were not described in Chap. 3, namely, conservation and transitivity of weight. The experimenter takes two identical balls of clay and puts one on each pan of a balance scale. The two pans remain horizontal, i.e., in equilibrium, and the subject agrees that the two balls weigh the same. The balls are then removed from the scale and one of them is deformed in some way, e.g., flattened into a pancake or rolled into a sausage shape. The subject would fail to evidence a belief in conservation of weight if he or she denied that the two pieces of clay would necessarily still weigh the same and still depress the two scale pans equally. A nonconserver of weight is therefore someone who does not understand that object weight remains unchanged when object shape is changed. An individual would fail to show a recognition of the transitivity property of weight if, having established by using the balance that object A weighs the same as object B and that object B weighs the same as object C, he denied that A had to weigh the same as C. The same would be true if "less than" or "more than" were substituted for "the same as" in the foregoing sentence. Hence, a person is said to recognize the transitive nature of weight relations if he understands that, for any weights A, B, and C, $A = B$ and $B = C$ always implies $A = C$, that $A < B$ and $B < C$ always implies $A < C$, and that $A > B$ and $B > C$ always implies $A > C$.

Recent evidence suggests that subjects' beliefs in both conservation and transitivity of weight, initially acquired during middle childhood, tend to become firmer as they move into adolescence and adulthood (Miller, 1973; Miller and Lipps, 1973; Miller, Schwartz and Stewart, 1973). Recall from Chap. 2 (p. 44) that infants' tacit beliefs in the permanence of objects have been assessed by presenting them with trick conditions which apparently violate the object-permanence rule. An infant who believes in object permanence ought to be and is surprised and perplexed if an object that had just been covered is nowhere to be seen when the cover is removed. Miller and his colleagues have similarly put older subjects' beliefs in weight conservation and transitivity to very severe tests by similar machinations. Their trick is to rig the scale balance with electromagnets so that it gives false weight information on any trial the experimenter chooses. What does a subject who has previously demonstrated both beliefs say when confronted with, for example, a flattened ball that now inexplicably appears to weigh more than what had just been its exact duplicate, or a series of pairwise weighings of three objects that yields the startling information $A = B$, $B = C$, and $A < C$? In the case of the conservation belief, only a minority of elementary-school subjects who had initially been diagnosed as weight conservers continued to maintain this belief in the face of such apparently disconfirming evidence. College students, on the other hand, showed considerably more fidelity to the conservation concept, although some of them did succumb. Transitivity of weight proved to be a sturdier concept. A minority rather than a majority of Miller's younger elementary-school subjects abandoned it when given false feedback, and a significantly smaller proportion of his older elementary subjects abandoned it. College students' beliefs in weight transitivity were not assessed in these studies, but presumably they would have been sturdier yet. Miller *et al.*'s (1973) conclusions speak to the idea of post-childhood consolidation and solidification of childhood acquisitions:

> . . . there may be developmental changes in the certainty with which a concept such as conservation of weight is held, changes which extend well beyond the point at which the child is usually considered to "have" the concept (p. 316).

Some Research Examples

Predictably, the most original and still the most interesting research in this area is described in Inhelder and Piaget (1958). The Piagetian formal-operational tasks and the behaviors they elicit are also summarized in Flavell (1963), Neimark (1975a), and numerous other places, with Neimark's (1975a) review chapter being the best source I know for subsequent research findings using these tasks. Her chapter also reports a number of other scientific results and conclusions not mentioned in the present chapter concerning the transition to adolescent-adult thought.

Shapiro and O'Brien (1970) assessed 6–13 year old children's understanding of logical necessity in a rather interesting way. They used test items of the following types:

1. If this is Room 9, then it is fourth grade.
   This is Room 9. Is it fourth grade?
2. If this is Room 9, then it is not fourth grade.
   This is Room 9. Is it fourth grade?
3. If this is Room 9, then it is fourth grade.
   This is not Room 9. Is it fourth grade?

The child could answer each question "Yes," "No," or "Not enough clues." When, as in items (1) and (2), the premises allowed a definite, logically necessary conclusion, even the younger children usually answered correctly. That is, they usually responded "Yes" to (1) and "No" to (2). On the other hand, they seldom gave the correct answer, "Not enough clues," to items of type (3), usually answering "No" instead. They failed to understand that no logically necessary conclusion concerning Room 9 followed from the premises in (3). It could even be argued, in fact, they may not have done much if any genuinely logical reasoning at all, even in the type (1) and (2) items (Knifong, 1974). The older subjects performed considerably better than the younger ones on these "open" items, as the authors call them, but even the 13 year olds got many of them wrong. Shapiro and O'Brien conclude: "The data from the present study suggest that hypothetical deductive thinking—at least that which is consistent with mathematical logic—cannot at all be taken for granted in students of elementary-school age" (1970, p. 829).

Bang and Lunzer (see Lunzer, 1968) have done some intriguing experiments on "false conservations." The objects and object transformations described below are not the ones actually used by Bang and Lunzer, but they illustrate the general point of their investigations. Suppose I show you two identical, circular wire hoops, lying flat on a table side by side. You agree that the two hoops have identical perimeters and enclose identical areas of table surface. Suppose I then compress one of the hoops a trifle, making it a bit ellipsoid in shape. Are the two perimeters still equal? Are the two enclosed areas still equal? Suppose I keep on compressing that hoop, bringing its two long sides closer together, and keep asking you these two questions. . . . Suppose instead I show you two sheets of $8\frac{1}{2} \times 11$ inch typing paper placed side by side on the table and you agree that their perimeters and areas are exactly the same. Then I cut a 2×11 inch strip off of one of those papers and lay it down so that its 2 inch base just touches the top edge of the $6\frac{1}{2} \times 11$ inch house with a 2×11 inch chimney on top of it. Is the perimeter of this house-plus-chimney still equal to that of the comparison, uncut piece of paper? Are their areas still equal?

The meaning of "false conservation" is undoubtedly now clear. In the first case, no wire is added or taken away during the compression transformation, and one might for that or other reasons (e.g., compensation arguments) expect that the perimeters and areas should remain identical. In fact, however, perimeter does but area does not. In the second case the opposite is true, in that the cutting and respositioning transformations "conserve" area but not perimeter. Clearly, one has to watch what one is about when being tested by Piagetians, among whom even conservation is no longer sacred.

Bang and Lunzer found that children of preoperational age tended to deny that either perimeter or area was conserved in either situation.

Middle-childhood subjects, on the other hand, tended to believe that both properties were conserved in both situations. Moreover, they often continued to adhere rigidly to these conservation beliefs in the face of increasingly disconfirming visual evidence. Adolescent subjects were likelier to sort out which property was conserved and which not, either at the outset or after a little experience with the transformation process. Moreover, they were often able to theorize about why one was conserved and the other not in a manner that Lunzer (1968) found compellingly formal-operational.

Finally, a more traditional investigation by Martorano (1974) is worth mentioning because it appears to be the most comprehensive follow-up to date of Inhelder and Piaget's (1958) research on formal-operational reasoning. The subjects were white, middle-class girls of 100–120 IQ, 20 from each of grades 6, 8, 10, and 12; the age range was 11–18 years. Each subject was individually administered 10 of Inhelder and Piaget's formal-operational tasks (previous follow-ups have not given anywhere near that many of their tasks to the *same* subjects, according to Martorano). Quality of performance on all tasks continued to improve across the entire age range, with the greatest improvement occurring between eighth and tenth grades for this particular sample. The tasks showed marked and fairly consistent (across subjects) differences in difficulty level. To take the most extreme discrepancy, 60 percent of the sixth graders were judged to handle one problem in a formal-operational manner, whereas only 15 percent of the twelfth graders were judged to do the same on another. Only two of the subjects appeared to be consistently formal-operational on all 10 tasks. The proportions of twelfth graders scored as formal-operational on each of the 10 tasks were: 0.15 (the difficult task just mentioned), 0.45, 0.50, 0.55, 0.55, 0.60, 0.60, 0.85, 0.90, and 0.95. One of Martorano's conclusions seems reasonable in view of these data, and also serves as a good bridge to the chapter section that follows: "Thus, formal operations thinking, while emerging during adolescence, cannot be said to represent the characteristic mode of thought for that developmental period" (1974, p. 43).

CONCLUSIONS ABOUT ADOLESCENT AND ADULT THINKING

Martorano's conclusion suggests that what I have said so far about adolescent-adult thinking may not be quite the whole truth; it implies that the developmental story here may not be quite as neat and clearcut as I have made it out to be. Certainly it is true that all the sophisticated forms of abstract thinking and problem solving described on previous pages really do occur in human beings. It is also true that when they do occur, the human being carrying them out is far likelier to be an adolescent or an adult than a child. There is, in other words, developmental-psychological reality in the picture I have been painting of adoescent-adult thought. That picture starts to become fuzzy, however, as soon as we ask how universal or even typical these forms of thought are among normal, mature members of our species the world around.

Neimark's (1975a) conclusion is similar to Martorano's, and it probably reflects the current consensus on this question:

> Logical reasoning, as reflected in consistent performance across a broad class of instances, does not appear until adolescence and even at that age is by no means a universal attainment of all adolescents (p. 570).

There is, I think, a tenable generalization about Piagetian development that would automatically raise questions about the universality of formal-operational and related types of mature cognition. The generalization is that the higher the Piagetian cognitive stage, the less inevitable its full attainment by normal individuals across all human environments. Full sensory-motor development must be universally completed, one would think. At least some degree of concrete-operational ability might also be universal or nearly so among normal adults, although it is hard to be really certain of even this on the basis of existing cross-cultural evidence (Dasen, 1972). The universality of formal-operational achievements would consequently be even less certain.

What exactly could be meant by "universal" here, and might not our degree of uncertainty concerning universality depend upon how rigorously and literally we construed the term? An extremely rigorous interpretation would have it that (1) all biologically normal (e.g., non-retarded) adults in all cultures and subcultures (2) can and (3) spontaneously do employ (4) all of the complex types of post-childhood thinking this chapter and other cited sources (e.g., Neimark, 1975a) have described (5) at a high level of expertise (6) in all problem situations and all content areas where such thinking is applicable. It can be quickly agreed that all six of these conditions or criteria do *not* simultaneously hold true in reality; we can be positive that there is nowhere near *that* much universality here. Nonetheless, a brief discussion of the factual status of these six criteria may help us obtain a more accurate conception of adolescent-adult cognition.

As to criterion (1), it seems almost banal to claim that the adult members of some human groups (cultures, subcultures, occupations, etc.) would for various good reasons exhibit less of this hypothetico-deductive, interpropositional, etc., thinking than the adult members of other groups. Some life circumstances simply provide more training in it, practice at it, and reasons for doing it than others, and people are nothing if not generally adaptive to their life circumstances. Similarly, an individual who is (2) capable of such thinking may not (3) actually use it in a given problem situation. Again, the possible reasons are myriad. For instance, he or she may misunderstand or fail to accept the task demands, may feel that a different approach is more appropriate to the situation, or may just be having an off day intellectually. If there is one truism in this field, it is that cognitive performance is seldom a wholly trustworthy index of cognitive capacity. In addition, an adult is likely to (4) find some types of reasoning operations more unnatural and difficult than others, and may therefore not perform them (5) efficiently, accurately, or at all. And finally (6), the specifics of the problem or content area are likely to make an enormous difference in the cognitive approach used, especially when considered in interaction with the previous five variables.

Here are some illustrations of the foregoing points. There is considerable evidence (e.g., Henle, 1962; Wason and Johnson-Laird, 1972) that even well educated adults are susceptible to all sorts of errors on reasoning problems. They generally appear to have more trouble with semantically "empty," purely formal-logical problems than with more substantive and meaningful problems. This may be true even when the latter are scientific problems dealing with physical causality, such as those used by Inhelder and Piaget (1958). Adults usually do better when thinking abstractly about real, concrete problems, even scientific ones, than when thinking abstractly about abstract, wholly logical problems that seem to have no reality outside of a logic textbook. Real problems with meaningful content are obviously more important in everyday human adaptation, and it is possible that these are the kinds of problems our cognitive apparatus has evolved to solve. In reviewing the Wason and Johnson-Laird book (1972), Hunt (1974, p. 23) says:

> What gives rise to such fallacious thinking? I conjecture it may be behavior with a survival value. Wason and Johnson-Laird have studied reasoning in the artificial laboratory situation in which things are true or not true. Let us call this the Boolean world. Their subjects do not live in it. Instead they must reason about things that are known only statistically, happen with multiple causes, and finally, happen in a world in which a thing may be partly true and partly false. . . . If this is everyday experience, is it surprising that subjects fail to adapt to Boolean reasoning immediately upon entering the psychologist's laboratory?

There are other sorts of errors that may also stem in part from a mismatch between certain kinds of formal reasoning problems and the kinds that mature people have become familiar with from everyday life (e.g., Wason and Johnson-Laird, 1972). Adults have trouble reasoning about negated propositions ("Not A implies . . ." versus "A implies . . ."). They may fail to interpert "or," "some," and other logical terms "correctly," i.e., as a logician would mean them to be understood. They are very likely to want to test a theory by adducing confirming evidence for it, rather than by seeing if anything that the theory says should not happen does, in fact, happen. (Many social scientists actually do the same thing, I strongly suspect.) And finally—shades of Shapiro and O'Brien (1970)—sometimes they will mistakenly interpret "if A, then B" as "if and only if A, then B," thereby thinking that if A implies B, B must also imply A.

Piaget himself (1972) is well aware that there are serious questions about the universality of formal-operational thinking as a developmental outcome. He suggests that most adults indeed may be capable of such thinking, but perhaps only in problem areas where their interest, experience, and expertise is greatest (criterion 6 above). An auto mechanic, for example, might engage in genuine hypothetico-deductive reasoning when trouble-shooting a car (controlling variables, testing hypotheses etc.), but perhaps not in most other daily activities. Piaget seems to have adults from industrialized societies in mind when making this interesting suggestion (pp. 9–11), although he does not explicitly exclude members of nonindustrial, nonliterate cultures. On the other hand, Tulkin and Konner (1973) very explicitly include the latter. They report that two Western scientists (Konner was one) participated in a series of informal "seminars" with several adult Kalahari Bushmen who were experienced and knowledgeable about hunting. What they observed and concluded seems germane to Piaget's suggestion:

> As scientific discussions the seminars were among the most stimulating the Western observers had ever attended. Questions were raised and tentative answers *(hypotheses)* were advanced. Hypotheses were always labeled as to the degree of certainty with which the speaker adhered to them, which was related to the type of data on which the hypothesis was based (p. 35).
>
> The process of tracking, specifically, involves patterns of inference, hypothesis-testing, and discovery that tax the best inferential and analytic capacities of the human mind. Determining, from tracks, the movements of animals, their timing, whether they are wounded and if so how, and predicting how far they will go and in which direction and how fast, all involve repeated activation of hypotheses, trying them out against new data, integrating them with previously known facts about animal movements, rejecting the ones that do not stand up, and finally getting a reasonable fit, which adds up to meat in the pot (p. 36).

Finally, it strikes me that there might be a substantial gain in degree of universality if we relaxed criterion (5) in the following way. As indicated above, there is abundant evidence that even well educated and sophisticated reasoners are prone to fallacies and other errors when dealing with certain kinds of formal reasoning problems. Nevertheless, I suspect that they and many other adolescents and adults have a sense of the general sort of cognitive enterprise these problems entail. Much more than middle-childhood subjects, I believe, they are likely to have at least some intuition that there exists an abstract realm of thought and discourse which has special, inviolable rules for getting from here to there, and that these rules are independent of content. They may mistakenly conclude that *B* implies *A* if *A* implies *B,* or commit other logical gaffes; indeed, they might refuse to work on such silly-looking problems at all. Nevertheless, they are likelier than the child to recognize that things *do* "have to" follow from other things in such problems, and also that what follows from what does *not* depend upon the meanings of *A* and *B*. In short, skill in actually playing the logic game and other abstract games may vary considerably from adult to adult, but even the poorer players may know something about the general *sort* of game it is. Consider the following logical problem: If the presence of either *A* or *B* or both implies the presence of both *C* and *D,* does the absence of *C* necessarily imply the absence of *B?* Trying to solve logical problems like these hurts my head and I do not always get them right, even when I take a lot of time and care. The same may be true of you. However, I think we both understand what general sorts of intellectual creatures such problems are, and I think this was probably not the case during the first decade of our lives. As I said, actually solving them is quite another thing: "At best, we can all think like logicians; at worst, logicians all think like us" (Wason and Johnson-Laird, 1972, p. 245).

SOCIAL COGNITION

As indicated in Chap. 2 (p. 49), social cognition takes humans and human affairs as its objects. Machines, mathematics, and moral judgments are all objects and products of human cognition, for instance, but only the latter would be considered a topic within human *social* cognition. Social cognition deals with the strictly social world, not the physical and logical-mathematical ones, even though all three worlds obviously have man's fingerprints all over them. The scientific investigation of this kind of cognition currently is of interest to psychologists, but its actual practice has undoubtedly been of even greater interest to practically everybody since the dawn of the species. Numerous motives ranging from self-preservation to idle curiosity, must continually impel people the world over to try to make sense out of themselves, other people, interpersonal relations, social customs and institutions, and other interesting objects of thought within the social world. And psychologists well ought to be interested in the nature and development of processes which are that significant in everyday mental life.

Needless to say, the social-cognitive achievements of infancy described in Chap. 2 are rudimentary in comparison with those which occur in subsequent years. There are a number of useful reviews of post-infancy developments in this area, including Flavell (1970a, 1974), Kohlberg (1969), Rest (1974), and especially Shantz (1975).

The Nature of Social Cognition

What are the major classes of objects and events towards which social cognitions are directed? Here is a good list:

> The observations or inferences we make are principally about intentions, attitudes, emotions, ideas, abilities, purposes, traits, thoughts, perceptions, memories—events that are *inside* the person and strictly psychological. Similarly, we attend to certain psychological qualities of relationships *between* persons, such as friendship, love, power, and influence. We attribute to a person properties of *consciousness* and *self-determination,* and the capacity for *representation of his environment,* which in turn mediates his actions (Tagiuri, 1969, p. 396).

I would add: that the persons in question include the self as well as others; that we think about social groups and people in general as well as about particular human beings (e.g., we think about human nature, and we think about governments or other social structures, with their constituent roles, rules, and institutions); that we ponder what individuals and groups *ought* to do (for moral, legal, or social-conventional reasons), and why, as well as what they actually *do* do; and that there are no doubt other interesting classes of social-cognitive phenomena psychologists have not yet identified for study. The possible objects of human social cognition are very numerous and very diverse, and psychology's present representation of them is almost certainly insufficiently rich and inclusive.

At least part of what social cognition includes is schematized in Fig. 4-1. *S* means the self and *O* means another person or group of persons. The dashed arrows represent acts and products of social cognition. They mainly include a person's inferences, beliefs, or conceptions about the inner-psychological processes or attributes of human beings, and are therefore represented in Fig. 4-1 as penetrating into the interior of their targets. The solid arrows represent overt social acts rather than covert mental ones, and consequently they cannot "penetrate" their objects in quite this sense. For instance, I may be able to infer what is

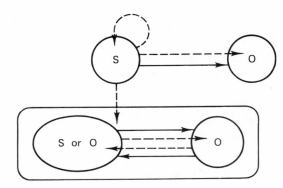

Figure 4-1. A representation of social cognition.

going on inside your head if given enough clues (social cognition), but I can affectionately pat only the outside of it (social act). The top part of Fig. 4-1 shows that the self can have all manner of cognitions about the self as well as about another person or group of persons. The bottom part shows that social cognition can also encompass various relationships and interactions among individuals or groups (Selman and Byrne, 1974). It further shows that the self can be one of the interacting individuals the self is mentally representing, and that the interactions represented can themselves include covert social cognitions as well as overt social acts. Thus, I may think about myself in isolation, about you in isolation, and also about the social acts and social cognitions each of us may carry out with respect to the other.

Another way to characterize the domain is to indicate some very general preconditions for the successful execution of any specific act of social thinking (Flavell, 1974; Flavell, Botkin, Fry, Wright, and Jarvis, 1968). There are at least three such preconditions: *Existence, Need,* and *Inference.*

Existence refers to the person's basic knowledge that a particular fact or phenomenon of the social world exists as one of life's possibilities. In order to think about something in the social world, one obviously first has to be aware of its very existence as a possible object of social cognition. If a young child has not yet become aware that people even *have* such psychological goings on as percepts, thoughts, and motives, for instance, he or she manifestly cannot try to infer their presence and detailed characteristics in particular people on particular occasions. The point is a most unprofound one: there scarcely can be any thinking about social-cognitive phenomena if the very existence of such phenomena is not yet represented by the thinker.

Need refers to the disposition or sensed need to attempt an act of social cognition. A person may know perfectly well that he and other people have experiences called feelings (Existence), and yet he may not even try to diagnose them when opportunities arise (Need). He may not think to, may not want to, or may not see any point to making such an effort.

Inference concerns the skill or capacity to carry off a given form of social thinking successfully. I may know of the existence of the type of thought or feeling you are currently having (Existence), and I may badly want to figure out what you are presently experiencing (Need), and yet I may simply not have the ability to identify it on the basis of the evidence provided (Inference). I can infer, perhaps, that you are feeling something unpleasant, and knowing even that much, of course, requires some Inference ability. However, lack of sufficient evidence, my general inadequacies as a people reader, or both, may prevent my obtaining a more detailed and precise understanding of exactly what sort of unpleasant affect you are experiencing.

The distinction between Existence and Inference is especially clear in the area of cognitions about visual percepts. I sit on one side of a random arrangement of complex objects (e.g., four vases of different shapes and colors, each containing a variety of different flowers) and you sit on the other. My task is to select, from a large number of different photographs of the array taken from different positions, that photograph which shows exactly how the array looks to you, from your vantage point. I am not allowed to walk around and look; I must figure out what you see from where I sit. The problem of computing (Inference) another person's visual perspective in such tasks can range from the trivially easy to the near impossible, depending upon the complexity of the array, the set of photographs used, etc. Even in the most difficult of these tasks, however, I know perfectly well that you have *some* visual experience of the array, just as I do (Existence). I also know some other things that require little or no on-the-spot computation, and therefore seem more Existence-like than Inference-like. For instance, I know at the outset that you have one and only one view of the array and that, whatever that view is, it is different from my own; consequently, only one photograph in the set can possibly be the right one, and any photograph depicting my own view can automatically be excluded (Salatas and Flavell, 1976).

To characterize the general nature of social cognition in these ways is implicitly to indicate what the child's developmental task is—what social-cognitive development is the development of. It is the developing awareness and general knowledge (Existence) of the enormous variety of possible social-cognitive objects alluded to in the first part of this chapter section. It is also a developing awareness (Need) of when and why one might or should try to take readings of such objects. Finally, it is the development of a wide variety of cognitive skills (Inference)— still largely unknown—with which to take these readings.

Parallels in the Development of Social and Nonsocial Cognition

There is a good mnemonic for reconstructing much of what happens during social-cognitive development. Just remember that the head that thinks about the social world is the selfsame head that thinks about the nonsocial world. It would therefore be astonishing if none of the developmental trends in nonsocial thinking already described could be seen in the area of social thinking. Their social vestments might disguise them a bit, but they ought to be detectable if one looks carefully. The following are the ones I think I have unmasked.

Surface to depth. We have seen (pp. 79–80) that cognition about nonsocial phenomena begins with surface appearances alone and only later gets beneath the surface to construct an inferred underlying reality. Social-cognitive development also proceeds from surface to depth. Children begin by reading only the most external, immediately perceptible attributes of themselves, other people, social interactions, and other social-cognitive objects. They pay attention to people's appearance and overt behavior, but they initially do not use these or other kinds of evidence to make inferences about the covert social-psychological processes, meanings, and causes which underlie them. The dashed arrows in Fig. 4-1 initially stop at the boundaries of those circles and ellipses, and only gradually penetrate into the interior.

Spatial and temporal centrations. The social cognition of younger children also shows spatial and temporal centrations (pp. 80–82). They are prone to attend only to the most obvious and highly salient features of a social object or situation, neglecting subtler but possibly more important features (spatial centration). For example, the young child can read the big, obvious signs of gaiety in another, but he will require additional social-cognitive growth before he can also pick up the little, nonobvious signs that indicate that this individual's gaiety is forced and false. Seeing through social facades is not the long suit of young children, any more than seeing through Piagetian-task nonconservation facades is. The same applies to temporal centration. The younger child is likely to hew closely to the immediately present social situation. It is only later that he will spontaneously infer its likely past antecedents and future consequences, e.g., what prior social experiences, motives, intentions, etc. led the people to act as they are now acting, and what will be the likely next steps in the episode. The child only gradually learns to integrate over time and events, to interlink states and transformations, and this is as true in the social domain as in the nonsocial one.

Invariant formation. Another parallel has been mentioned already (pp. 47–48, 72), namely, that there is a good deal of invariant formation in both worlds. Children gradually come to think of themselves and others as stable human beings who conserve, over time and circumstances, their personhoods, personalities, social and sexual roles and identities, and many other attributes. Day to day changes in one's own or another's mood and behavior come to be construed as variations on an enduring theme, rather than as a succession of unrelated melodies. The cognitive construction of these social invariants can, of course, be viewed as a special type of temporal decentration, one which identifies important personal continuities which persist over time.

Quantitative attitude. The child was said (pp. 85–86) to acquire a quantitative attitude toward physical phenomena, entailing a conception of how to measure things in a precise fashion. Similarly, in the social realm the child develops a quasimetric conception of rewards and punishments. He gradually comes to believe that rewards and punishments should be doled out in strict proportion to the recipient's deserts, however these be ascertained (the criteria become more sophisticated with age). This conception includes ideas about "fair" versus "unfair" distribution or exchange of goods ("fair" shares and "fair" trades), "fair" versus "unfair" punishments, etc., and all of these ideas seem to have a semiquantitative cast to them.

Metacognition. As indicated earlier (p. 107), there is a sense in which interpropositional, "second degree" thinking is automatically social-cognitive in nature: propositions are stated thoughts rather than physical objects, and hence thinking about such thoughts represents a kind of social cognition. During the adolescent years, especially, people are likely to develop a heightened consciousness of their own and other people's psychological processes (metacognition). These processes gradually become "objects of contemplation" (p. 39)—things to think about rather than merely things to do. Accordingly, the individual becomes more introspective, much given to scrutinizing his own thoughts, feelings, and values. He also spends more time wondering about those of significant others. In particular, he may wonder what they think of his outer appearance and behavior (self-consciousness), and also what they might know or guess about his inner world.

Abstract and hypothetical thinking. Similarly, the abstract and hypothetical quality of mature thinking is also visible when its cognitive objects are social. The person becomes capable of thinking about groups, institutions, and people in general (concepts of "human nature," etc.) as well as specific individuals. Moreover, specific individuals, both self and others, become endowed with more general, enduring traits and dispositions as well as more specific and transient processes. Likewise, the mature thinker may think about all manner of abstract ideas and ideals in such areas as morality, religion, and politics. Finally, the hypotheses he makes in a Piagetian task situation have their social-cognitive counterparts in the speculations he makes about his personal future. Elkind (1967) has written insightfully about these and other social-cognitive expressions of formal-operational intellectual capacity.

Cognitive shortcomings. It was stated earlier in this chapter (pp. 116–17) that even mature thinkers are vulnerable to all sorts of errors and fallacies when reasoning about impersonal phenomena. The same is true for social reasoning. Social psychologists and personality theorists (e.g., Kelley, 1973; Mischel, 1973) have shown that our inferences about ourselves and other people, although by no means wholly inaccurate, are subject to various biases and distortions. For example, we probably tend to overestimate the degree to which a person's behavior is governed by stable, internal traits versus variable, external circumstances. This is especially true when trying to explain another's behavior rather than our own (Mischel, 1973, p. 264): you tripped because you are clumsy (a stable trait) whereas I tripped because it was dark (a variable circumstance).

The ailment that most plagues social cognition, however, is what Piaget calls *egocentrism*. Piagetian egocentrism can be roughly defined as a failure to differentiate or distinguish clearly between one's own point of view and another's. For instance, my assessment of your opinions and feelings about something is egocentric to the degree that I have unwittingly misattributed my own opinions and feelings to you. Piagetian egocentrism is often assumed to be very prevalent in early childhood social cognition and to decline thereafter, much like logical errors in nonsocial cognition. While there is something in this assertion, it does not represent the whole truth about egocentrism, as Piaget and his followers have been well aware (e.g., Elkind, 1967).

The following is only one psychologist's ideas about egocentrism, and should therefore not be read uncritically. Unlike, say, nonconservation of number, I believe we are "at risk" (almost in the medical sense) for egocentric thinking all of our lives, just as we are for certain logical errors. The reason lies in our psychological design in relation to the job to be done. We experience our own point of view more or less directly, whereas we must always attain the other person's in a more indirect manner. Furthermore, we are usually unable to turn our own viewpoint off completely when trying to infer the other's. Our own perspective produces a clear signal that is much louder to us than the other's, and it usually continues to ring in our ears while we try to decode the other's. It may take considerable skill and effort to represent another's point of view accurately through this kind of noise, and the possibility of egocentric distortion is ever present. For example, the fact that you thoroughly understand calculus constitutes an obstacle to your continuously keeping in mind my ignorance of it while trying to explain it to me; you may momentarily realize how hard it is for me, but that realization may quietly slip away once you get immersed in your explanation. Thus, we can no more "cure" ourselves of our susceptibility to egocentrism than we can cure ourselves, say, of our difficulties in understanding two simultaneously-presented messages. Both cases represent a human information processing limitation with respect to a certain class of cognitive task.

A sense of the game. Unlike the young child, however, the mature thinker knows that others do have cognitive perspectives which differ from his own, that his own perspective may interfere with his representation of them, and other Existence-type truths about social cognition. Therein lies a final parallel with nonsocial cognition. Grown-ups the world around surely have developed some "sense of the game" of people-reading, just as they have in the case of impersonal thinking games (p. 118). As with the latter, the disposition and ability to play this kind of game no doubt shows enormous individual and cultural differences. Once again, however, even the poorer and less motivated players have a sense of the enterprise, and that sense is the product of development. Moreover, it is my guess that the average quantity and quality of adult play may, in fact, be higher here than in the impersonal realm. For the majority of people, I suspect, other human beings and their activities constitute the most interesting and challenging objects of thought that their daily lives afford, and therefore much of their richest and most complex cognition may be social cognition.

SPECIFIC TOPICS

Percepts

This topic concerns the child's developing knowledge and inferential ability concerning people's perceptual acts and experiences. He or she gradually must come to understand, for instance, that other people also see things, and that the nature of another person's visual experience at a given moment can often be inferred from various clues (e.g., the apparent direction of the person's gaze or the spatial relation between him and what he is looking at). Recent evidence suggests that there may be at least two, roughly distinguishable developmental levels or stages of Existence-type knowledge about visual percepts (Flavell, 1974; Masangkay *et al.*, 1974).

At the higher one, called Level 2, the child has a symbolic-representational (i.e., not merely sensory-motor) understanding of the fact that the selfsame object or array of objects presents different appearances when viewed from different spatial locations. The Level 2 child basically understands the idea of people having different, position-determined perspectives or views of the same visual display. He is aware that even though he and another person both see the very same object, they nonetheless see it differently—have different visual experiences of it—if located at different observation points.

The younger, Level 1 child has acquired the very fundamental and important insight that another person need not always see the same object that he himself currently sees. For instance, he is likely to realize that, if a picture of an object is held vertically so that the picture's face is towards him and its back towards another person seated opposite him, he sees the depicted object but the other person does not. Similarly, he probably would be aware that, if he placed an object on the other person's side of an upright opaque screen, the other person would see it even though he himself no longer could. What he fails as yet to represent, however, is the Level 2 idea that an object which is currently seen by both is seen differently from different spatial perspectives. What is addressed at Level 1 is the global, all-or-none question of *whether* someone does or does not see something; *how* that something looks from here versus there, assuming that it is visible from both positions, is probably not yet a meaningful question. The Level 1 child thinks about viewing objects, according to this theory, but not yet about views of objects.

Masangkay *et al.* (1974) found that 2–3 year olds can usually solve very simple Level-1 type problems, such as the vertical-picture problem just mentioned. It is not until 4–5 years of age, however, that children get to be equally facile with very simple Level-2 type problems, such as the following. Child and experimenter sit facing one another and a side-view picture of a turtle is placed flat on a small table between them. The child is first shown repeatedly that the turtle appears "right side up" (i.e., standing on its feet) to him when the picture is placed in one horizontal orientation, and "upside down" (i.e., lying on its back) when the picture is rotated 180° from that orientation. He is then queried about which of these two perspectives of the turtle he and the experimenter see in each of a series of these 180° picture rotations. Only 9 out of 24 of Masangkay *et al.*'s three year olds were consistently correct in attributing the upside down view to the experimenter when they saw the right side up view and vice-versa, although all 24 were always accurate in describing their own view. In contrast, 35 out of their 36 4–5½ year olds were consistently accurate in their inferences about how the turtle looked to the experimenter. As indicated earlier in our example of the flowers-and-vases perspective task (p. 121), however, it is one thing to know in general that object appearance covaries with observer position (Level 2 Existence knowledge) and quite another to construct an accurate, detailed representation of exactly how something appears from a position other than one's own (Inference skills). The turtles task was the easiest, least taxing perspective problem Masangkay *et al.* could think up. While it may indeed have required some genuinely Level 2 Existence knowledge for its solution, as intended, it certainly required next to no Inference skill. Numerous other studies (e.g., Coie, Costanzo, and Farnill, 1973; see Shantz, 1975) have shown how very much more Inference skill acquisition the four year old has ahead of him before he reaches his zenith as a visual perspective taker.

We have recently studied the genesis of Level-1 type knowledge and skill, and thus, presumably, the very beginnings of children's cognitions about percepts (Lempers, Flavell, and Flavell, in press). A large battery of simple tasks was administered to 12–36 month old children in their homes with the help of their mothers. The tasks were designed to assess various skills within each of three major categories of Level 1 ability: (1) *percept production* or provision, where the child causes another person to have a visual percept of an object that the other person did not previously have, e.g., by showing him an object picture or pointing to an object; (2) *percept deprivation* or prevention, where the child hides an object or otherwise prevents the other from seeing it; (3) *percept diagnosis,* where the child infers what object the other is visually attending to by interpreting the other's eye or finger orientation, as indicated by his looking where the other looks or points, rather than simply staring at his eyes or outstretched finger.

There were a number of interesting results. The favored method of showing pictures at 18 months seems to be to "share" the percept, e.g., holding the picture flat or while standing directly beside the other. This method gives way at 24 months to the adultlike procedure of holding the picture vertically, turning it around, and thrusting its face toward the other so that only the other sees it. If the other holds his hands over his eyes at the time, the 18 month old may and the 24 month old will uncover the eyes before showing the picture. The latter can also solve showing problems that he or she has presumably had little experience with in everyday life, such as showing a picture which is glued to the inside bottom of a hollow cube. Percept deprivation skills (e.g., hiding objects) are acquired later than percept production ones, but they seem well developed by age three. Children of 1½–2 can usually look where the other looks when the other's eyes and face both point in the same direction, and older children can usually do so even when they are divergent (e.g., face straight ahead but eyes facing to the right). Infants of 12 months point to objects and correctly interpret others' pointing gestures. In general, the results of this study suggest that at least some elementary forms of cognition about visual percepts may develop toward the beginning of the early childhood period.

The reader may have noticed that "percepts" has been unobtrusively rendered as "visual percepts" throughout this section. The reason is that we simply know nothing at all about the child's developing knowledge and inferential skill concerning audition or other types of perception. More generally, students of social-cognitive development have not yet investigated children's ability to assess others' *attention* to external stimuli, regardless of the participating sense modality or modalities. Higher forms of this sort of social cognition would include the ability to detect feigned attention ("You're not *really* listening, Mommy!") and feigned inattention ("You're just *pretending* not to notice, Mommy!"). "Metattention development" is a verbal barbarism, but what it refers to would be very interesting to study (see Chap. 5).

Feelings

If an 18 month old looks at his mother's face, and then immediately looks where she is staring (Lempers *et al.,* in press), must we conclude that he is consciously representing the fact that she is having a certain visual experience? Surely not, and we always have to be very careful not to overestimate the young child's social-cognitive competence regarding other people's percepts on the basis of such isolated pieces of evidence. His perception of her demeanor certainly led to his achieving the same visual experience she had, but that alone does not prove that he was aware of the fact and content of her visual experience.

A similar situation obtains in the area of cognitions about feelings. Another person may give conspicuous evidence of experiencing some intense negative feeling, say, and a young child observer may straightaway display a similar feeling. As Hoffman (1972) and others have pointed out, however, it is possible in such cases that the child's feeling may have not been accompanied by any sort of mental representation whatever of the other's feelings. Simple conditioning mechanisms could plausibly explain the child's distress, for instance. There might even be an innate, unlearned component. On the other hand, such a cognitive representation might have been present. And if it had been present, it may have been either a cause or a consequence of the distress (Feshbach, 1973)—or, conceivably, just a functionally unrelated concomitant of it. It is apparent that there are a number of possibilties here, and I believe they all occur at one age or another, in one interpersonal situation or another.

Three of the possibilities are of particular interest. The first, illustrated above, might be termed noninferential or unenlightened empathy: the expression of the other's feelings somehow triggers off similar or related feelings in the child—a sort of emotional contagion phenomenon —but no relevant social cognition accompanies these induced feelings. The child's emotional reaction may, for example, be a "passive and involuntary one, based upon the 'pull' of the cues emitted by the victim which are perceptually similar to cues associated with his own past painful experiences" (Hoffman, 1972, p. 2).

The second could be called inferential or enlightened empathy (or empathic inference). In this case the child has inferred something about the other's feeling state in addition to having some sort of related feeling himself. Of course, the empathy would still be "enlightened" in this sense (or the inference "empathic") even if he happened to be dead wrong about how the other actually felt; inaccurate social cognition is still social cognition. If the child really "felt with" the other, we might be inclined to call his response "empathy," whereas if he only "felt for" the other, we might label it "sympathy"; the differentiation is often a difficult one, however, and may not be all that important to make.

The third possibility could be called nonempathic inference. It means an inference about the other's feeling unaccompanied by any relevant feeling of one's own, or perhaps by any feeling at all. There might exist a natural and appropriate affective response to the other's feelings (e.g., pleasure at the other's happiness), or there might not (e.g., dispassionately noting that the tennis player on the TV screen appears a bit winded after a longish rally). Even in the former case, the social cognition can be and often is relatively affectless.

The following are some of the main things presently known or surmised about the development of cognition concerning feelings and emotions (Shantz, 1975). Noninferential empathy probably has its origins in early or middle infancy, and it is certainly observable in very young children (Hoffman, 1972). For example, Kreutzer and Charlesworth (1973) found that babies of six months and older are likelier to react negatively (e.g., frown, cry) when an adult displays anger and sadness than when the same adult acts happy or neutral; no developmental psychologist I know, however, would interpret that as evidence that six month olds can have conscious representations of people's inner states.

By preschool age, children show some capacity for both nonempathic and empathic inference. For the former, they can accurately interpret certain facial expressions of emotions, and they can correctly infer how another person is likely to feel when certain things happen to him or her (Borke, 1971, 1973; Shantz, 1975). These inferences and interpretations can naturally be quite affectless. For example, the child who understands, from strong facial-expression cues, that the stranger in the picture is "happy" is seldom overcome with joy himself in consequence. Why on earth should he be? However, the preschooler's seeming capacity to make such dispassionate inferences and interpretations suggests that, unlike the infant and toddler, when he is observed to feel with or for other children, his feeling may, in fact, be enlightened by some knowledge of their emotional state. Thus, evidence for nonempathic inference in early childhood buttresses evidence for empathic inference. As Shantz (1975) points out, however, the cognitive level of these inferences need not be very high. For instance, the child knows he would feel unhappy if someone took his toy, and hence he assumes that this toyless child feels unhappy.

At first, the child seems only to distinguish global positive affect from global negative affect: in effect, the other "feels good" if he wears a broad smile, or "feels bad" if something obviously unpleasant has happened to him. It is only later that, for instance, the other's negative affect will be differentially interpreted as "mad," "sad," "scared," etc., depending upon how he looks or what happened to him. There are also other major changes with age (e.g., Flapan, 1968; Rothenberg, 1970; Savitsky and Izard, 1970). Older children and adolescents are more likely than younger children to try to infer feelings spontaneously, without explicitly being asked to (a development in the Need category). They become increasingly accurate at diagnosing emotional states, and they need fewer obvious cues to do it. They also become more disposed and able to explain the feelings they have diagnosed. Furthermore, their explanations will eventually include the actions and feelings of other alters as causes (e.g., "He is unhappy because she doesn't love him") as well as impersonal causes (e.g., "He is unhappy because he lost his watch"). Predictably, their affect inferences can also be more complex, abstract, and broad-ranging. For instance, an adolescent may represent and sympathize with the chronic, silent plight of some distant group as well as the temporary, noisy distress of a familiar individual (Hoffman, 1972). Finally, they must eventually discover the possibilities of intentionally monitored and guided emotional expression, e.g., pretended or disguised feelings, both in themselves and in others ("meta-emotion"?). As would be expected, adults differ considerably in their disposition and ability to consciously monitor and shape the expression of their own feelings (Snyder, 1974). Essentially nothing is known as yet about the development of this and other advanced forms of affect inference, however.

Thoughts

The child's acquisitions in this area of social cognition appear to be very rich indeed, and we are still a long way from having a full and accurate description of the whole developmental sequence. The most interesting and detailed attempt to characterize it is to be found in a recent theoretical model by Selman and his student Byrne (e.g., Byrne, 1973; Selman, 1974, 1976; Selman and Byrne, 1972, 1973, 1974). Their model is partly based on earlier theory and research on the development of role taking skills (e.g., Feffer and Gourevitch, 1960; Flavell *et al.*, 1968; Miller, Kessel, and Flavell, 1970) and of moral judgment (e.g., Kohlberg, 1969). The model has to do primarily with the knowledge-in-general, Existence aspects of cognition concerning thoughts. It does not say much, for instance, about how disposed (Need) and competent (Inference) an individual will be to successfully achieve any particular social-cognitive objective involving people's thoughts. It is broad in other respects, however. That is, it attempts to deal not only with the child's developing knowledge about "thoughts" in the narrow sense, but also with his simultaneously developing conceptions of society and social reality, social roles and relations, personality structure, intentions and motives, cognitions about the self, and other related phenomena (Selman and Byrne, 1972, 1973). Some of their ideas about these topics will be mentioned here or in subsequent chapter sections.

A cautionary note before describing the Selman-Byrne model. Although some developmental data have already been gathered in support of it (Byrne, 1973; Selman and Byrne, 1974), a very great deal still needs to be done in the way of both conceptual clarification and empirical validation of its theoretical claims. I have made it the centerpiece of this section because I think that most of it is extremely creative and seminal, and that at least some of it will prove to be scientifically valid. For other research not described here, see Shantz (1975).

According to the Selman-Byrne model, there are six major stages or levels (0–5) which emerge in fixed sequence between about four years of age and cognitive maturity. Only Levels 0–2 will be described in any detail here.

Level 0: egocentric perspective taking (roughly 4–6 years of age). At the beginning of this stage, the child already recognizes that he (*S*) and others (*O*) are different entities, but he does not yet clearly represent either as a true *subject*. That is, neither *S* nor *O* is really conceptualized as a *person,* a thinking, evaluating being who makes judgments about situations and acts in the light of these judgments. *S* represents *O*'s overt actions and such relatively "overt" inner states as strongly-expressed emotions, but he does not represent cognitive perspectives, either his own or *O*'s. At the end of this stage he begins to do so, but still does not distinguish very clearly between one person's perspective and another's. For example, the typical Level 0 child does not think to himself that he believes toys are fun (*S*'s perspective) and that his mother also does (*O*'s perspective). In other words, he does not consciously represent two perspectives and then consciously decide that they must be identical. Rather, there is simply an unreflective, Piagetian-type egocentric assumption that "toys are fun," and that his mother will, of course, also find them so. In his mind there is only *the* reality; there are no personal constructions or interpretations of reality.

Level 1: subjective perspective taking (roughly 6–8 years). The child now recognizes the basic *subjectivity* of people, and that they have individual cognitive perspectives. Both *S* and *O* are seen as active processors and evaluators of data. He recognizes that different people may have different thoughts and attitudes about things—even about the very same things—based upon the information available to them, their individual motives and goals, and so on. Whereas the Level *O* child may sense that people perceive social events and obtain information from them, the Level 1 child also knows that they interpret and make judgments about these events. He now distinguishes between intended and unintended behaviors, and has the concept of "personal reasons" as subjective causes of a person's choice of action.

Level 2: self-reflective perspective taking (roughly 8–10 years, or perhaps later). Towards the end of Level 1, the child begins to understand not only that people have cognitive perspectives, but also that they can make inferences about one another's perspectives. Initially, he only represents one *O* making such inferences about another *O* (*S* infers that O_1 thinks that O_2 thinks such and such). At the beginning of Level 2, he also recognizes that he himself may be the object of *O*'s perspective-taking, just as *O* may be the object of his own or another *O*'s inference. Moreover, *S* comes to understand that *O*'s taking of *S*'s perspective may have important implications for how *S* behaves towards *O*. For example, your perspective regarding another person whose thinking you are trying to read may have to change if you sense that he is also trying to read your thinking. Toward the end of Level 2, he has the additional insight that O may likewise be aware that S understands that O may be inferring S's thoughts. Finally, he may sense that this "I think that he thinks that *I* think . . ." chain would go on forever, at least in principle.

A task originally devised by Flavell *et al.* (1968, pp. 44–55) illustrates these complexities (see also Miller, Kessel, and Flavell, 1970). The child is presented with two cups placed upside down on a table. One has a nickel glued to its upturned bottom to show that it conceals a nickel inside; the other is similarly marked to show that it contains two nickels. The child is told that another person will shortly enter the room, select one or the other of the two cups, and get to keep any money that may be hidden under it. The child's task is to fool the person by taking the money out of one cup, whichever one he thinks the person will select. He is also told that the person knows full well that the child is going to try to fool him in this way. The child is encouraged to think hard, pick a cup, and explain why he thinks the person will choose that one. In the Selman-Byrne model, the Level 0 S would have no way of making a rational choice, because he attributes no thoughts and motives to O. The Level 1 child can, and therefore might guess that O would pick the two nickel cup because it contains more money (i.e., S infers that O has a monetary motive which leads him to make that particular choice). The less advanced Level 2 child recognizes that O might assume S would attribute that motive and choice to him, decides that O would consequently choose the one nickel cup to outwit S, and counters by removing the money from that cup. In other words, S guesses that O will also make inferences about S's own inferences, and S knows that any such reciprocal role taking activity on O's part has important implications for what he, S, should do in relation to O. A more advanced Level 2 child might go on to assume that O could even attribute this whole line of reasoning to S, decide that S would indeed empty the one nickel cup, and therefore decide to choose the two nickel one. Again, the child realizes the implications of O's inferences about S for his own behavior: he should empty the two nickel cup, not the one nickel one.

The reasoning process just described is, of course, extremely tortuous and may in practice present serious computation (Inference) problems, even for an intelligent adolescent or adult. However, younger subjects may at least sense that such chains of social cognition can happen (Existence), because they may have discovered that one person's thinking can include another's as its object. The fundamental insight of Level 2 may come down to this: I know I could conceivably tune in on your cognitive perspective because we are both subjects or persons rather than objects; I also know that you could do the same to me for the same reason; it follows that you may be doing so at the very moment I am, and that your tuning may therefore pick up my tuning. Such an insight, whenever it comes, must represent a giant step in the development of social cognition.

Levels 3, 4, and 5 (preadolescence and older). At these higher levels, the *Ss, Os,* and their cognitive perspectives become progressively less concrete, individualized, and limited to the here and now. At level 3, *S* understands that he and others can assume a third-person, impartial-spectator perspective on a two-person interaction, even if he is himself one of the participants. It becomes possible for him to view himself, *O,* and the mutual perspective-taking both may be simultaneously doing in a relatively detached and objective way, as if watching two actors playing their parts (see the vertical arrow in Fig. 4-1). At Level 4, the perspectives considered become those of whole groups rather than of concrete individuals (e.g., consideration is given to what "everybody" would think about a certain act). At Level 5, the individual comes to recognize the essential relativity of all cognitive perspectives, e.g., that different cultures may construe or evaluate the same social act differently. As suggested above, these more elaborate forms of perspective-taking are largely confined to adolescence and adulthood. Middle-childhood subjects may try to put themselves in *O*'s shoes, but neither *O* nor his shoes are likely to be very abstract:

> Tom (10, 0): You should take the other person's opinion. Like say you're about to step on an ant, and you get in the ant's shoes and you wouldn't want to be killed or something; so I wouldn't really step on the ant (Selman, Damon, and Gordon, in press).

Intentions

This topic has to do with purposes and purposefulness; with dispositions, intentions, and motives; with the personal, psychological causes and reasons assumed to instigate human actions. Why did that person do what he just did? Was his act intentional or accidental? What motive or goal, if any, prompted it? What implications would various different answers to these questions have for our evaluation of his act, and therefore of him as a person? That is, should we regard him as praiseworthy, blameworthy, or neither, on the basis of these answers. The following are some educated guesses about the nature and course of development in this area (see also Shantz, 1975).

Children are likely to know some things about human motives and intentions by the time they enter kindergarten or first grade. In the case of motives, they surely recognize the distinction between wanting to and having to do something, and they may also be aware of a variety of possible wants and wishes. Additionally, they will probably comprehend the fundamental distinction between unintended, accidental behaviors and intended, "done on purpose" ones, although they may not always diagnose actual cases correctly (e.g., King, 1971). Surprisingly, psychologists know practically nothing about the dawning of these basic insights, but a few things can be suggested concerning subsequent developments. Predictably, the growing child gradually becomes both more sensitive or attuned to the presence of peoples' covert motives and intentions in social situations, and more skilled in interpreting them accurately. If shown an aggressive television program, for example, younger children are likelier to notice and remember only the aggressive acts, or only the aggressive acts plus their consequences for the actor, whereas older children are likelier to apprehend and retain the entire causal sequence of motive-act-consequence (Collins, Berndt, and Hess, 1974).

Moreover, the young child still has a lot to learn about the applications and implications of intentionality and motivation. As Berndt and Berndt put it: "Children seem to be learning to apply the intentional-unintentional distinction correctly for several years after the distinction itself is understood" (1974, p. 17). One kind of error of application young children may make is to overapply or overattribute personal motives and intentionality. For example, a young child might wrongly attribute his father's inability to do something for him to an unwillingness to do it, despite all attempts at explanation; that is, he persists in making a motivational interpretation where a capacity interpretation is called for (Berndt, 1973, p. 8). Contrariwise, he may wrongly attribute positive personal motives to people whose nice behavior towards him actually has an impersonal, "in-role" cause, e.g., the warm and smiling toy salesman. Presumably, the child learns only gradually that if a person is acting under strong internal or external influences (the father's inability, the salesman's job requirements), his true motives and intentions may not match his behavior. The young child may sometimes even confuse physical and psychological causality, mistakenly attributing wants and purposes to inanimate, purely physical entities, as in the artificialistic and animistic causal explanations first observed by Piaget (Flavell, 1963, pp. 279–90; see also Shultz, 1974a).

As to underapplication, the Collins *et al.* (1974) study just cited is, of course, one illustration: their young subjects did not spontaneously attribute motives where motive attribution was in fact clearly possible and appropriate. Flapan (1968) has obtained similar results. The best researched example of underattribution, however, more directly concerns the evaluative implications of the intentional-unintentional distinction. An adult is likely to believe that positive and, especially, negative evaluations should be largely confined to intentional actions.

If a person did a good deed voluntarily and intentionally, he and his action deserve more praise than if he did it involuntarily and unintentionally. Conversely, only intentional, malicious harmful acts are thought to be really bad; unavoidable accidents are wholly blameless, while avoidable, careless accidents are evaluated somewhere in between. Piaget long ago reported that young children, in contrast to older ones and adults, regard as more worthy of blame ("naughty") those acts that have the most serious objective consequences, with no consideration given to the motives and intentions of the actor (Flavell, 1963, pp. 292–293). A girl who steals food for a hungry friend is accordingly judged to be naughtier than one who steals a cheaper ribbon for herself. A boy who breaks 15 cups through an unavoidable accident is believed to be more guilty than one who accidentally breaks a single cup in the course of deliberately doing something he was not supposed to do. Subsequent research, however, suggests that children as young as kindergarten age may, in fact, have some intuitive understanding that motives and intentions are relevant to evaluation, but they may not understand this as clearly or use motives and intentions in evaluating as consistently as, say, 8–9 year olds (Shantz, 1975). In particular, large differences in the seriousness of the outcome (e.g., 15 broken cups versus 1) may not affect the older child's judgment of blameworthiness much, but they may distract the younger child and cause him to ignore motive and intention considerations he might otherwise have used in making his judgment.

What else develops? Children seem to acquire some intuitive understanding of unconscious intentions and motives of the Freudian defense-mechanism variety during middle childhood (King, 1971; Whiteman, 1967). A child's mother promises to buy her some ice cream but then forgets to do it; later in the evening the girl spanks her dolls, something she has never done before. Why did she do such a thing? Because the dolls were naughty, says the kindergartener. Because the girl was mad at her mother and took it out on the dolls, says the third grader. Selman and Byrne (1973) hypothesize a number of interesting insights that the child or adolescent is likely to attain. He or she is likely to learn that people have whole hierarchies of motives; that one motive may conflict with another in a given situation; and that others may try to infer your motives and intentions as well as your thoughts and feelings. He may also discover that there is a large error factor in these and other types of social-cognitive inference. For instance, he is apt to find out that he and other people may be wrong about their own motives or may be unaware of their true intentions; he discovers that they may also misread his purposes or, if they do read them correctly, may evaluate them less favorably than he does.

Personality

The counterpart of this section in Shantz' (1975) excellent review of social-cognitive growth has a homely but apt title: "What is the other like?" How, in other words, do children of different ages construe and characterize the personal characteristics of other people? What are the salient developmental changes in the way they describe human personalities? Good reviews of this topic can be found in Shantz' chapter (1975) and in a book by Livesley and Bromley (1973). Their book also contains an extensive and insightfully discussed empirical investigation which will serve to illustrate the way research is commonly done in this area. The subjects in their principal study were 320 English boys and girls, 40 at each of 8 age levels between 7 and 15 years. Over a series of sessions the children wrote descriptions of themselves and other people they knew well. They were very carefully and repeatedly instructed to indicate what sort of person the individual is, what he is like and what they think of him, and *not* to describe his physical appearance, clothing, etc. Although such free description procedures have their problems (Shantz, 1975), Livesley and Bromley appear to have managed both method and data analyses intelligently; moreover, their results and conclusions seem convincing and also accord well with other research evidence. The following developmental sketch is a synthesis of their findings and those of other studies (e.g., Flapan, 1968; Hill and Palmquist, 1974; Peevers and Secord, 1973; Rosenbach, Crockett, and Wapner, 1973).

The child of 6–7 years or younger is very prone to describe the other person's general identity, appearance, family, possessions, environment, etc., despite the experimenter's explicit instruction to the contrary. Almost 50 percent of Livesley and Bromley's seven year olds failed to mention even a single psychological quality (1973, p. 210). Likewise, Peevers and Secord found that "kindergarten children scarcely recognized a person as such, and described him in terms that failed to differentiate him from his environment or his possessions" (1973, p. 126). If any personal traits do get mentioned they are apt to be global, stereotyped, and highly evaluative ("He is very bad"). Children of this age are also likely to describe the other in rather egocentric, self-referential terms ("She gives me things"). This excerpt from a seven-year-old's description of a woman she likes illustrates some of these properties:

> She is very nice because she gives my friends and me toffee. She lives by the main road. She has fair hair and glasses. . . . She sometimes gives us flowers . . . . (Livesley and Bromley, 1973, p. 214).

During middle childhood the subject's descriptions become more focused on traits and dispositions, his trait vocabulary increases considerably, and the trait-descriptive terms he selects seem less global and stereotyped, more abstract, and more precise in meaning than before ("nice" gives way to "considerate," "helpful," etc.). The other person is often endowed with attitudes, interests, abilities, and other psychological qualities seldom found in the younger child's description. The more external types of attributions (possessions, etc.) also occur, however, and will continue to do so into adulthood. [Peevers and Secord (1973, p. 127) make the interesting observation that nonpsychological descriptors do sometimes seem to help create a vivid impression of the essence of an individual.] The middle-childhood subject's character sketch is still likely to be rather poorly organized, however, with different attributions just strung together in a more or less random sequence. In the same vein, opposite or contradictory qualities are simply juxtaposed with no attempt at reconciliation; more generally, there is not apt to be much explanation and integration in his descriptions. Here are two ten-year-olds' descriptions that illustrate these points:

> She is quite a kind girl. . . . Her behaviour is quite good most of the time but sometimes she is quite naughty and silly most of the time. . . . (Livesley and Bromley, 1973, p. 218).

> He smells very much and is very nasty. He has no sense of humour and is very dull. He is always fighting and he is cruel. He does silly things and is very stupid. He has brown hair and cruel eyes. He is sulky and 11 years old and has lots of sisters. I think he is the most horrible boy in the class. He has a croaky voice and always chews his pencil and picks his teeth and I think he is disgusting (Livesley and Bromley, 1973, p. 217).

There are some interesting novelties that become increasingly prominent during the adolescent years. The subject flexibly and planfully selects ideas from a wide range of possibilities, and carefully shapes them into an organized, integrated portrait of the other. He knows that his impression of the person is only *his* impression, and may therefore be inaccurate or different from other people's. He or she is sensitive to the presence of seemingly contradictory traits and of different levels or depths within the individual's personality; the individual may be both this and that, or may appear to be this but really be that "underneath." For example, a thirteen year old acquaintance of mine began his written character sketch of a friend this way (it was an English class assignment, and was therefore judged to require fancy vocabulary—this too represents a bit of social cognition): "He may appear a joker in class because of his unique style of eloquence, but in reality he feels a deep responsibility towards the advancement of his own personal knowledge." The adolescent also feels that a human personality represents a unique blend of qualities and therefore deserves an idiosyncratic, nonstereotypic characterization. Because he is aware of these considerations, he tries to explain and justify, not merely describe, and he tries to particularize and qualify, not just baldly assert. That is, since there are apparent contradictions within or between levels of an individual's personality, he knows one must appeal to dispositions, motives, personal history, or other causes to explain and reconcile them. And since each individual is believed to have a unique personality, he feels one should search out (and explain) unexpected combinations of traits, unusual blends of feelings, etc. The best examples of these higher forms of personality description are of course to be found in great literature, not in Livesley and Bromley (1973). Nonetheless, Livesley and Bromley and other investigators have obtained some fairly impressive specimens from lesser mortals: "She is curious about people but naive, and this leads her to ask too many questions so that people become irritated with her and withhold information, although she is not sensitive enough to notice it" (Livesley and Bromley, 1973, p. 225).

Self

This topic may deserve a lengthy presentation, but there are several reasons why we can get by with a brief one here. First, while there has certainly been a great deal of theoretical speculation over the years concerning the development of ideas and knowledge about the self, most aspects have been "subjected to negligible empirical investigation" (Guardo and Bohan, 1971, p. 1909). In addition, a few things have already been explicitly stated about self-cognition in Chap. 2 (initial differentiation of the self, p. 49), Chap. 3 (self identity and sex-role identity, pp. 74–76), and the present chapter (the brief sections on metacognition and invariant formation, p. 123). But above all, a lot has already been said about it implicitly because, not surprisingly, the development of self-cognition has much in common with that of other-cognition. Recall, for example, the parallels between the child's conception of himself and of other people in Selman and Byrne's (1975) developmental model, as when he credits both self and other with subjectivity at Level 1 and with reciprocal perspective-taking abilities at Level 2. Similarly, Livesley and Bromley's subjects' personality descriptions of themselves tended to be on the same cognitive-development level as their descriptions of others (1973, pp. 236–241). Their younger children's self-descriptions showed the same dearth of personal-psychological attributions, for instance, that their descriptions of others did. Characterizations of others also become less global and more differentiated with age, and the same has been shown to be true of characterizations of the self (Katz and Zigler, 1967; Mullener and Laird, 1971).

There are two research articles on the topic that might be mentioned briefly, however. Guardo and Bohan (1971) have made the intriguing suggestion that there are at least four basic dimensions to an individual's sense of self-identity: (1) *humanity*—the feeling of having distinctively human capacities and experiences; (2) *sexuality*—the sense of one's femaleness or maleness; (3) *individuality*—the awareness of being a singular and unique being, the one and only "you" ever; (4) *continuity*—the related sense of being somehow the same "you" over time (identity in the Piagetian sense—see pp. 72–76). In other words, the child must acquire an awareness "that he is one being with a unique identity who has been, is, and will be a male (or female) human person separate from and entirely like no other" (Guardo and Bohan, 1971, p. 1911). Guardo and Bohan's own attempt to assess the development of this sort of awareness was not very successful (there are formidable measurement problems here), but their ideas are most interesting and worthy of further research effort. For another thoughtful discussion of the early development of cognitions about personal identity, especially sex-role identity, see Kohlberg (1966).

The second article (Amsterdam, 1972) deals with the question of when the child first acquires a rudimentary, physical self-concept, i.e., some sense that he is, or inhabits, that particular dynamic object we call his body. The answer to such a question will likely depend upon the method of assessment used as well as the researcher's criteria for deciding that the concept has been acquired. Amsterdam's method was to put a spot of rouge on an infant's nose, and then put the infant in front of a mirror. The use of a similar method showed that chimpanzees (but not monkeys) do seem to interpret what they see in the mirror as an image of themselves, as evidenced by such behaviors as preening and touching their faces rather than the mirror (Gallup, 1970). In the case of young humans, Amsterdam found that:

> The first prolonged and repeated reaction of an infant to his mirror image is that of a sociable "playmate" from about 6 through 12 months of age. In the second year of life wariness and withdrawal appeared; self-admiring and embarrassed behavior accompanied those avoidance behaviors starting at 14 months, and was shown by 75% of the subjects after 20 months of age. During the last part of the second year of life, from 20 to 24 months of age, 65% of the subjects demonstrated recognition of their mirror images (Amsterdam, 1972, p. 297).

Morality

This is a much, much bigger topic than can be adequately presented in the space available. A great deal of work has already been done on moral judgment development and it continues to be a very active research area at this writing. As with Piagetian theory and research, the reader has no choice but to look elsewhere if he really wants to understand this most important aspect of cognitive development. Fortunately (true also of the Piagetian work) he will not have to look far. The principal theorists are Piaget himself (who else?) and Lawrence Kohlberg (e.g., 1969), and their highly influential ideas are summarized in practically every introductory psychology textbook on the market. Research studies of closely related topics, such as children's developing conceptions of religion, law, society, and politics, have also been summarized (Flavell, 1970a, pp. 1030–1032; Tapp, 1971, 1974).

The following is a brief summary of Kohlberg's developmental stages 1–6 of moral reasoning, prefaced by a Stage 0 recently described by Damon (Damon, 1973; Selman, Damon, and Gordon, in press).

Stage 0: no morality-relevant orientation. At this stage, the child's choice in any morality-relevant situation is essentially undifferentiated from his reason for that choice. He elects one course of action rather than another "because I want to"; he thinks a person shouldn't be punished for a transgression "because he won't like it." There is, in other words, no distinction as yet between what is desirable and what is morally right. At the end of this stage the child takes the crucial step of looking beyond the act and one's wants with respect to it, although the reasons he finds are still ethically irrelevant (the girl should receive more "because girls are better than boys").

Stage 1: obedience and punishment orientation. Things are wrong, no longer just because the subject does not like them (Level 0), but because authority figures say they are wrong. One obeys unquestioningly because of fear of punishment.

Stage 2: naively egoistic orientation. The child's morality is now one of instrumental hedonism and reciprocal exchange. He no longer believes in any absolute moral authority, and moral decisions are based largely on pragmatic considerations. Right acts are those that benefit the self and occasionally others. Favors are done for others with the expectation that they will be returned—a kind of "you scratch my back and I'll scratch yours" orientation. It can be seen that Stages 1 and 2 are also largely premoral, although not as obviously and completely as Stage 0. They are also called *preconventional,* in comparison to Stages 3 and 4.

Stage 3: Good boy orientation. Moral acts are done to please and help others, rather than to be repaid in kind. The social approval of others, the maintenance of reciprocal social relationships such as mutual friendship, and the inner sense of being a nice person are sufficient rewards for the Stage 3 subject. A person's motives and intentions are very clearly recognized as being crucial to one's moral evaluation of his actions.

Stage 4: Law and order orientation. The Stage 3 sense of obligation to maintain stable, positive relationships between himself and other individuals becomes generalized to the whole society. The individual is oriented towards doing his duty, respecting authority, and obeying the law without question, because such behavior on everyone's part is believed necessary for the maintenance of the social order. The morality of Stages 3 and 4 is called *conventional* because the rules and norms of one's own society are never called into question. For instance, the Stage 4 subject believes that the maintenance of his own particular social system is an absolute good, to be done for its own sake.

Stage 5: Contractual legalistic orientation. Stages 5 and 6 are called *postconventional* or *principled*. In Stage 5, the subject recognizes that the existing social order is only one variety among many possible, and that the ideal society should have laws and institutions based upon certain abstract principles of justice (e.g., they should be democratically arrived at, and they should maximize social utility). Laws are still seen as necessary and usually to be obeyed, since they represent a kind of social contract. Laws may be unjust, however, and such laws may be changed through orderly, democratic procedures. Stage 5 is the official morality of the United States government and its constitution.

Stage 6: Conscience or principle orientation. The emphasis is more inner-directed here than in Stage 5. Although the Stage 6 individual is aware of the importance of Stage 5 legal and social-contract reasoning, he gives more weight to the dictates of an enlightened individual conscience and the search for universally valid, ultimate principles of justice and right action. The Stage 6 subject feels obliged to do what he believes to be morally right "deep down inside" (e.g., never to take a human life), regardless of circumstances, law, or the behavior of others "out there." Thus, although both are equally principled in comparison to earlier stages, Stage 5 is more societally oriented and Stage 6 more individually oriented.

Kohlberg's provocative stage-developmental approach to morality bristles with problems which are currently receiving research attention (Rest, 1974). His work has also come in for some strong criticism recently (Kurtines and Greif, 1974). How psychologically "real" are his stages? What is the best way to decide which stage a subject is "in"? Can a person be "in" more than one stage at a time? What warrant is there for claiming that, say, Stage 6 is "higher," "more advanced," or "more developmentally mature" than Stage 5? What relations might there be between a person's moral reasoning level and his other cognitive abilities, social or nonsocial? For example, does one need to have attained a certain Selman-Byrne level of cognitive perspective taking ability before a certain Kohlbergian level of moral thinking even becomes an intellectual possibility (e.g., Byrne, 1973; Selman, Damon, and Gordon, in press)? What causes the developing child to abandon one way of thinking about moral questions in favor of a different, "more developmentally mature" way? What is the relation, if any, between a person's assessed moral reasoning stage and his level of moral behavior in real situations? Is it possible to teach people to think at higher Kohlbergian moral levels? And if so, do the teaching effects endure, and are there any consequent changes in actual moral behavior? These are the sorts of questions that psychologists working in this area are presently asking.

What has just been suggested for morality is equally true for social-cognitive development as a whole, namely, that the present review has not even mentioned a number of important questions in this area (Shantz, 1975). As examples, to what extent are various social-cognitive abilities related to one another and to other cognitive measures, such as intelligence-test scores and Piagetian task performance? What are the important antecedents and consequents of social-cognitive acquisitions? On the antecedent side, what childhood experiences facilitate and inhibit the growth of social cognition? The variables of interest here include the child's social-cultural milieu, his parents' child-rearing attitudes and practices, possible educational interventions (e.g., can social-cognitive skills actually be taught?), and the child's social experiences with peers and others. On the consequent side, there has been considerable interest in the possible role of social-cognitive abilities as mediators of effective verbal communication (Glucksberg, Krauss, and Higgins, 1975) and other adaptive forms of social behavior (Shantz, 1975). For instance, if, in fact, one could teach children to be more sensitive to others' thoughts and feelings, would their social adjustment and ability to solve everyday interpersonal problems improve as a consequence (e.g., Spivak and Shure, 1974)?

OTHER ASPECTS OF THE DEVELOPMENT OF THINKING AND KNOWLEDGE

Chapters 2-4 have dealt with the development of thinking and knowledge. Some of that thinking and knowledge has been impersonal and relatively dispassionate: the development of sensory-motor schemes, number concepts, logical reasoning abilities, and the like. Some of it has been personal and less dispassionate: the development of various forms of social cognition. Has anything been left out? Some thinking and knowledge of both kinds, actually. On the more dispassionate side, not a word has been said so far about the development of "intelligence" of the IQ test variety. A recent textbook on child development has one chapter called "Cognitive Development" and another called "Intelligence" (Mussen, Conger, and Kagan, 1974). Although such a division sounds peculiar, it is commonly made and there are several justifications for it. The main one is that responses to standardized intelligence tests simply do not tell us much about what cognitive structures and processes the child has acquired—about where he "is" in his cognitive-developmental odyssey. These tests were simply not designed to measure qualitative, structural changes in the way children think and reason as they grow older, or to assess the extent to which fundamental, theoretically significant concepts have been acquired (e.g., the infantile object concept, or the middle-childhood concept of a measurement unit). As Green put it:

> Psychometric models have rarely enabled one to say much about the course of intellectual development, although they are based on the assumption that the components of intelligence grow in quantity during childhood. Test theory has made dramatic progress in the past 50 years, but it has not concerned itself with the mechanisms of intellectual growth (Green, 1971, p. 215).

The less dispassionate side also has its omissions, because social cognition does not cover all forms of emotionally-charged thinking and knowledge. Needless to say, logic, mathematics, and science are cases in point for some cerebral types, but there are better examples:

> Most research into human cognition has been concerned with what might be called serious or adaptive processes. . . . Historically, psychologists have tended to neglect the lighter, more playful side of cognition, although some recent interest can be detected in topics such as humor, play, and aesthetics (Schultz, 1974*b*, p. 100).

Consider two of these topics, aesthetics and humor. Howard Gardner has recently proposed a cognitive-development based theory of how children acquire the ability to create and appreciate works in the various art forms (Gardner, 1973). As he says in the preface of his book, ". . . research about the development of artistic capacities can provide an important corrective to the one-sided study of 'scientific' skills that presently pervades the psychological literature (Gardner, 1973, p. ix)." He rightly believes that the psychologist's conception of the mind and its development has been too narrow, too exclusively focused on the more anemic forms of cognition. Similarly, it is now recognized that the child's attained level of cognitive growth partly determines what he finds funny. A small developmental literature is also building about this improbable-looking area, bearing titles like "The role of operational thinking in children's comprehension and appreciation of humor" (McGhee, 1971*a*) and "Cognitive development and children's comprehension of humor" (McGhee, 1971*b*). What I have been trying to suggest in these last paragraphs is that "cognitive development" potentially includes a very broad and very diverse assortment of childhood acquisitions, some of which psychologists have just begun to recognize and explore. How could it be narrower, when one stops to think about it? How many aspects of child behavior and development, after all, have nothing to do with the child's "thinking and knowledge"? The chapters which follow should further extend our concept of cognitive development.

SUMMARY

The chapter begins by describing the typical differences between middle-childhood and adolescent-adult cognition. The comparison made are largely based on Piaget's account of the transition between *concrete-operational* and *formal-operational* thought. When confronted with a problem, the younger, concrete-operational subject mostly confines his thinking to the problem data as presented (the *real*). In contrast, the older, formal-operational subject begins by imagining a variety of potential realities (the *possible*), and then tries to verify, often by systematic experimentation, which one is actually "real" or true in the present case. His thinking is *hypothetico-deductive* rather than *empirico-inductive,* because he creates hypotheses and then deduces the empirical states of affairs that should occur if his hypotheses are correct. Unlike the younger subject, his thinking in certain problem situations bears a close resemblance to scientific reasoning, involving as it does the systematic generation and experimental testing of hypotheses. Moreover, while the child formulates isolated propositions about reality (*intra-propositional* thinking), the adolescent or adult also thinks about the logical relations that may hold among two or more propositions (*inter-propositional* thinking), e.g., that one proposition implies a second but is contradicted by a third. The older individual's thinking can therefore be totally abstract, totally formal-logical in nature. For instance, he understands that one can reason about the validity of statements that have no external, real-world referents at all. "If *A* implies *B,* then not *B* implies not *A*" is such a statement, true solely by virtue of its logical form.

Piagetian formal-operational reasoning is also said to include the ability to generate all possible *combinations* and *permutations* of a set of elements in a systematic, planful fashion. It likewise entails the ability to understand how the two forms of concrete-operational reversibility, *inversion* and *compensation*, may have equivalent effects within a single physical system. Adolescents and adults also show more sophisticated *information processing strategies* in a wide variety of tasks and problems. Finally, concrete-operational acquisitions may undergo further *consolidation* and *solidification* during adolescence. Other examples of recent research on mature thinking were also briefly described.

Formal-operational and other types of adolescent-adult thinking well illustrate the generalization that the higher the cognitive-developmental stage, the less universal its attainment is likely to be. For a variety of good reasons, these types of mature cognition are decidedly not "universal" in the extreme sense of meaning that all normal adults of all cultures can and will use them skillfully in all applicable problem situations. It has been suggested instead that many adults may exercise what formal-operational capacities they possess only in certain limited areas of their cognitive functioning. It is also possible that an adult may have some feeling for the general nature of abstract, formal reasoning, even though he may lack the motivation or ability to do it well.

Chapter 2 described the development of social cognition during infancy; this chapter takes up its subsequent development. Figure 4-1 (p. 120) is one representation of what social cognition entails. Another emphasizes three preconditions for successfully identifying any social-cognitive object (e.g., another person's feeling state): knowing that such states can exist in people (*Existence*); being motivated or disposed to identify them (*Need*); being able actually to identify them on the basis of the available evidence (*Inference*). Because social and nonsocial cognition are the products of the very same mind, naturally there are many parallels in their developmental courses. Like its nonsocial counterparts: social-cognitive growth proceeds from *surface* (people's appearance and behavior) to *depth* (their inner thoughts, feelings, etc.), and also shows *invariant formation;* immature social thinking is plagued with *spatial* and *temporal centrations;* mature social thinking is *abstract, hypothetical,* and *metacognitive,* has characteristic *cognitive shortcomings* (e.g., *egocentrism*), but clearly has *a sense of the game* of people-reading.

Specific developmental trends in the area of social cognition can be described under such (overlapping) headings as *percepts, feelings, thoughts, intentions, personality, self,* and *morality.*

Recent theory and research suggest that there are at least two developmental levels of cognition concerning visual *percepts:* at Level 1, the young child only represents *whether* another person sees a given object; at Level 2, he also represents *how* an object that the person sees looks to that person from his particular spatial perspective. Some Level 1 understanding seems to be present toward the beginning of early childhood, some Level 2 understanding toward the end of this period.

Preschool children can correctly attribute global positive and negative *feelings* to another person on the basis of his facial expression or his immediately prior experience (e.g., someone just gave him a present). The intellectual processes mediating these attributions may not be very high level, however. As the child grows older, he progressively differentiates the emotional domain ("bad" is partitioned into "sad," "mad," "afraid," etc.), becomes more attuned to others' affects, seeks to explain as well as describe people's feelings, and can abstractly represent the plight of a whole group of unfortunates (e.g., the populace of some distant country which is stricken with drought). He also will probably learn to monitor and shape his own affective expression (e.g., consciously feign a certain emotion), as well as to detect such behaviors in others.

It has been suggested that the development of cognition about *thoughts* also proceeds through a sequence of distinguishable levels. At *Level 0,* the child does not yet fully represent either himself or other people as *subjects* or *persons* (as opposed to objects), each of whom actively interprets and evaluates experiences from his own point of view. The child acquires this sort of representation at *Level 1,* and people are henceforth credited with *subjectivity.* At this level the child realizes that the other has thoughts and may try to infer them. At *Level 2,* he realizes that the other may similarly try to infer the child's thoughts, and that the other may even infer that the child is thinking about the other's mental events. "I think he suspects that I'm trying to figure out what his decision will be" is an elaborate example of Level 2 social cognition. At still higher levels, his attributions of ideas and opinions become more abstract, impersonal, and oriented towards groups or "people in general" rather than specific individuals.

By the beginning of formal schooling, children seem to have at least some understanding of psychological causes such as *intentions* and motives, but they become much more sensitive to their presence in others during middle childhood and adolescence. They also learn more about the proper applications and implications of intentionality and motivation. The most frequently researched case in point is the developing inclination to pay attention to and heavily weight a person's intentions and motives when assessing merit or blame. Other developmental acquisitions include: an intuitive understanding of Freudian defense mechanisms; the knowledge that people have hierarchies of motives, some of which may conflict; the recognition that people frequently try to read and evaluate one another's intentions, and sometimes err in the process.

There are striking ontogenetic changes in the way children conceptualize and describe another individual's *personality*. Up to 6–7 years or thereabouts, a child is likely to characterize another person in terms of "surface" rather than "depth"—the person's appearance, possessions, overt behavior (especially toward the self), etc., rather than his inner, psychological qualities. During middle childhood there is considerably more emphasis on these internal aspects, and the child acquires a larger and more differentiated set of trait-descriptive terms, but his personality descriptions still tend to lack organization. They become increasingly well organized and integrated during adolescence, however. The other's seemingly conflicting and idiosyncratic combinations of traits are mentioned, and attempts are made to explain, justify, and qualify what is said about him.

Developing conceptions of the *self* generally appear to parallel those of other people fairly closely, e.g., both become more differentiated and more "psychological" with increasing age. There has, however, been relatively little research done as yet on certain interesting aspects of this topic.

In contrast, much more work has been done on the cognitive-developmental aspects of *morality* than a small chapter section can begin to cover. Most current research on the topic deals with Kohlberg's structural-developmental stages of moral reasoning: *Stage 1—obedience and punishment orientation; Stage 2—naively egoistic orientation; Stage 3—good boy orientation; Stage 4—law and order orientation; Stage 5—contractual legalistic orientation; Stage 6—conscience or principle orientation.* There are a number of issues concerning Kohlberg's thought-provoking theory that current research is attempting to answer. Similarly, there are important questions about the correlates, antecedents, and consequents of social-cognitive development in general that this chapter can do no more than mention.

Finally, it is important to emphasize that the development of thinking and knowledge is a broader topic than Chaps. 2–4 suggest. On the more coldly cerebral side, there is also the development of "intelligence" of the psychometric, IQ variety. Unfortunately, the intelligence-test literature has not proven very useful so far in our attempts to characterize human cognitive growth. On the warmer-blooded side, there are likewise other things to study besides the genesis of social cognition. Two examples were briefly mentioned, namely, the cognitive-developmental aspects of aesthetics and of humor. There is simply not much that human beings do that does not implicate their "thinking and knowledge."

5

perception
and
communication

PERCEPTION

The Role of Innate and Experiential Factors
in Perceptual Development

As Gibson defines it:

> Perception, functionally speaking, is the process by which we obtain
> firsthand information about the world around us. It has a phenomenal
> aspect, the awareness of events presently occurring in the organism's im-
> mediate surroundings. It also has a responsive aspect; it entails discrimina-
> tive, selective response to the stimuli in the immediate environment. (Gib-
> son, 1969, p. 3).

What is the origin of that "process," that "awareness," that "discriminative, selective response"? The question has been asked for centuries, and
the answers given have ranged from those of extreme nativism to those
of extreme empiricism (Hochberg, 1962; Pick and Pick, 1970). Are our
adult perceptual abilities and our perceptual knowledge of objects,
events, and space provided by initial, inborn biological "nature" (nativism), or are they the products of years of postnatal psychological "nurture" (empiricism)? They might be available right at birth or they
might require a shorter or longer period of biological maturation to

become completely functional; in either case, the extreme nativist assigns no developmentally formative role to experience. Alternatively, the organism might begin with the classical empiricist's tabula rasa, or blank slate, and have to construct all perceptual abilities and knowledge through countless experience with the external environment. Which view of perceptual development is the correct one, the nativist's or the empiricist's?

When stated in such extreme and uncompromising terms, neither view is correct. All perceptual processes (like all other psychological processes) are mediated by biological structures evolved by the species and inherited by the individual. Conversely, these structures require sensory input from the world if the processes are to function and develop. Recall the favorite cliché of introductory psychology texts: Development is always a matter of heredity *and* (or *times*) environment, never heredity *or* environment. The nativists and empiricists of old were clearly addressing a real issue, however, even though their questions and answers concerning it now may strike us as too extreme, too much all nature or all nurture. Contemporary students of human and animal perceptual development would prefer to get answers to more precise and differentiated questions such as the following. How much of exactly what kind of experience during exactly what period of ontogeny is necessary and/or sufficient for the emergence of exactly what component of perceptual knowledge or skill? Is a lot of experience needed, or only a little? Will any of a wide variety of experiences do the developmental job, or is a particular, specific kind required? Is there a so-called "critical period" involved, namely, a particular age period during which the necessary experience must be had if the perceptual component in question is to develop fully, or even develop at all?

Very seldom are we able to answer questions as precise as these in the case of human perceptual development, although progress is clearly being made (Banks, Aslin, and Letson, 1975; Cohen and Salapatek, 1975). Take the case of the development of space perception in infancy, an area in which people are currently doing some ingenious experimentation (Bower, 1974; Yonas and Pick, 1975). The problems are formidable. In the first place, what exactly do we mean to attribute to the infant when we say he can "perceive space" (Yonas and Pick, 1975)? Do we mean a full, adult-like apprehension of spatial layout in three dimensions, in which objects are perceived as being at various real-world positions, directions, and distances in relation to the perceiver and one another? Or do we simply mean an automatic sensory pickup of this or that visual cue for spatial depth, say—a visual experience as yet devoid of any interpretation by the infant as to the real sizes of objects seen and their actual distances from the observer?

Even if we use criteria of this last-mentioned, weaker sort, there is considerable controversy at present as to when the infant first meets such criteria. In general, Bower and his associates have obtained evidence for very early spatial-perceptual competence, whereas Yonas, Campos, and other investigators have obtained what seems to me to be more convincing evidence for later acquisition, e.g., towards the middle or latter part of the first year (Yonas and Pick, 1975). If the former group is correct, a fairly strong nativistic position would be tenable with respect to the origins of "space perception," at least in its minimal definition. If the latter group is correct, a more empiricistic position is possible but—to complicate our lives—by no means mandated. "Space perception" might be neither wholly innate and therefore present at birth, nor acquired as a function of subsequent perceptual experience; instead, it might develop gradually during infancy, but by means of some largely endogenous, biological-maturational process.

We are nearer to a precise answer in the case of certain other species, thanks to some extraordinary recent animal experiments (see Blakemore, 1974; Ganz, 1975). In the normally-reared, adult cat, individual neurons in the visual cortex have been found to show "preferences" for stimuli presented in particular spatial orientations. For instance, one neuron is likeliest to fire if a vertical line (bar, stripe) is presented, another neuron is tuned to lines oriented about 45° from vertical, and so on. Each orientation from 0° to 360° has one or more neurons that are primarily sensitive and responsive to it. A variety of such primitive "feature detectors" have been identified in several species; contour and color detectors are other examples. The cat's orientation detectors presumably help it analyze and discriminate object shapes. Prior to visual experience, on the other hand, the young kitten's visual-cortical cells tend to respond weakly to visual input and nonspecifically to orientation. What role, if any, does visual experience play in the genesis of the adult cat's cortical pattern?

Blakemore and his coworkers (Blakemore, 1974) reared kittens in darkness, except for a few hours a day spent in a most unusual environment. It consisted of a tall, cylindrical chamber painted with black and white stripes which were either horizontal or vertical. A ruff around the kitten's neck prevented it from seeing its own body. All it could see was either vertical or horizontal stripes, depending upon which chamber it was reared in. After several months of such experience, recordings were taken from each kitten's visual cortex. Blakemore (1974) describes the results as follows:

> Despite their very strange early visual diet, we found virtually no visually unresponsive neurons or nonoriented cells and no regions of silent cortex.

The neurons were quite normal and adult in all their properties. Only one thing was really unusual: We could find no neurons that had a preferred orientation within 20 deg of the angle orthogonal to the stripes the kitten had been reared in. Nearly all the cells responded best to orientations within 45 deg of that which the kitten had seen early in life. (p. 109)

In other words, visual experience with stimuli in particular orientations modifies cortical cells so that they become selectively sensitive to those particular orientations. Kittens reared with vertical stripes appear to develop the ability to discriminate only vertical or near-vertical contours with normal acuity. (Just what, if anything, they would actually see if presented with a horizontal rod or grating is still uncertain.)

Students of human perceptual development would be very happy if they had that type of fact. They would be even happier if they had the human counterpart of the rest of Blakemore's developmental story. First, further research has shown that there is a critical period for these experiential effects on the cat's visual development. The sensitivity of the kitten's cells to such orientational polarization by specific visual input is dependent upon its age. Sensitivity increases rapidly around 3 weeks of age, remains high from 4 to 7 weeks, and then diminishes gradually until about 14 weeks, after which time the cells become wholly unmodifiable by visual experience. Second, during this critical period very little visual experience is needed to effect polarization—as little as 1 hour. Finally, polarization seems to become fixed and irreversible after about 10 hours of visual exposure. That is, additional experience with differently-oriented stripes does not reverse the initially-acquired orientational preference of the cells. We have here, then, an almost ideal example of the kind of detailed understanding researchers would like to have concerning the interplay of innate and experiential variables in perceptual development. A specific amount and kind of experience has a definite, permanent effect on a particular type of perceptual ability, providing the experience occurs sometime during a delimited period of ontogeny. Banks, Aslin, and Letson (1975) have recently obtained less precise data of the same general kind concerning the development of binocular vision in humans. One hopes there will soon be more such evidence about human perceptual growth.

A Theory of Perceptual Learning and Development

There are a number of theories of perceptual learning and development (Gibson, 1969, Chaps. 2–5; Pick and Pick, 1970, pp. 824–828). Of particular interest to us is the theory of Eleanor J. Gibson (1969) (see also James J. Gibson, 1966). Her theory is more detailed and carefully worked out than others, has been and continues to be very productive of research, and is probably the most salient and influential theory on the contemporary scene. As will be explained subsequently, it is also the most pertinent to those aspects of perceptual development that will be emphasized in this chapter.

E. J. Gibson's theory addresses two basic kinds of questions concerning perceptual learning and development. First, *what is it that gets acquired whenever perceptual learning or development takes place?* What is the nature of the change or progression that occurs? How is the organism different at the end of the growth period than it was at the beginning? What is the characteristic product or outcome of the change process? Second, *what processes or mechanisms are responsible for this change?* What does the organism do and experience in order to get from the initial, lower level of perceptual competence to the later, more advanced one? The first set of questions asks how perceptual advances should be *described;* the second, how they should be *explained.*

Descriptive aspects.   The change process is said to consist of:

> . . . an increase in the ability of an organism to get information from its environment, as a result of practice with the array of stimulation provided by the environment. This definition implies that there are potential variables of stimuli that are not differentiated within the mass of impinging stimulation, but which may be, given the proper conditions of exposure and practice. As they are differentiated, the resulting perceptions become more specific with respect to stimulation, that is, in greater correspondence with it. There is a change in what the organism can respond to. The change is not acquisition or substitution of a new response to stimulation previously responded to in some other way, but is rather responding in any discriminating way to a variable of stimulation not responded to previously. The criterion of perceptual learning is thus an increase in specificity. What is learned can be described as detection of properties, patterns, and distinctive features. (Gibson, 1969, p. 77).

There is a lot of Gibson's theory packed into that excerpt. The first part of it reflects her belief that the outside world is exceedingly rich in physical information (optical, acoustic, etc.) of a type which reliably specifies the real nature of objects and events, and that this information is directly available to us through our senses. We do not have to *construct* our world *intellectually* because sense data are so impoverished and distortive of reality, as some psychologists have argued. We can *detect* its structure *perceptually,* according to this theory, because the sensory stream turns out to carry richer and more accurate information about the outside world than anyone thought. Philosophically, this view is a form of "realism," but it is hardly "naive realism": J. J. Gibson (e.g., 1966) has spent his professional life showing that there is, indeed, much more valid information about the world directly available to us via the senses than had been suspected. In fact, his contributions here are widely accepted as milestones in our understanding of perception.

However, to say that something is directly perceptible is not to say that it is automatically perceived. On the contrary, the essence of E. J. Gibson's theory is that with perceptual experience and practice we gradually isolate and attend to (differentiate, discriminate, selectively "pick up") information that was always "there" in the sensory input but not initially detected. What comes to be detected through this process are stimulus features and complexes of stimulus features that distinguish one object or event from another—hence, "distinctive features." According to this theory, we do not build up holistic mental copies, templates, or prototypes of things repeatedly perceived. Rather, we learn the specific features or feature combinations that differentiate those things from other, similar things. What is acquired, then, is an increased perceptual sensitivity to stimulus information that allows the perceiver to discriminate between similar things which he did not initially distinguish. In many cases, this information consists of patterns or relations which remain invariant under various transformations that preserve the identity of the thing (object, event) in question. (Recall from previous chapters the notion of *invariant formation* and its importance in cognitive development.) Much of what gets detected in the course of perceptual experience and practice could, in fact, be described as invariants in the sensory input which specify exactly what is being perceived. Depending upon the case, these invariants may be extremely simple or extremely complex—so complex that considerable scientific research may be required to identify them.

It is time for some examples. In one experiment (Gibson, 1969, pp. 77–80), subjects were presented with a standard, coil-shaped scribble and asked to indicate which of a number of other scribbles were exactly like it. The other scribbles were constructed so that they looked very much like the standard at first glance. They were also designed to differ from the standard on one or more of three dimensions or factors: number of coils, degree of horizontal compression (how "squashed" the coil was), and whether its center was to the right or to the left.

The subjects became more and more accurate with repeated comparisons between the standard and each other figure, even though they were given no feedback by the experimenter as to the correctness of the same-different judgments they were making. Moreover, their pattern of errors in the course of this miniature perceptual-learning experience was by no means random. The more dimensions differentiating a scribble from the standard, the likelier the subject was to recognize that the two were not the same. If the scribble differed from the standard in both number of coils and horizontal compression, for instance, the subject was less likely to err than if it differed on only one of these two dimensions. What the subjects appear to have been gradually learning were the features which were critical in distinguishing one novel form from other, similar-looking ones. It is likely, moreover, that they progressively differentiated out these critical features, finally identifying the set of three simple "invariants" which perceptually defined the standard as contrasted with its various "transformations" (the other scribbles):

> Detection of properties was illustrated in the scribble experiment, as the subjects discovered the dimensions of difference. It would be hard to over-emphasize the importance for perceptual learning of the discovery of invariant properties which are in correspondence with physical variables. (Gibson, 1969, p. 81).

The complexes of invariant properties and relations that specify what is being perceived can be incredibly complicated. Learning to distinguish among those scribbles is no perceptual feat at all compared to some that humans (and other animals) accomplish. For example, what exactly are the invariant features in the visual input that tell you ("perceptually specify") that an object is coming directly toward you at a roughly constant rate of speed, as when someone throws a basketball at your face, hard, from 10 feet away? Optically, the features consist of a continuous, symmetrically expanding closed contour, with the expansion accelerating at a certain rate (Gibson, 1969, p. 271). If the expansion is not continuous, the movement will be seen as jerky (hardly the behavior of a thrown basketball). If the expansion is not symmetrical, within the visual field, the ball will be perceived as heading to one side, about to miss you. If the expansion of the contour were uniform in speed, or insufficiently accelerative, you would perceive the ball as magically slowing down more and more as it neared your face. Thus, the physics-type invariants that specify this versus that perceptual experience-over-time ("event perception") can be surprisingly complex. These are the sorts of subtle, "higher order" invariants that the Gibsons and their students have been trying to identify. Note that they really are "out there" in the complicated and changing patterns of light that the eye detects. Gibsonian theory is decidedly stimulus oriented.

We do not yet know the extent to which the perception of object looming and similar events is dependent upon perceptual learning and experience; the problem is currently under investigation (Yonas and Pick, 1975). However, there are many other examples of very complex invariant detection that we know require months or years of learning (Gibson, 1969). The ability to land a plane smoothly, identify bird songs, and judge the quality of wine all presuppose considerable perceptual learning of the Gibsonian sort. So also does the ability to read radar screens, aerial photographs, X-rays, pathologists' slides—and, especially important, written language. For a recent application of the theory to the problem of how children learn to read, see Gibson and Levin (1975).

Explanatory aspects. An interesting feature of E. J. Gibson's theory is its explicit rejection of external reinforcement as a significant explanatory factor in perceptual learning and development: ". . . reward and punishment undoubtedly influence behavior, but it is very doubtful if they play an important role in perceptual learning, and certainly they do not play a necessary role" (Gibson, 1969, p. 136). Rather, the processes which result in Gibsonian perceptual differentiation and critical-feature identification are typically set into motion by intrinsic cognitive motives of the sort described at the beginning of Chap. 2. Gibson identifies three such processes—abstraction, filtering, and peripheral mechanisms of attention. The subject abstracts or extracts invariant features and relations among features in the course of perceptual experience with a variety of objects and events. To say that the subject abstracts and retains certain constant features or feature patterns is to imply that other, irrelevant or variable features are being ignored or filtered out. Filtering is a necessary complement of abstraction whenever the information reaching the senses exceeds that which is singled out for further processing by the central nervous system. Finally, the subject may or may not bring his sense organs into peripheral receptive contact with a potential stimulus in the outside world. In the case of vision, for instance, his eyes may actively explore the environment, scrutinizing some things slowly and with great care, inspecting others only fleetingly and superficially, and focussing on still others not at all. Perceptual learning and development thus is explained by the processes of making peripheral sensory contact with one thing rather than another, and of centrally abstracting out this and filtering out that within the thing contacted. To summarize the central tenets of the whole theory in Gibson's own words:

> It has been argued that what is learned in perceptual learning are distinctive features, invariant relationships, and patterns; that these are available in stimulation; that they must, therefore, be extracted from the total stimulus flux. The processes which are relevant for extraction include orienting responses of the sense organs; abstraction of relations and invariants; and filtering relevant features from irrelevant stimulation. . . . (Gibson, 1969, p. 119).

Perceptual Development as the Development of Perceptual-Attentional Selectivity

E. J. Gibson's theory represents a useful introduction to this chapter's treatment of perceptual development because of its emphasis on the selective character of perceptual processing and attentional deployment. Much of perceptual and other aspects of cognitive growth can be characterized as the development of selectivity (Pick, Frankel, and Hess, 1975). At any given moment, our sensory receptors do not even contact more than a fraction of what could be perceived in our immediate environment. This is Gibson's "peripheral mechanisms of attention" and constitutes an initial form of perceptual selectivity. As Gibson's "abstraction" and "filtering" concepts suggest, there is further selectivity once peripheral contact has been made—at the receptor level and upstream in the central nervous system. In the visual case, for instance, we cannot look everywhere at once, visually discriminate and identify everything we do look at, and simultaneously give full, cognitive attention to everything we can discriminate and identify. The notion of perceptual-attentional selectivity has been encountered previously in this book, e.g., the selective tuning of the cat's visual system to specific orientations which was cited earlier in this chapter and the Piagetian concept of centration in Chap. 3. A little reflection should convince you that this multilevel selectivity is an adaptational necessity. An organism that could, and had to, perceive and attend equally to everything in its surroundings simultaneously is scarcely imaginable, let alone viable. Perception and attention do not merely involve selectivity, they absolutely presuppose it.

The following sketch of human perceptual ontogenesis will emphasize the development of selectivity, particularly in the case of visual and auditory perception. Good sources for readers who want more than just a sketch include the following, some of which have already been cited: Bond (1972), Bower (1974), Bronson (1974), Cohen and Salapatek (1975), Gibson (1969), Hagen and Hale (1973), Kessen, Haith, and Salapatek (1970), Pick, Frankel, and Hess (1975), Pick and Pick (1970), and Salapatek (in press). Salapatek (in press) provides an especially helpful overview.

INFANCY

Fifteen years ago, Hochberg said that it would be highly desirable to study young infants' visual abilities, but that "the human infant displays insufficient behavior coordination to permit its study to give us very much useful information" (1962, p. 323). Since that time, Robert Fantz and other psychologists have developed a number of ingenious methods for assessing the perceptual abilities and dispositions of infants—even newborns. It does not seem an exaggeration to say that we have witnessed a methodological revolution here in the past fifteen years. The new order it produced is a flourishing area of psychological inquiry called infant perception. The idea that there could ever be a two volume book on infant perception (Cohen and Salapatek, 1975) would have been almost unthinkable when Hochberg wrote those words.

The young infant is an essentially helpless, poorly coordinated, behaviorally undeveloped creature—certainly a most improbable looking subject for a perception experiment. The key to studying infant perception proved to be the discovery and experimental exploitation of measurable response systems that partially track or reflect the infant's perceptual-attentional activity. By tapping into these response systems, it was discovered that we had underestimated the infant's perceptual capabilities because of his motoric ineptness. The infant turns out to be able to perceive the world a lot better than he can act on it.

The three major indices used have been looking patterns, sucking patterns, and heart rate patterns. Let us first examine how looking patterns can be used to gain information about infant attention. The experimenter displays a certain stimulus figure and a special camera tells him that the infant's eyes almost always fixate on particular parts of the figure rather than on other parts. He displays two figures and discovers that the infant systematically tends to look at one longer than the other. He repeatedly shows pairs of figures, one member of which always remains the same while the other keeps changing from pair to pair, i.e., consists of a new figure on each new presentation trial. As the trials continue, the infant devotes more and more of his looking time to the novel figure, as if he had gradually gotten used to and bored with the unchanging figure. More technically and less anthropomorphically, we would say that the infant "habituated" to it.

This process of *habituation* also figures importantly in the use of heart rate and sucking patterns to index infant attention patterns. The experimenter presents a certain visual array, or a particular sound, over and over again. At first the infant becomes alert and actively attends to the stimulus. If he is sucking on a pacifier nipple when the stimulus is presented, he may show this heightened attention by slowing down his sucking rate. Similarly, special recording devices might indicate a slowing down of his heart rate. Except in very young infants, such heart-rate deceleration is widely accepted as reflecting an orienting, attentional response. (Heart-rate *acceleration* would mean startle, upset, etc.) After repeated presentation, perceptual interest in that stimulus may gradually appear to wane (habituate), as indexed by the gradual recovery of sucking and heart rate to their initial, prestimulus levels. The experimenter then presents a new visual array or a different sound. The infant may signal his recognition of the change and his heightened interest in the new stimulus by once again reducing sucking and heart rate. This is referred to as recovery from habituation, or *dishabituation*. Even a newborn baby is capable of habituating to a repeated stimulus, and then dishabituating when it is replaced by a new one (Horowitz, 1974).

Without saying exactly what we mean to attribute to the infant psychologically in using the term, it is useful to think of all these measures as indices of infant perceptual "preferences." The measures may variously show that he "prefers" to look at or listen to this rather than that stimulus or stimulus component, or "prefers" a newly presented stimulus to the very same stimulus after it has been presented repeatedly (habituation). Such preferences tell us two very important things about the infant's perceptual system. First, they tell us what the system can perceptually distinguish or discriminate. Preferences logically imply discriminability: An organism could not systematically attend to ("prefer") one thing rather than another unless it could somehow perceptually discriminate the one from the other. If an infant prefers to look at a pattern of fine black and white stripes rather than at a homogeneous gray pattern of equal total brightness, for instance, that preference tells us that he has at least sufficient visual acuity to see the stripes. His visual acuity may, of course, be better than that, but it must be at least that good or there could have been no perceptual preference for the one pattern versus the other. Second, preferences tell us about themselves, that is, what the infant is more and less disposed to attend to, and thereby something about the design of the infant's perceptual-attentional and related psychological systems. Recall the discussion of cognitive motivation in Chap. 2 (pp. 19–24). It was said that human beings may be designed to be selectively attentive to certain absolute and relative properties of stimuli, such as movement and novelty. If a young infant usually looked at a moving object rather than an identical stationary one, we could say both that he can perceptually discriminate movement from nonmovement and that his visual system is so constructed as to be more attentive to movement than nonmovement. In summary, research methods now exist that can detect systematic attentional preferences in infants of different ages, including neonates. Inferences about both the powers and the propensities of the infant's perceptual system can then be made from these preferences.

As always, I have made things sound more simple and straightforward than they really are. The recording and interpretation of looking, sucking, and heart-rate patterns in infants are fraught with problems. Young babies are unstable little creatures, subject to changes in physiological state from one time period to another. Imagine how that fact can complicate the interpretation of, say, changes in heart rate over time. The evidence obtained from one measure may not always accord with that obtained from another. The infant may, in fact, be able to discriminate between two stimuli perceptually but not show any attentional preference for one versus the other, with the result that his discriminative ability goes undetected. That is, preference logically implies discrimination but discrimination certainly does not imply preference. Finally, even if it can be shown (e.g., by preference data) that the infant can discriminate one thing from another, it still may be very difficult to establish the exact basis on which the discrimination was made. Stimuli are likely to differ from one another in a variety of ways simultaneously, and it may be very hard to prove exactly which differentiating feature or combination of features the baby is attending to.

Despite these problems, the new methods have produced a number of provisional facts about infant perceptual development. Most of the evidence concerns vision and audition, probably the two most important sensory instruments of human learning and development. The following synopsis therefore deals only with infant visual and auditory development.

Vision

One of the most striking recent findings concerning infant visual development is that the visual abilities and propensities of very young babies (0 to 1 or 2 months) differ considerably from those of older ones (1 or 2 or 3 months and beyond). The visual system is still quite neurologically immature at birth, both within the eye itself and within the parts of the brain that mediate vision. In both places, furthermore, the areas that are most immature appear to be those which govern form or pattern perception (the visual cortex in the brain and, less certainly, the foveal region of the eye's retina). This is a significant fact, as will be shown. Nonetheless, the newborn can indeed see and even exhibits visual selectivity ("preferences") of a sort. However, his visual system has three conspicuous deficiencies, all of which are at least partly remedied in the next several months of life. These are poor visual acuity, inflexible visual accommodation, and imperfect binocular convergence.

First, his acuity has been very roughly estimated at only about 20/600 (normal adult vision is, of course, about 20/20); it will improve to around 20/150 at four months of age (Salapatek, in press). Second, unlike the older infant and adult, the lens of his eye does not reflexively change its shape (accommodate) when objects are presented at different distances, so as to focus them most sharply and clearly on the retina. Instead, the lens tends to remain fixed in a shape that would produce the clearest retinal image for an object presented somewhere within 13 inches from the eye; this fixed focal point varies from infant to infant, but it has an average value of about 7 inches from the eye. Finally, the two eyes do not always move together and fixate on the same thing (converge). It appears, then, that the very young baby cannot make really fine visual discriminations (poor acuity), often sees things out of focus and blurred (fixed accommodation), and may—we do not know—even experience double vision sometimes (occasional lack of binocular convergence). It might be mentioned parenthetically that the convergence problem alone could limit the newborn's innate capacity (if he has any) to perceive spatial depth and distance. The reason is that some of the cues for depth are binocular rather than monocular, i.e., require that both eyes focus on the same thing. His acuity and accommodation problems may impose similar constraints on space perception.

Bronson (1974) and others have recently conceptualized early visual development in the following way. They distinguish between a phylogenetically older "second visual system" and a more recently evolved "primary visual system." Very roughly, the second visual system tells the organism *where* visible objects are in the immediate environment and the primary one tells it precisely *what* those objects are (Salapatek, in press). The second visual system reflexively turns the eyes to fixate an object when it enters the periphery of the visual field, and it also causes them to track it if it continues to move across the field. It thus uses eye movements to bring peripherally-detected targets into central, foveal vision and to keep them there. The system does these two things much more reliably and effectively in the case of visual targets that are large and perceptually salient. This is the visual system that allows an organism to move adaptively through its environment: to avoid obstacles, pursue prey, evade looming predators, and the like.

In contrast, the primary visual system is concerned with a precise, fine-grained visual analysis and encoding of forms and patterns. It examines and identifies the detailed perceptual properties of the targets that the second visual system brings into foveal vision—that is, their patterns of contours, colors, and other features. Central feature detectors of the sorts mentioned earlier in this chapter play an important role in this fine visual analysis. This is presumably true in humans as well as in other species. Bronson (1974) also believes that it is the primary rather than the second visual system that permits the organism to fixate and track small versus large objects, and to scan or redirect its gaze intentionally rather than just reflexively.

The developmental hypothesis is that the visual behavior of the very young human infant is mediated primarily by the second visual system, with the primary visual system becoming progressively more functional and more perceptually important during subsequent months. A number of facts seem consistent with this hypothesis. Among these are the newborn's neuroanatomical immaturities and his visual deficiencies which were mentioned earlier, all of which suggest only a minimally functional primary visual system. His or her gaze does get reflexively "captured" by large, moving stimuli, especially if they appear in the peripheral visual field. His patterns of visual preferences or selectivity also have a second- rather than primary-visual-system ring to them. The stimuli that tend to attract the most visual attention seem to be those that possess the most contour. It is only the sheer size or number or density (we are not sure just which) of contoured elements that appear to matter for the very young infant, not the specific shapes and configurations of those elements. If one introduces the outline of a triangle into his visual field, for instance, he is likely to fixate his gaze on one corner and keep it there. That is, he looks only at one, contour-rich fragment of the stimulus, rather than explore and analyze the entire stimulus pattern. Similarly, he does not seem to process the interior components of complex forms. If presented with a pattern consisting of a square with a smaller square inside it, he is likely only to fixate a corner of the outer square, even though he is easily capable of fixating the smaller square if it is presented in isolation (Salapatek, in press).

As the infant grows older and the primary visual system matures, his visual analysis becomes progressively finer and more extensive. He becomes able to direct his gaze voluntarily, and to inspect all the different components—inner as well as outer—of entire complex figures. Moreover, he attends to the interrelationships among these components, i.e., whole patterns of visual features. This eventually makes it possible for the baby to recognize and discriminate among objects and events. With increased visual experience, what he has seen in the past comes to influence what he sees and wants to look at in the present. Absolute stimulus properties like movement and amount of contour continue to influence visual selectivity, but experience stored in memory plays an increasingly dominant role (see Chap. 2). As Salapatek describes it: "The infant is changing from an organism that began by selecting patterns and shapes solely on the basis of amount and size of contour present towards a conscious human with memory for visual events who now selects where he will look, on the basis of memory as well as reflexes" (in press). Or in Bronson's words, "the infant becomes an internally directed, historically guided, pattern-organizing individual" (1974, p. 887).

The development of the infant's responses to the human face illustrates these points. The face is a potent elicitor of visual attention, even in very young infants. At one time it was thought that babies might be endowed by evolution with an inborn, unlearned visual preference for the human face per se. While this idea is not biologically implausible, recent research suggests that it is almost surely wrong. Faces seem to elicit visual attention at first only because they are mobile and have lots of perceptually salient contour. They are not inherently more attention-getting than nonface targets which have equivalent stimulus properties. Initially, the baby is likely to fixate only some piece of external contour, such as the hairline, behaving much as he does with the embedded squares. Later, he becomes capable of analyzing and storing information about inner features (eyes, mouth, etc.) and their spatial relationships. The infant can now see face as a whole, i.e., as an entire stimulus configuration. The rest of the story is largely that of the development of social attachment and infant social cognition (Chap. 2). That is, the baby gradually discriminates faces from nonfaces, then one face from another, and so on, with visual preferences and attentional selectivity changing accordingly.

There are other developing visual abilities of considerable adaptive significance, but their ontogenesis is still poorly understood. The development of space perception is a case in point, as was indicated at the beginning of this chapter (Yonas and Pick, 1975). A "visual cliff" is a device invented by Walk and E. J. Gibson for assessing an organism's depth perception abilities (see Gibson, 1969, pp. 240, 319–321). On one side, a horizontal plate of glass rests just above a textured surface. On the other, deep or "cliff" side, the surface lies a considerable distance beneath the covering glass. The young of several species (e.g., rats) have been found to possess an innate ability to perceive depth, as evidenced by a differential tendency to avoid traversing the deep versus the shallow side of the Walk and Gibson visual cliff. Campos and his coworkers have observed that two-month-old human babies show greater heart-rate deceleration when placed on the deep side than when placed on the shallow side. In contrast, they found that while the shallow side continues to elicit heart-rate deceleration in nine month olds, the deep side now causes not deceleration but acceleration (Yonas and Pick, 1975). The younger infants' differential deceleration suggests that some kind of depth-related discrimination must be taking place, but its interpretation is problematic. On the other hand, the heart-rate acceleration of the older infants indicates that they are clearly responding to the deep side *as* a deep side, i.e., as a drop off that quite properly induces some heart-racing fear. This and similar lines of evidence led Yonas and Pick (1975) to be quite confident that a baby of, say, six months has considerable spatial sensitivity by anyone's definition. But they were a lot less confident about just what younger infants possess in this important area of visual perception.

In keeping with our emphasis on perceptual development as the development of perceptual-attentional selectivity, the following excerpt from Bond (1972) seems an appropriate way to conclude this section on infant vision:

> The selective attention of the infant serves the purpose of directing his gaze toward certain kinds of stimulation in the environment. At a very early age, the basic neural structure of the organism may take primary responsibility for this direction. Gradually, however, the effects of experience grow in influence, and stimuli become recognizable and meaningful. The selective attention of the infant becomes tempered by the kinds of stimuli to which he has been exposed (and to which he has exposed himself). (p. 243)

Audition

Less is known about infant auditory development than about infant visual development (Pick, Frankel, and Hess, 1975). It is certain that the neonate can hear as well as see (Pick and Pick, 1970; Salapatek, in press). However, we are less certain about precisely how well he can hear, exactly how he may differentially react to different kinds and intensities of sound, and how these auditory abilities and preferences may change with age. The very young infant appears to be able to hear a sound at least as soft as 40 decibels (and probably softer). He is likely to be startled and upset by very loud, sudden noises. On the other hand, at least certain sounds of moderate intensity seem to be experienced as pleasureful or pacifying. For instance, the sucking response can be operantly conditioned using music or speech as the sole reinforcer; that is, if sucking is followed by such sounds, the sucking increases. Parents often report that low, rhythmic sounds tend to soothe and quiet their babies, and the research evidence suggests that they are probably right (Kessen *et al.*, 1970, p. 321).

There have been reports that newborns will automatically look in the direction of a punctate sound, like a click. In general, however, evidence for good visual-auditory coordination or integration during the earliest months is uncertain at best. In one experiment using 1-, 4-, and 7-month-old subjects, baby and mother sat facing one another while the mother spoke continuously to the baby through a microphone (McGurk and Lewis, 1974). Louspeakers attached to the microphone made her voice appear to come from different places at different times—now from her mouth—now from the baby's right, now from its left. Babies at all three ages tended to turn their heads more when the voice came from a side rather than from the center, but only the four- and seven-month-olds tended to localize the sound accurately, i.e., turn to the correct side. An earlier study (Aronson and Rosenbloom, 1971) had reported that babies as young as one month old become disturbed if their mother's voice appears to originate elsewhere than from her mouth, perhaps suggesting some inborn ability to perceive events as belonging to a common auditory-visual space. McGurk and Lewis (1974) saw no such disturbance, however, even in their two older groups. Once again, we know very little about the young infant's perception of space.

During the first six months of life, babies become understandably more attuned to and interested in a certain class of auditory input, namely, the human voice and human speech. Horowitz and her co-workers (1974) have shown that babies as young as two months of age are capable of perceptually discriminating between two voices reading the same passage (their mother's and that of an adult female stranger), and even between the same voice reading the same passage in a "soft" versus a "harsh" intonation.

Far and away the most dramatic research on infant audition nowadays, however, has to do with the perception of elementary phonological speech units, such as consonant sounds. Recent studies by Eimas (1975) and others in this area can only be described as astonishing. It is necessary to say something about the nature of speech perception in adults before the infant findings can be understood and appreciated. Someone once told me that there are only two levels of understanding of the field of international trade and finance: One takes about five minutes to achieve and the other about five years. The same is true of speech perception. I will only try for the five-minute variety here; you are referred to Eimas (1975) if you want to get started on the five-year course.

The purely physical, acoustic difference between an auditory stimulus that sounds like "ba" and one that sounds like "pa" is a completely quantitative, continuous one. The acoustic dimension involved is a continuum, just like length or weight. Supposing we were to vary the auditory stimulus on that dimension. We start on the "ba" end of the dimension and gradually, continuously change the stimulus until we get to the "pa" end, much as we might gradually, continuously lengthen a line by slowly moving our pencil along a straightedge. What should happen perceptually? The "ba" should come to sound more and more "pa"-like, and there should be a broad zone in the middle of the dimension where the listener cannot easily say which of the two consonants the sound most resembles. He might be inconsistent in his choice from trial to trial within this broad zone, or report blends of "ba" or "pa."

The major discovery of the last decade or so of speech perception research is that we do not perceive certain speech sounds in this expected, continuous fashion. What happens instead is that suddenly, abruptly —almost at a single point on that continuous dimension—the stimulus is heard as "pa" instead of "ba." As the stimulus continuously varies, the listener discontinuously reports . . . "ba," "ba," "ba," "pa," "pa," "pa". . . . Thus, consonant perception tends to be discontinuous or "categorical" rather than continuous, in marked contrast to most other forms of perception. For instance, a tiny change in light wave length does not abruptly change the color category reported, e.g., from a clear, unequivocal blue to a clear, unequivocal green. Similarly, my pencil line will not suddenly and thereafter be perceived as "long" rather than "short" when it reaches, say, 8.23 inches.

Not all languages distinguish between the consonantal sounds "b" and "p," as does English. However if a language does use this particular phonetic contrast to distinguish one word from another, the small region on that acoustic dimension where the abrupt shift from "b" to "p" perception occurs is likely to be the same as in English. Is this just happenstance, or might it be that all human beings are built alike in certain important respects in regard to perceiving speech? Of course, childhood experience with a particular language will profoundly affect speech perception, but it might still be true that this experience builds upon some natively given, evolved perceptual biases or proclivities. The latter might importantly aid the child in learning some of the phonological distinctions that the people around him make, because they allow him to hear these distinctions easily—to make the same "perceptual cuts in the physical-acoustic stream" that they do.

What Eimas (1975) and other investigators have recently shown is that very young infants (e.g., one month old) also exhibit categorical perception of consonantal sounds. To illustrate the nature of their evidence, let us suppose that our "ba"-"pa" acoustic dimension was arbitrarily marked off into equal physical segments, like this: 1–2–3–4–5–6. Let us further suppose that adults hear stimuli 1, 2, and 3 as "ba" and stimuli 4, 5, and 6 as "pa," since the dimension's small transition zone lies between stimuli 3 and 4. While sounds 1 and 3 are no more different from each other from the physicist's standpoint than 3 and 5 are from each other, a listener hears the members of the first pair as the same sound ("ba") and the members of the second pair as two different sounds ("ba" and "pa"). This is a clear instance of categorical speech perception. If a young infant is exposed to 1 until he habituates to it, he will continue to show habituation if 1 is replaced by 3. In contrast, if initially habituated to 3 and then presented with 5, he shows dishabituation. In other words, the baby acts as if he does not hear the difference between 1 and 3, just as adults do not, but as if he does hear the difference between 3 and 5, just as adults do. Eimas (1975) also has evidence that infant categorical speech perception may be mediated by linguistic feature detectors in the brain, akin to the visual feature detectors discussed earlier in this chapter. He further argues that the infant would find it exceedingly difficult if not impossible to acquire speech without these specialized instruments for perceiving human language.

The young infant therefore shows auditory as well as visual selectivity but, as in the visual area, only subsequent experience will endow that selectivity with meaning and purpose:

> Finally, it is clear that as one moves beyond one and two months of age, an increasingly powerful determinant of attention comes into play—mind. As the cortex matures, and as the infant encodes the events with which he has been confronted, his interests change. What is strange or known, or interesting, fearful, or boring changes. . . . At this point mind controls attention more than the physical properties of stimuli. (Salapatek, in press).

CHILDHOOD AND ADOLESCENCE

As in other areas of functioning, we still know relatively little about perceptual-attentional development during the period between late infancy and early preschool age (Pick, Frankel, and Hess, 1975). However, changes from about age three on have received considerable study (Gibson, 1969; Goodnow, 1971; Hagen and Hale, 1973; Maccoby, 1969; Pick, Frankel, and Hess, 1975; Pick and Pick, 1970). As "mind" comes increasingly to "control attention" (Salapatek, in press) during the post-infancy years, it becomes harder and more unnatural to think about perception in isolation from other cognitive categories, such as memory and thought. It is apparent, for instance, that selective attention gradually becomes deployable over the inner world as well as the outer one (Pick *et al.*, 1975), The older individual can mentally attend to things before and after, as well as during, their perceptual presence. Similarly, with the advent of "mind," knowledge becomes more abstract and amodal, less specifically "visual," "auditory," or "tactile" in nature (Goodnow, 1971). What is typically stored in memory is the essential information about the world derived from a perceptual act; the fact that the information came in through this sensory gate rather than that is generally of little consequence for the individual, and will not necessarily even be remembered. While our focus here is still on perceptual-attentional selectivity rather than on, say, selectivity in memory (see Chap. 6), it should be borne in mind that such distinctions are largely convenient fictions.

The developmental picture I am about to draw has elements of best guess as well as fact in it, but I believe it is generally accurate (cf. Gibson, 1969, Chap. 20). There is a good mnemonic for remembering the highlights of childhood perceptual-attentional development, which is somewhat reminiscent of the one proposed for cognitive motivation in

Chap. 2. Imagine what properties a good, adaptive attentional system ought to have, and then assume that the child's system increasingly tends to resemble this ideal as a function of attentional experience and general cognitive growth.

Environmental Influences

Pick *et al.* (1975) suggest that a rough distinction can be made between environmental contributions to attentional selectivity and those provided by the subject himself. Much of the existing developmental literature deals with environmental contributions, often considered in conjunction with the child's attentional dispositions. For instance, we may be able to guide and control a young child's attention by careful instruction, by perceptually highlighting the stimuli to be attended to, and so on. What he cannot do on his own, the child may be able to do if we structure his perceptual environment for him in such ways. In addition, he is likely to walk into our task situation with his own, preexisting attentional biases and preferences. Some stimulus dimensions (e.g., color, shape, size) are likely to be more noticeable or perceptually salient for him than others; indeed, there may be whole hierarchies of dimensional salience (e.g., Odom and Guzman, 1972). These preexisting attentional dispositions, like the instructions, highlighting, etc., may be important in influencing what the child processes, learns, and remembers in a task situation. For instance, he is likely to learn more easily that a certain dimension is the "correct" one in a discrimination or concept learning task, to sort on the basis of it in a classification task, and so on, if that dimension has high perceptual salience for him. Perceptual salience is undoubtedly a factor to be reckoned with at any age, but it seems to be particularly important in affecting the young child's attentional deployment. What stimulus features or dimensions are most salient may also change with age, as well as differ from subject to subject and from task setting to task setting at any given age.

Perhaps more interesting than the foregoing, however, are developmental changes in other attentional abilities and dispositions within the subject. These are the changes for which the above-mentioned mnemonic is most useful.

Control

As children develop, they generally become more capable of deliberately directing and controlling the deployment of their own attention. They become better able to focus their attention in an active, controlled fashion on just those external data which are relevant to their task objectives, while disregarding task-irrelevant data that are also present and equally perceptible. The process of disregarding irrelevant data may vary from a relatively effortless ignoring of nonsalient features to an active and effortful shutting out of unwanted input, as when a person consciously forces himself not to attend to clamorous, distracting, attention-compelling stimuli. One thing that seems to develop, then, is the capacity for controlled selective attention to wanted information coupled with controlled selective inattention to unwanted information. As indicated earlier in this chapter *(Perceptual Development as the Development of Perceptual-Attentional Selectivity)*, such selectivity can occur at more than one stage of information processing. To paraphrase a statement made in that earlier section, a good attentional system will look where it wants to, discriminate and identify only the wanted portion of what it sees, and give full, cognitive attention (in perception, thought, or memory) only to the wanted portion of what it discriminates and identifies. There is much that we still do not know about how, where, and when these selection or filtering processes operate, and also just what does and what does not develop in these respects. But almost certainly an overall developmental trend exists toward greater voluntary control over one's perceptual-attentional processes.

Adaptability

This increase in attentional control serves as a means to the end of attentional adaptability. An attentional system is adaptive if it can flexibly, efficiently, and economically adjust itself to what the situation requires (Hagen and Hale, 1973; Gibson, 1969). As the individual matures, he uses his control capability to shape and accommodate his attentional behavior to the idiosyncracies of the task or problem before him. In one study (Hale and Taweel, 1974), for instance, eight year olds were shown to be more apt than five year olds to attend to two features of a stimulus when that was the adaptive (efficient, economical) thing to do and to attend to only one feature when that was the better strategy. The older children spontaneously broadened or narrowed their attentional tuning, depending upon what the task seemed to call for. Similarly, sixth graders have been found to be better than second graders at rapidly adapting their attentional strategy to trial-to-trial changes in task demands (Pick and Frankel, 1974). As the authors indicate: "This finding is in accord with the hypothesis of a developmental trend toward greater flexibility and adaptability of strategies of selection or of attention" (p. 1164).

My own mental image of a cognitively mature information processor is that of a conductor who directs his ensemble of musicians (attentional processes and resources)—now calling forth one instrument, now another, now a blended combination of several or all, depending upon the effect desired. I think we do not so much "pay attention" as "play our attentional system." That is, we intentionally exploit and deploy it in a flexible, situation-contingent, adaptive fashion.

Planfulness

"Intentionally exploit and deploy" suggests that mature attending is planful and strategic, and this is indeed often the case. The conductor obviously has a plan in mind as he shapes the behavior of his orchestra (control) to make its musical product accord with the composer's intentions (adaptability). A mature attentional system may foresightedly pretune itself to process a specific kind of information efficiently and economically, if it knows beforehand that this information rather than some other kind is coming its way. If second graders and sixth graders are told what to attend to before rather than after a stimulus array is presented, both groups respond more quickly, i.e., benefit from the foreknowledge. More importantly, however, the older children derive relatively more benefit from this foreknowledge than the younger children do (Pick, Christy, and Frankel, 1972).

Similarly, an older child is more apt than a younger one to search for information in a planful, systematic fashion. (Recall what was said on this point in the *Information Processing Strategies* section of Chap. 4.) Vurpillot (1968) gave children of different ages the task of comparing pairs of houses to determine whether or not they were identical. Some were, in fact, identical, while others showed differences in one or more pairs of corresponding windows. For instance, the top left window of one house might have a different appearance from the top left window of the other. Older children proved likelier than younger ones to approximate the ideal perceptual-attentional strategy for this task: Scan corresponding windows pair by pair in some systematic, planful fashion that ensures that none will be missed, e.g., scan column by column. If a difference is detected, stop—the houses are nonidentical. If no difference is detected after all pairs have been compared, stop—the houses are identical. The perceptual search of the young child is often, as here, incomplete (centered versus decentered, in Piaget's terms) and unsystematic in relation to what the task demands. It is, in a real sense, less "intelligent" than that of the older child in its lack of planfulness. In Maccoby's words: "With increasing age, the child's perceptions are more and more dominated by organized search patterns that are related to sustained 'plans' or ongoing behavior patterns of the perceiver" (1969, p. 94).

Not all planful-looking behavior need be accompanied by conscious awareness that a plan is being followed, but this is surely the case sometimes. I believe that future research will show that older subjects are more aware than younger ones of their own ongoing patterns of attentional deployment. In Chap. 4 (*Percepts* section) the term "metattention" was coined to describe a (probably) developing awareness of the attentional behavior of others. It could equally apply to the conscious monitoring and guiding of one's own planful attentional behavior, which also (probably) develops.

Attention Over Time

One of the principal characteristics of attentional behavior in real life is that it is extended in time. Everyday attentional deployment does not ordinarily consist of single, isolated acts of noticing and processing this rather than that, as the existing research literature would sometimes lead one to believe. Rather, it commonly entails a complex sequencing and interweaving of interrelated attentional acts over whole stretches of time, with feedback from earlier acts affecting the nature and course of subsequent ones. The cognitively mature individual uses his capacity for control, adaptability, and planfulness to impart an integrated and patterned character to his attentional deployment over time. He maintains an attentional strategy if it continues to work, but is liable to change it when he discovers that it was—or has now become—inappropriate to his objectives. He avoids hasty perceptual decisions based on an inadequate or incomplete sampling of the pertinent information, as Vurpillot's (1968) study illustrated. He also resamples or rescans stimulus elements already investigated if he believes he may have missed or misinterpreted something. Both illustrate his ability to avoid premature attentional closure. Finally, he is capable of enacting multiple as well as single attentional sets or plans, maintaining and continuously updating several perceptual search enterprises at once over a considerable period of time. Future research in this area would do well, in my opinion, to investigate the development of these more complex, extended, multiset patterns of attentional deployment.

OTHER TOPICS

There is more to perceptual development than the development of perceptual-attentional selectivity (cf. Pick, 1971; Pick and Pick, 1970). Other topics include developmental aspects of: time perception; space and object perception (object orientation, spatial frames of reference, etc.);

cross-modal integration of information coming from different senses; the coordination of sensory and motor systems; eidetic imagery (visual "photographic memory"); perceptual illusions; and picture perception. As examples, some visual illusions increase with age while others decrease with age. Interesting explanations have been proposed for these developmental patterns (e.g., Pollack, 1972), but none seems wholly adequate at present. Similarly, children can usually discriminate visual and auditory patterns perceptually long before they can copy or imitate them accurately. Why this "developmental lag between perceiving and performing," as it has been called (Olson and Pagliuso, 1968, p. 155)? Finally, there are unresolved questions concerning the development of picture perception (Hagen, 1974). When you think about it, a picture is an odd perceptual object. To perceive what a picture depicts, the viewer must somehow extract a three-dimensional visual representation from a flat, two-dimensional object. At the same time, however, he must also perceptually register the picture's flatness; otherwise, he would think he were viewing a real scene, not a depicted one. Not much is known as yet about the ontogenesis of this dual competence—to see *what* is depicted, and to see that it *is* depicted, rather than really there.

COMMUNICATION

Communication Development as an Aspect of Language Development

The original plan had been to title this section "Language" rather than "Communication." Language development is clearly part of cognitive development. Furthermore, it is one of the most active and exciting research topics in psychology today. Like Piaget's theory, speech perception, and other topics, however, language development as a whole unfortunately does not lend itself well to brief presentation. On the other hand, it is possible to be both brief and comprehensible about a particular aspect of language development, namely, the acquisition of verbal communication skills.

The child more or less simultaneously learns two things in the course of language development. He learns language itself, and he learns how to use language. The first means that he acquires his native language per se—as a language. He comes to "know" it in the sense that you "know English." But what does it mean to say that you "know English," or that a child has "acquired language"? Basically, it means that you and he in some sense possess an incredibly complex system of implicit linguistic rules for producing and comprehending novel but phonologically and grammatically correct English utterances. Further questions then arise:

What is this system of linguistic rules like, what could "in some sense possess" mean, and how do children acquire the system? It is at this point that the story of language development must either stop or else become much longer. Dale's text (1972) provides a good, readable introduction to the rest of the story.

We can roughly distinguish between the private-cognitive and the social-communicative in regard to language use. The former refers to the use of language as any sort of aid to one's own thinking, remembering, emotional control, or other nonsocial endeavors. The latter refers to the use of language to send and receive messages in interpersonal situations. The past decade has seen two main types or traditions of research on the development of the communicative uses of language.

Two Research Traditions in the Study of Communication Development

Research in the earlier of the two traditions grew out of some pioneering studies by Piaget (1926), and generally it exhibits the following characteristics (e.g., Flavell, Botkin, Fry, Wright, and Jarvis, 1968; Glucksberg, Krauss, and Higgins, 1975). First, much of it is rather narrowly focused on the development of what are called referential communication skills. Essentially this means the child's developing ability to describe something so that his listener could identify, from among a set of available alternatives, exactly which thing the child had in mind. Second, the communication problems presented to the child usually are of the nonnaturalistic, laboratory-task variety. The child is told what the communicative problem is (e.g., impart information about X to listener Y under communication conditons Z) and is asked to solve it, much as one might ask him or her to solve any kind of arbitrary problem in a psychological experiment. Finally, efforts are made to identify the underlying cognitive abilities and inabilities responsible for the child's communicative performance on such tasks. A frequently explored possibility, for instance, is that because of the child's egocentrism, he fails to construct his message with his listener's informational needs in mind. An extreme example of communicative egocentrism would be to say, "this thing (point) does that (gesture)," to a listener who cannot see you. A common finding of studies done in this tradition is that children of elementary school age or even older perform inadequately, e.g., egocentrically, on the communication tasks used. Research in this tradition still continues, and Glucksberg *et al.* (1975) provide a useful review and analysis of it.

The second research tradition is still in process of formation, and it is difficult to find any single, comprehensive account of it (Bates, 1974; Dore, in press; Ervin-Tripp, 1974; Garvey and Hogan, 1973; Halliday,

1973; Shatz and Gelman, 1973). This tradition contrasts with the first on almost all the above dimensions. First, communication development is taken to mean far more than the acquisition of referential communication skills. It also includes the child's developing ability to use language to request, demand, command, promise, deny, greet, comment, converse, and perform numerous other communicative acts or functions (e.g., Halliday, 1973). Researchers in this tradition might ask, for instance, when the child first uses or comprehends indirect requests, such as understanding "It's rather noisy in here" to mean "Please stop making so much noise" (Ervin-Tripp, 1974). The term "sociolinguistic" is often used to describe this sort of research. While some studies in the earlier tradition have dealt with persuasion, for example Flavell *et al.* (1968, pp. 135–47), most have operationally defined "communication" to mean only the attempted transmission of information about perceived objects from one head to another. Second, the research methods used in the second tradition tend to be either systematic observations of children's spontaneous communications or "tasks" which closely mimic the natural, real-life communication situations the child encounters at home or at school. Third, there has been somewhat less explicit concern with the cognitive processes underlying communicative performance than in the earlier tradition, although such concern seems to be increasing. Finally, as we shall see, the development of communicative competence looks much more precocious in this tradition than in the earlier one. Children of *grade* three or four often communicate egocentrically in the tasks of the first tradition; children of *age* three or four often communicate non-egocentrically in the contrived or uncontrived situations of the second.

Cognitive Processes in Communication

Research of the first tradition has suggested the existence of several cognitive processes that help to mediate effective communication (Glucksberg *et al.*, 1975). Several processes appear to show developmental increases with age, and generally can be detected in the behavior of adult subjects.

One of these is a sensitivity to the referent-nonreferent array, i.e., to the similarities and differences between what you are trying to get the listener to identify (the referent) and other things he might confuse it with (the nonreferents). "The red block" will obviously not identify the referent if all the objects in front of the listener are red blocks. "The one with a chipped corner" will obviously serve the listener very well indeed if there is only one such block in the referent-nonreferent array. Of course, in some situations the child may not possess the necessary vocabulary or verbal fluency to produce a description that adequately distinguishes referent from nonreferent. More interesting are the cases where he does have the necessary linguistic resources but fails to detect the problem, e.g., by ignoring the nonreferents entirely in composing his communication.

A second process is a sensitivity to the listener and his communicative situation. One often has to be more explicit to a stranger than to an intimate, to a young child than to an adult, to someone on the phone than to someone in the room.

A third is sensitivity to feedback from the listener as to how one's communicative attempts are faring. A puzzled look or an "I'm not sure I understand" on the listener's part may not be interpreted by a child speaker as an implicit mandate to augment or reformulate his original message.

Finally, there are important processes on the listener side. A listener needs to be sensitive to possible message inadequacies or ambiguities, and he must know how to clarify them by appropriate questions or other feedback to the speaker.

It is apparent that all of these processes (except adequate vocabulary and the like) can implicate the social-cognitive abilities described in Chap. 4. A skillful speaker or listener tries to diagnose or predict the cognitions of his interlocutor from all available data (the referent-nonreferent array, the nature of the speaker and his situation, etc.) in order to achieve his communicative goals. There are different types and levels of sensitivity here, only a few of which have been investigated developmentally. For instance, a listener needs to know when to turn a nonspeaker into a speaker as well as when to turn an unclear speech into a clear one; that is, he needs to know when he ought to seek information in the first place, as well as when he ought to seek clarification of information already delivered (Cooper, 1972). A sensitive listener may intuit that the message he has just received is ambiguous, as indicated earlier. But the person who sent it also may be sensitive enough to detect its potential ambiguity and, knowing his listener, anticipate exactly that intuition. On the other hand, the same speaker may predict that a different sort of listener, e.g., a small child, will not detect the potential ambiguity at all, but instead will pick up only the one meaning the listener intended he should. As with the social cognition that helps mediate it, there is no obvious end to the development of communication skills.

Contrasting Research Findings From the Two Traditions

Consider the striking difference in results between these two, formally similar studies. Flavell *et al.* (1968, pp. 82–102) taught second- and eighth-grade subjects how to play a board game by silently playing it with them, rather than by explaining it verbally. The subjects, however, then were given the task of explaining the game verbally to two supposedly naive adults in turn, one of whom was sighted and the other blindfolded. The eighth graders appropriately produced longer, more explicit descriptions when talking to the listener who could not see the game materials. In contrast, the second graders did not seem to try to tailor their messages to the very different informational needs of these two listeners. Instead, their two game descriptions tended to be much the same. Similar developmental differences were found when subjects who communicated only to a sighted listener were compared, at each age level, with subjects who communicated only to a blindfolded listener.

In the other study (Maratsos, 1973) a wooden hill with a toy car on the top was placed on the table between the experimenter and the child. For subjects in the blocked-vision condition the instructions were:

> We're going to play a game with this hill and this car and some toys. This is how the game works: I want you to sit there and catch the car coming down the hill, O.K.? Now I'm going to put some people and animals on top of the hill and then I'll close my eyes, and you tell me which one I should put in the car. (p. 697)

For subjects in the normal-vision condition, the instructions were identical except that the phrase "and then I'll close my eyes" was omitted. On a given trial the experimenter would put, say, a red duck and a green duck on the hill, put her hand over her eyes (in the blocked-vision condition only), and say, "O.K., now who gets a turn?" After the child indicated his choice she took her hand away, put the chosen duck in the car, and sent it down the hill for the child to catch. The subjects in the normal-vision group usually indicated their choice to the sighted experimenter by mutely pointing to it. In the blocked-vision group, on the other hand, the subjects usually told the unsighted experimenter which toy to put in the car. Moreover, their verbal messages were usually adequate to her communicative requirements, e.g., "The red duck" or "The green one." In other words, Maratsos' (1973) subjects nonegocentrically adapted their communications to their listener's situation and informational needs, much as Flavell *et al.*'s (1968) eighth graders did. However, Maratsos' subjects were about ten years younger than Flavell *et al.*'s eighth graders—they were only three years old.

Nonegocentric, listener-adapted communication in preschool children has also been documented in other investigations of the second tradition. You are on one side of a small wall and a four year old is on the other. If you say, "Is the X (e.g., hidden object) on *this* side of the wall or on *that* side of the wall?" he is very likely nonegocentrically to interpret "this side" to mean your side and "that side" to mean his (de Villiers and de Villiers, 1974). When a four year old tells a two year old rather than a peer or an adult about a toy, he is likely to "talk down" to his young listener, e.g., use shorter utterances (Shatz and Gelman, 1973). Adult *A* and preschooler are in room *X* (Menig-Peterson, 1975). Adult *A* "accidentally" spills a cup of juice on a table cloth. The two discuss how best to clean it up and eventually do so. A week later preschooler returns to room *X* with either adult *A* or supposedly naive adult *B*. The empty cup is present and the adult asks, "I wonder what that cup is doing there," and similar queries (if adult *B*), or "Look at that cup. Do you remember what happened when we were here before?" (if adult *A*). Menig-Peterson (1975) found that her preschool subjects appropriately varied their recounting of the spilling incident as a function of which adult was the listener.

Factors Influencing Communicative Performance

How can the markedly discrepant developmental findings of the two traditions be reconciled? At this writing, nobody in the field seems to be really sure, but at least some educated guesses can be made. First, the sheer information-processing demands of the earlier-tradition tasks are often considerably greater. Recall the idea proposed in Chap. 4 that children and adults alike are continually "at risk" for lapses into ego-centrism. That risk undoubtedly gets greater as the information-processing load increases, and the load is surely much heavier in Flavell *et al.*'s (1968) game-description problem than in Maratsos' (1973) object-identification "task." It might be very difficult to keep your listener's inability to see continuously in mind throughout an extended verbal description of a novel, complex game that you had just learned without benefit of any verbal description. Prolonged attention to the game materials for purposes of encoding them into a verbal description could imply prolonged inattention, and hence possible forgetting, of that all-important blindfold. It is possible that Flavell *et al.*'s (1968) second graders did understand clearly that the two listeners had different informational needs, but that they could not maintain and use this understanding when actually communicating because of task-induced cognitive overload.

A second possibility is the greater naturalness of the communication situations used in the more recent studies. Explaining a game to a blindfolded adult is probably more unnatural-seeming, more test-like, for a child than playing a game with an adult who briefly covers her eyes from time to time as part of the game. Surely, it is less like everyday life than communicating to people of different ages (Shatz and Gelman, 1973), or to people who have versus people who have not shared a vivid previous experience with you (Menig-Peterson, 1975). The ability to communicate differently to different categories of listeners is a formidable cognitive accomplishment, and how children acquire it is still a mystery. Furthermore, those recent demonstrations of just how precocious it can be may not surprise you, but they certainly surprised me. At the same time, it makes sense to suppose that such communicative differentiation should first appear in the context of natural communicative interactions with familiar, frequently-encountered categories of listeners.

Finally, there is a third, more speculative possibility. The term "metalanguage" is sometimes used to describe the ability to be aware of and reflect upon language (e.g., Gleitman, Gleitman, and Shipley, 1972; Papandropoulou and Sinclair, 1974). Its meaning is analogous to that of "metacognition" and other "metas" mentioned in Chap. 4. We might coin the term "metacommunication" to refer to one type of metalanguage, namely, the ability to take a verbal-communicative message as a cognitive object and analyze it. Bates (1974, p. 109) has proposed the term "metapragmatics" to mean roughly the same thing. ("Pragmatics" is the linguist's term for actual language use, such as communicating with others.)

My speculation is as follows. Certain communicative behaviors may require metacommunication ability. Metacommunication ability, like other "metas," is likely to be fairly late-developing. Any communicative behaviors that require metacommunication would consequently also be relatively late-developing. There are several such behaviors that come to mind, and all of them seem to develop fairly late (Glucksberg, Krauss, and Higgins, 1975). One is carefully shaping and tailoring a message under novel, unfamiliar conditions or constraints, as in some of those problem-solving type communication tasks of the earlier tradition. If you have to "solve" a "communicative problem," rather than just "say what comes naturally" in a familiar communicative interchange, then you may have to consciously analyze, evaluate, and edit candidate messages. Similarly, if your listener indicates that he did not understand your message, you may have to reanalyze and reevaluate it in order to construct a more adequate one. In both cases you are thinking about the message (metacommunication) rather than sending it (communication). Similarly, metacommunicative ability seems required for skillful listening, especially in sensing possible message inadequacies or ambiguities. There is reason to suspect that a preschooler, say, would be unlikely to evaluate or query any message he can achieve *some* meaningful reading of, whereas an older individual would be likelier to recognize that certain ones need clarification or amplification.

To recapitulate, at least three factors may affect the level of a child's communication performance: (1) the task's information-processing demands; (2) its naturalness, familiarity, or meaningfulness to the child; (3) more speculatively, the extent to which it requires metacommunicative ability. I am not sure how well the following communicative exchange (Glucksberg *et al.*, 1975, p. 321) illustrates these variables, but I know I cannot resist citing it. Two four year olds are seated on opposite sides of a screen and cannot see one another. They have identical referent-nonreferent arrays in front of them. One is trying to communicate to the other which stimulus in the array he is looking at. The task is thus a vintage "problem" of the earlier tradition. The dialogue goes like this:

> Speaker: It's a bird.
> Listener: Is this it?
> Speaker: No.

SUMMARY

Are our adult perceptual abilities and perceptual knowledge the products of inborn biological *nature* or of childhood experiential *nurture*? There are two answers to this question. The first is that, here as elsewhere in psychological development, both factors play a vital role. The other is that this ancient question is not precise and differentiated enough for the present day student of perceptual development. The student would prefer instead to ask this sort of question: How much of exactly what kind of experience during what specific period of childhood is necessary and/or sufficient for the acquisition of precisely what kind of perceptual knowledge or ability? This question is easier asked than answered, however, especially in the case of human perceptual development; current controversies about the early development of space perception illustrate some of the problems. The evidence from animal studies is somewhat clearer. For instance, recent experiments have shown that even brief exposure to stimuli in particular spatial orientations (e.g., vertical stripes) will cause a young kitten's visual-cortical cells to become almost exclusively responsive to those particular orientations for the rest of its life. Moreover, the development of such orientational *feature detectors* has a definite *critical period:* The cells are maximally susceptible to such environmental modification when the kitten is between 4 and 7 weeks of age (the critical period).

One of the most important contemporary theories of perceptual learning and development is that of Eleanor Gibson. Her theory attempts both to *describe* and to *explain* perceptual growth. To describe it, for Gibson, means to specify what gets acquired whenever perceptual learning or development takes place, including the general *nature* of the changes that occur and their characteristic *products* or *outcomes*. To explain it means to identify the *processes* or *mechanisms* responsible for those changes. On the descriptive side, with perceptual experience and practice, we gradually *differentiate* perceptually the *distinctive features* and *invariants* that distinguish one object or event from another. These distinguishing properties vary greatly in complexity, and often consist of relations among a number of stimulus attributes. What gets acquired, therefore, is an increased perceptual sensitivity to that stimulus information which permits the individual to discriminate among similar objects and events that he did not initially distinguish. As to explanation, Gibson identifies three processes that bring about the changes just described: *abstraction, filtering,* and *peripheral mechanisms of attention.* The individual perceptually abstracts invariant features and feature relations, filters out irrelevant or variable features, and selectively orients his sense organs towards one thing rather than another.

As Gibson's theory illustrates, perceptual development can be usefully conceptualized as the development of *perceptual-attentional selectivity.* There now exist powerful research methods for studying perceptual-attentional selectivity in infants, even newborns. Changes in the baby's patterns of looking, sucking, and heart rate may tell us what he or she tends to select for attentional processing—what he or she "prefers" to perceive, so to speak. These preferences in turn tell us what the infant is capable of discriminating perceptually, since to show a perceptual preference between two things obviously implies that one must have perceived at least some kind of difference between them. These new research methods have shown that the human visual system undergoes considerable development during the first several months of life. According to a recent theory, the visual system of the newborn is mediated primarily by the *second visual system,* which mainly localizes and tracks large, perceptually salient objects that enter the visual field. During the next several months the *primary visual system,* capable of making more precise, detailed visual analyses of forms and patterns, becomes increasingly functional and increasingly important in the baby's perceptual life. But the baby is also storing information about his world all the while that his visual system is maturing, and this stored information eventually becomes the most powerful determinant of his visual-attentional behavior.

Newborns can also hear as well as see, and as in the case of seeing, appear to show both initial and acquired auditory preferences. The most interesting evidence on infant auditory perception has to do with speech perception. Unlike the perception of most things, the perception of speech consonants in adults is discontinuous or *categorical* rather than continuous: A very small change at a certain point on the relevant acoustic dimension results in the hearing of an entirely different consonant from the one heard just before the change. Recent studies have shown that very young infants also perceive consonantal sounds categorically, a capability that will undoubtedly help them considerably when they begin to learn language.

A useful way to remember at least some of the changes that take place after infancy may be to imagine what properties an effective perceptual-attentional system ought to have, and then assume that the growing child's system becomes progressively more similar to this ideal. One such developing property is the ability to *control* the deployment of one's attention deliberately, especially to attend selectively to wanted information in the sensory input while disregarding or "tuning out" unwanted information. Acquiring this ability to control his attention voluntarily allows the child to make his attentional deployment more flexible, more *adaptive* to the situation he is in. For example, he becomes able to deploy his attention more broadly so as to pick up several stimulus features at a time, if the situation should call for that strategy; and he can also tune it narrowly to a single feature, if the situation seems to demand that approach. A third developmental trend is towards greater *planfulness* in the child's attentional behavior. Perceptual search strategies become more systematic and planful, for instance. A fourth outcome of development in this area is the ability to use these acquired capacities for control, adaptability, and planfulness to monitor, guide, and modify *attention over time,* even to the extent of managing several, temporally extended, attentional enterprises simultaneously.

Language development consists of simultaneously learning one's native language as a language *(language per se)* and learning how to use it for *private-cognitive* and *social-communicative* purposes *(language use).* During the past decade there have been two traditions of research on the development of the social-communicative uses of language. Studies in the earlier tradition deal mostly with referential communication skills, tend to use nonnaturalistic, laboratory type communication tasks, and try to identify the underlying abilities and processes responsible for the child's overt communicative performance. Research in the later tradition examines a wider variety of communicative skills, studies communicative performance in more natural, everyday-life type situations, and has been less process oriented.

Some of the developing processes or abilities identified by research in the first tradition are: (1) sensitivity to the differences between the referent the speaker is trying to communicate and other, nonreferent objects that the listener also perceives; (2) sensitivity to the listener and his communicative situation; (3) sensitivity to feedback from the listener as to the adequacy of one's message; (4) on the listener's part, sensitivity to possible message inadequacies or ambiguities and knowledge of how to get the speaker to clarify them. These processes appear to be the products of social-cognitive development (Chap. 4).

Studies in the later tradition make communication development appear to be considerably more precocious than do studies in the earlier one. At present we can only guess at possible reasons for this discrepancy. One possibility is that the earlier tradition's tasks make heavier information-processing demands on the child than do the later tradition's. A second is that the former tasks' nonnaturalistic, "test-like" quality makes them more difficult for the young child. A third, and more speculative, possibility is that many of the tasks used in the earlier tradition research require the ability to take a message as a cognitive object and consciously analyze it, edit it, etc. Since this is a type of *metacognitive* ability, we would expect it to be relatively late in developing.

6

memory

Suppose I were to read aloud to you a random sequence of numbers at the rate of one per second. Your task is to reproduce the sequence exactly, just as soon as I stop reciting it. I might begin, for instance, with "3–5–4–9", and you immediately respond "3549". I then try a 5-digit series, then a 6-digit one, and continue making them longer and longer until you reach your limit, sometimes referred to as your *memory span* for this kind of input. Simple memory problems such as this *digit span* task have been included in intelligence test batteries for over half a century. They correlate moderately well with other measures of intelligence, and performance on such tasks definitely improves with chronological age throughout childhood. A four year old is likely to have a digit span of about three or four, a twelve year old one of about six or seven.

It is only a slight exaggeration to say that, prior to the past dozen years or so, our knowledge of memory development consisted of little more than a few descriptive facts of that sort. We knew, in effect, that if we fed younger and older memory machines the same amount of information, the older machines usually could give more of it back to us than the younger ones could.

But *why* could they? Possibly because the older ones were thinking and doing something different or better than the younger ones were in the period between the beginning of our learning input to them and the conclusion of their memory output to us. We were, in retrospect, surprisingly late in asking this question and in formulating that sort of possible answer. The study of memory development began to quicken when researchers started inquiring into age differences in the kinds of cognitive processes and knowledge that might underlie and account for these more superficial age differences in sheer memory output. Memory development is currently one of the liveliest research areas in the field of developmental psychology, and this redirection of attention from overt memory products to the cognitive activities that generate them is largely responsible. Good secondary sources on memory development include Brown (1975), Hagen, Jongeward, and Kail (1975), Meacham (1972), and especially Kail and Hagen (1976).

Some Concepts and Distinctions

Let us begin with some concepts and distinctions that are useful in thinking about memory and its development. Consider first the following three assertions: (1) I remember seeing a particular object fall off my kitchen table yesterday; (2) I remember that that object and all others of the same sort are called "cups"; (3) I remember that cups and all other objects normally continue to exist when I stop looking at them (Piaget's object permanence) and continue to weigh the same when broken into pieces (Piaget's conservation of weight). You are likely to feel an increasing urge to substitute the word "know" for the word "remember" as you progress from assertions (1) to (2) to (3). Yet the retention and recovery of knowledge acquired in the past is somehow involved in all three cases, and hence "memory" is somehow implicated in all three cases. In fact, it is difficult to make a clear-cut demarcation between what is ordinarily meant by "memory" and what is ordinarily meant by "knowledge" (including cognitive concepts, operations, skills, and the like). Moreover, as we shall see, the two interact with one another in important ways.

Piaget and Inhelder (1973) have something like this memory-knowledge contrast in mind when they distinguish between *memory in the strict sense* and *memory in the wider sense*. Memory in the strict sense essentially means the remembering of a specific event, accompanied by the definite feeling on the rememberer's part that this event occurred at a particular time and place in the past and that he personally experienced it. Assertion (1) above illustrates this ordinary-usage, conventional meaning of "memory". Essentially, memory in the wider sense means the retention of all the products and achievements of one's cognitive development to date. The two cognitive-developmental attainments mentioned in (3) above would certainly be good, Piagetian examples of memory in this wider, less conventional sense. As Piaget and Inhelder (1973) put it, the subject "conserves" in memory his previously acquired cognitive "schemes".

Tulving (1972) has a somewhat similar dimension in mind when he contrasts *episodic* and *semantic* memory. Assertion (1) would exemplify the first, assertion (2)—and perhaps (3)—the second. Assertions (2) and (3) illustrate the point that, at the knowing versus remembering end of the dimension, what is retained in memory can be as specific and unremarkable-looking as an isolated vocabulary item (cups are called "cups"), or as general and conceptually momentous as a Piagetian developmental milestone (object permanence, conservation of weight). How we remember or activate any sort of stored knowledge whatever, important or unimportant, is a question of great interest to contemporary students of human memory. Furthermore, it is becoming clear that the nature and development of "memory" even in the narrower, episodic sense simply cannot be understood without taking the structure and content of the rememberer's entire knowledge system into account.

Students of memory also distinguish between *storage* and *retrieval* activities. As their names suggest, storage activities put information into memory while retrieval activities recover information from memory. Storage means attending to, encoding, memorizing, studying, and the like: "learning" is sometimes a good synonym. Retrieval means recognizing, recalling, reconstructing—the "remembering" of what had previously been stored. It would seem to be unnaturally constraining and restrictive to consider only the storage and retrieval activities that transpire between the subject's ears (Flavell and Wellman, 1976; Kreutzer, Leonard, and Flavell, 1975). If you want to store information for later retrieval you will, of course, often do nothing else but memorize it mentally and later recall it from your internal memory store. But you may also opt to take notes on it (tape-record it, store it in a computer) or ask others to help you remember it. People use external storage and retrieval resources all the time in real life mnemonic undertakings, and it would be foolish for psychologists not to study the nature and development of such intelligent behavior on the grounds that it is not "memory" (or not "*real* memory"). Such a claim would generally be untrue as well as irrelevant, since most mnemonic scenarios of this kind involve a sequential, back-and-forth movement between internal and external memory stores. For example, you remember (internal) that you made a note on your calendar and so you go look at it; it explicitly spells out (external) certain information, which in turn reminds you (internal) of yet other information not contained in the note.

There are a few other concepts to mention on the retrieval side of memory. Something that reminds you of something else is called a *re-

trieval cue in the trade, since it leads to or "cues" the retrieval from memory of that something else. Two kinds of retrieval are commonly distinguished: *recognition* and *recall*. You may recognize as familiar something which is presently perceived or thought about, i.e., identify it as identical to, similar to, or reminiscent of something previously experienced. There must be some sort of enduring representation of the previously-experienced something in memory that is somehow contacted in the course of your experiencing of the present something, and this contact somehow gives rise to the feeling of recognition. In recall, on the other hand, the familiar something is not initially present in conscious thought or perception. Rather, *recall* is the term we use for the very process of retrieving a representation of it from memory and presenting it to consciousness. In recognition, there is something already there in immediate experience to assist the retrieval process. In recall, the subject has to do more of the retrieval job on his own (but, not necessarily all of it, since there may be retrieval cues present to lend a hand). In clear cases of recall, the subject consciously experiences an internal representation (e.g., an image, an idea) of something experienced earlier. There need be no such conscious mental representation involved in an act of recognition, although of course there may be.

Piaget and Inhelder (1973) have identified an intermediate, hybrid form of retrieval called *reconstruction*. Suppose I ask you to study and remember an unfamiliar, geometric design built out of wooden rods of different lengths. I could test your memory of it later by asking you to *recognize* it from among a set of similar designs. I could also ask you to *recall* it from scratch, perhaps by having you draw it as accurately as possible. Finally, I could put all the rods used in the design in front of you and ask you to reassemble them from memory, i.e., *reconstruct* the design. As in the recognition test, all the design elements are physically present to help the rememberer. As in the recall test, the spatial relationships among the elements have to be retrievd from memory. All three types of memory may be involved in the same retrieval problem. For example, you think you vaguely *recall* how two rods might have been related in that geometric design, so you physically *reconstruct* them that way. Then you *recognize* your now-perceptible rod configuration as an accurate or inaccurate reproduction of the original.

There are four categories of phenomena that it is useful to distinguish in analyzing memory development (Flavell and Wellman, 1976). The first, *basic processes,* includes the most fundamental operations and capacities of the memory system, e.g., the processes by which an object is instantly and automatically recognized as familiar. The second, *knowledge,* refers to the more or less automatic effects of what you have come to know on what you will store and retrieve—roughly, the effects of memory in the wider sense on memory in the strict sense. The third is a special class of storage and retrieval activities which are called memory *strategies.* Deliberately rehearsing someone's name in order to memorize it would be an example of a memory strategy. Unlike the basic processes, strategies are voluntary and potentially conscious. In computer terminology, the basic processes are more like the computer's electronic circuitry or "hardware," while the strategies are more like its programs or "software." The fourth category is called *metamemory,* and it refers to an individual's knowledge about anything pertaining to memory (e.g., that certain kinds of information are harder to learn and remember than others). The nature and course of memory development will be summarized by considering each of these four categories in turn.

BASIC PROCESSES

This is the least interesting category of the four for a developmentalist. The reason is that much of the basic "hardware" of our memory system may not change much or at all during ontogenesis (Olson, 1976). Moreover, it is my guess that what development of basic capacities and processes does occur may be largely completed by the end of the sensory-motor period (circa 1½–2 years of age), and probably has a strong maturational component to it. Therefore, it is important to begin by examining what little is known about memory in early infancy (Cohen and Gelber, 1975; Olson, 1976) and then proceed from there.

Do babies have any sort of memory capabilities? You already know the answer (indicating the presence of some metamemory on your part), although you may not realize you do (absence of metacognition concerning that metamemory). Recall from Chap. 2 that novel stimuli tend to elicit more interest and attention in the infant than familiar ones. Similarly, Chap. 5 described how even young infants show habituation (response decrement) to repeated visual and auditory inputs. But, obviously, an organism cannot respond to a stimulus as "familiar" or "previously presented" unless it has something resembling a memory for past events. Hence, the same behavior that informs us of the infant's cognitive motivation (Chap. 2) and perceptual abilities and preferences (Chap. 5) testifies to the existence of a memory capability.

What sort of memory capability would the infant have to possess to show habituation behavior? Clearly, full-fledged, conscious recall of past presentations of the stimulus would not have to be present to account for habituation effects. Those repeated stimulus presentations just modify the cognitive organization of the infant so that he now assimilates the stimulus differently than he did initially. This sounds suspiciously like some form of recognition memory. There are even some speculations as to how this modification process might work (Cohen and Gelber, 1975; Olson, 1976). However, everyone seems to agree that no higher form of memory than recognition memory would be needed to explain habituation phenomena. Indeed, Piaget and Inhelder (1973, p. 380) suggest that no higher form than recognition memory is even possible for the child during most of infancy.

Although it may only be recognition memory, it is still fairly impressive. Habituation studies have demonstrated that a 4–6 month old can see a photograph of a face for only a couple of minutes and show measurable recognition effects as long as two weeks later. It is anyone's guess how long the retention interval could be for much more familiar patterns, such as his mother's face. Also, the nature and number of the stimulus features the baby is disposed and able to store for later recognition changes markedly with age during infancy (Olson, 1976). This is, of course, the same developmental story about the infant's progressive cognitive differentiation of the environment that was told in Chap. 5, but here it is looked at from the point of view of memory rather than perception.

Surprisingly little attention has been given so far in the infant memory literature to the really central question of how the baby develops from a creature that can only recognize to one that can also recall (Cohen and Gelber, 1975). The ability to recall certainly falls into the "basic process" category, and it certainly must develop during infancy, as Piaget has pointed out. In the following passage, Piaget uses the term "evocation" where we would say "recall":

> Recognition can rely on perception and sensori-motor "schemes" alone, while evocation requires mental imagery or language, that is, some form of the symbolic function, some form of operational or preoperational representation. For this reason, there is no evocative memory in children before the age of 1½ or 2 years, while recognition memory is present during the first few months of life. (Piaget, 1968, p. 11).

Unfortunately, virtually nothing is known about any developmental intermediaries or transitional forms that may precede the full capacity for recall or "evocative memory." It seems plausible that there might well exist some kind of primitive imagery prior to age 1½ or 2 years, a sort of protoform of conscious representation and recall. However, I know of no research that has identified and described such phenomena.

Once the full capacity for conscious recall is acquired—whenever and however—the development of basic memory processes or the "hardware" of memory may be essentially complete. In adults, for instance, the recall of one thing can trigger the recall of another, associated thing (the "retrieval cue" notion mentioned earlier). Goldberg, Perlmutter, and Myers (1974) have shown that the same basic process occurs in two year olds. Similarly, adults automatically store information about temporal order and temporal duration. That is, they often have a mnemonic sense of which of two events occurred earlier in time and of roughly how long ago a single event occurred or began. Under some testing conditions, seven year olds are every bit as good as adults at remembering temporal order (Brown, 1973). Indeed, even young infants may have some capacity to store information about temporal duration (Fitzgerald, Lintz, Brackbill, and Adams, 1967).

KNOWLEDGE

A person's acquired knowledge, or his "memory in the wider sense" (Piaget and Inhelder, 1973), powerfully influences what he stores and what he retrieves from storage, or his "memory in the strict sense." As an example, master chess players and amateurs show an interesting pattern of similarities and differences in their ability to reconstruct from memory the positions of chess pieces on a chessboard (Chase and Simon, 1973). If the pieces are arranged randomly, both groups perform equally poorly. If the arrangement of pieces is one that could legitimately occur in an actual chess game, the masters' ability to remember the positions is far better than the amateurs'. A further illustration is the fact that one item of information can hardly serve as a retrieval cue for another if the two are unrelated in a particular rememberer's system of knowledge. Similarly, inputs that have little meaning for the individual—that do not fit readily into his acquired knowledge structure, that cannot easily be assimilated into his existing cognitive schemes, etc.—tend to be hard to store and retrieve.

Thus, what the head knows has an enormous effect on what the head learns and remembers. But, of course, what the head knows changes enormously in the course of development, and these changes consequently make for changes in memory behavior. The point is a simple but very important one:

> Older individuals will presumably store, retain, and retrieve a great many inputs better or differently than younger ones, for example, simply because developmental advances in the content and structure of their semantic or conceptual systems render these inputs more familiar, meaningful, conceptually interrelated, subject to gap-filling, or otherwise more memorable for them. (Flavell and Wellman, 1976.)

There have been two lines of research that fall under this category of memory development. Although the two have proceeded independently of one another, their basic conceptions of the nature and development of memory are quite similar.

Piagetian Research

The first line of research includes a series of studies by Piaget and his coworkers (Piaget, 1968; Piaget and Inhelder, 1973), plus attempted replications of those studies by others (Liben, 1976). The Piagetians make two related claims about the dependence of an individual's memory on his or her attained level of cognitive development. The following experimental situation will illustrate both claims. The experimenter displays a row of 10 parallel sticks which regularly increase in length from one end of the row to the other, thereby forming an ordered series (Piaget and Inhelder, 1973, p. 34). The child subject is asked to take a good look at the sticks and try to remember what he sees. He is subsequently asked to draw the array of sticks from memory, first about one week later, and again about eight months later.

The first and less startling of Piaget's claims is that the child's memory for the array on the first test will depend upon his basic understanding of seriation or asymmetrical relations, an important cognitive-operational achievement in Piaget's theory. In other words, the child's general knowledge about the nature of ordered series (Piagetian memory in the wider sense) helps him accurately store and subsequently retrieve from memory the appearance of that specific ordered series (Piagetian memory in the strict sense). For example, a child who does not yet grasp the basic concept of a graded series might simply recall seeing two groups of sticks, "big ones" and "little ones." The effect of general knowledge on specific memory in this case is somewhat reminiscent of the master versus amateur chess players example (Chase and Simon, 1973) cited earlier. It is another instance of the generalization that what the head stores and retrieves is heavily influenced by what the head has come to know and understand in the course of its development.

Suppose that a child in this experiment happens to improve his general understanding of seriation between his one-week and his eight-month memory test. That is, simply as a consequence of normal cognitive growth he attains a more mature, more concrete-operational grasp of asymmetrical relations in the long interim between the two tests. Piaget and Inhelder's second and more startling claim is that his memory for that specific 10-stick array may actually *improve* from first to second testing, because of his improved general understanding of seriation. That is, his eight-month reproduction might be more faithful to the original than his one-week reproduction, despite the fact that he has not seen the original since its initial presentation. Piaget and Inhelder suggest some situations in everyday life where such a paradoxical-seeming improvement in memory over time might occur:

> It is quite conceivable that the memory of a lecture or a long passage should be better once progress in reflection has enabled the subject to reconstruct certain connections, not merely forgotten but unnoticed in the first place; or, again, that practical experiences gained in the meantime (for instance in horticulture or mountaineering) should lead to the improvement, by reorganization, of defective memories. (Piaget and Inhelder, 1973, p. 384).

Piaget and Inhelder (1973) have obtained experimental evidence which they take to be supportive of both claims. Follow up research by Liben (1976) and others raises questions, however. In general, subsequent research findings seem to support the first claim more strongly and unequivocally than they do the second. At the same time, that second claim does seem as if it could have some truth to it; for instance, those examples of memory improvement in everyday life quoted by Piaget and Inhelder (1973) do not really strike one as wholly implausible or counterintuitive. Perhaps long term improvements in memory caused by intervening cognitive growth sometimes occur and sometimes do not, for reasons we do not yet understand. Perhaps improvement can even occur when there has been no real intervening "cognitive growth" in the usual sense; Piaget and Inhelder's lecture example above may be a case in point. It is hard to know what to conclude about this aspect of Piaget's theory of memory development on present evidence, except that we clearly need more and better research evidence before firm conclusions are warranted.

Research on Constructive Memory

As indicated earlier, this second line of research is animated by a view of memory and its development very similar to Piaget's (Paris and Lindauer, 1976). It, too, stresses the essential role that the subject's general knowledge and cognitive activities play in specific acts of memory. Students of constructive memory share with the Piagetians and others the view that memory is "applied cognition" (Flavell, 1971*b*, p. 273), i.e., the application to mnemonic problems of whatever intellectual weaponry the individual has so far developed.

Most of the things we remember in everyday life, say the proponents of constructive memory, are meaningful, organized events or bodies of structured information. They are not the isolated, largely meaningless "items" of the classical laboratory study of rote learning. Pairs of nonsense syllables, random sequences of digits, or lists of unrelated words are not usually the objects of everyday, extralaboratory learning and remembering. Moreover, these meaningful, structured inputs are not just copied or printed into memory at storage time and equally literally and faithfully recopied or reproduced at retrieval time. Rather, the act of comprehending and encoding into memory is a Piagetian assimilation-type process of *construction* of an internal conceptual representation of the input (hence, "constructive memory"). What is usually constructed and stored in memory could variously be described as a sensible (to the subject) interpretation of what he has perceived, an integrated rendering of it, or an organized representation of its gist. The mnemonic construction disregards some features of the input, highlights others, integrates or reorganizes still others, and even adds information not actually present in the input.

Similarly, retrieval is conceptualized as an equally active and assimilatory process of *reconstruction,* rather than as a passive, unedited copying out of what is stored in memory. It is somewhat akin to the archaeological reconstruction of an ancient civilization based upon building fragments, bits of pottery, and other artefacts, plus a lot of logical inference, conceptual integration, and just plain guessing on the archaeologist's part. These constructions and reconstructions which are so ubiquitous in everyday, meaningful memory are usually more automatic, involuntary, and unconscious than I have made them sound here, although they certainly can be, and sometimes are, very conscious and intentional (very "strategic," very "metamnemonic"). The point is that, automatic or deliberate, the memory machine is nothing at all like a tape recorder or camera. We most emphatically do *not* simply take mental photographs of inputs at storage and then simply develop them at retrieval.

It is time for an example. The following story certainly qualifies as a meaningful input to memory:

> Linda was playing with her new doll in front of her big red house. Suddenly she heard a strange sound coming from under the porch. It was the flapping of wings. Linda wanted to help so much, but she did not know what to do. She ran inside the house and grabbed a shoe box from the closet. Then Linda looked inside her desk until she found eight sheets of yellow paper. She cut up the paper into little pieces and put them in the bottom of the box. Linda gently picked up the helpless creature and took it with her. Her teacher knew what to do. (Paris, 1975a).

A person could not really understand Linda's adventure, let alone recall it, without doing a lot more than simply copying its constituent sentences into memory. Consider the eight memory questions Paris (1975a) asked his subjects after reading them the story:

1. Was Linda's doll new?
2. Did Linda grab a match box?
3. Was the strange sound coming from under the porch?
4. Was Linda playing behind her house?
5. Did Linda like to take care of animals?
6. Did Linda take what she found to the police station?
7. Did Linda find a frog?
8. Did Linda use a pair of scissors?

You may have noticed a difference between questions 1–4 and questions 5–8. The first four could be answered by a tape recorder type of memory machine, since the answers are literally "there" in the surface structure of the story. In sharp contrast, questions 5–8 can only be answered by a human type of memory machine, since they require the subject to draw inferences from what is on the surface. The ability to make those inferences clearly depends, in turn, upon Piagetian memory in the wider sense, including stored knowledge about the world (e.g., that birds have wings but frogs do not) and reasoning abilities (e.g., a person who would do what Linda did probably likes to take care of animals).

The constructivist's argument is that we are constantly making spontaneous inferences and interpretations of this sort in processing, storing, and retrieving information. Such additions and elaborations are the rule rather than the exception, and they are believed to be of the very essence of cognition and memory. The argument is buttressed by the fact that we may not even be able to distinguish on a later memory test what we have constructed or elaborated from what had actually been initially presented (Bransford and Franks, 1971). For instance, after hearing sentences like "The box is to the right of the tree" and "The chair is on top of the box," the subject may falsely believe that "The chair is to the right of the tree" was one of the presented sentences, because it is semantically consistent with the mental representation of the input he has constructed (Paris and Mahoney, 1974). A similar but nonconsistent sentence like "The chair is to the left of the tree" will likely be identified as nonpresented, on the other hand. Under some circumstances, the subject actually may be even *more* confident that he remembers hearing a semantically consistent but never-presented proposition than one that was presented (e.g., Bransford and Franks, 1971). These sorts of memory effects also can be obtained when the meaningful input is pictorial rather than verbal, by the way; constructive memory is amodal or transmodal.

We have so far said quite a lot about constructive memory but nothing about its relation to children. Do children construct and reconstruct in this fashion when they store and retrieve information? Are there developmental changes in constructive memory?

The answer to the first question is an unequivocal "yes." Studies by Paris and others (Paris, 1975*a*; Paris and Mahoney, 1974; see Paris and Lindauer, 1976) have found that grade-school children show the sorts of constructive-memory phenomena described above. They are apt to believe that Linda found a bird, used scissors, etc. Similarly, they are likely to think they previously had heard semantically consistent but nonpresented sentences, while correctly denying that they had heard nonpresented sentences that were not consistent with their semantic integration of the input. As Hagen, Jongeward, and Kail (1975) point out, children could scarcely carry on everyday conversations if they could not make the kinds of spontaneous inference, integrations, elaborations, and reorganizations we have been talking about. A great deal has to be assumed, presupposed, or otherwise added by a listener in understanding and remembering what a speaker says; a surprising amount of what gets said in an ordinary conversation is inexplicit and elliptical.

The first few developmental studies of constructive memory failed to find clear cut age differences, but some solid evidence for developmental changes now seems to be emerging (Paris, 1975*b*; Paris and Lindauer, 1976). As children grow older, they generally seem more prone and able to make the sorts of inferences that allow for a full, integrated, and meaningful memory representation of what they experience. During the middle-childhood years, at least, "the ability to spontaneously apply inferential processes to discourse increases with age" (Paris, 1975*b*, p. 9). In addition, older children seem to manage what appear to be more complex and difficult inferences better than younger ones do. However, it must be admitted that exactly what is meant by "more complex and difficult" here is not yet wholly clear. For instance, the "lexical inferences" needed to answer Paris' (1975*a*) questions 7 and 8 seem to be easier for the younger child to make than the "contextual inferences" needed to answer questions 5 and 6. Beyond those two statements, with all their cautionary "seems" and "appears," there is little to say at present about the ontogenesis of constructive memory. But then, scientific investigation of this highly interesting and important topic has just begun.

STRATEGIES

This category encompasses the large and diverse range of potentially conscious activities a person may voluntarily carry out as means to various mnemonic ends. Verbally rehearsing a telephone number during the brief interval between looking it up in the phone book and going to the phone to dial it is a clear example of a mnemonic strategy. Others include: (1) taking notes in class; (2) underlining key expressions in a textbook; (3) noting tomorrow's dentist appointment on your calendar; (4) reorganizing any sort of information so that related elements are studied and stored together; (5) trying to reconstruct your day's events step-by-step in hopes of recalling where you may have left that missing watch; (6) and attempting to remember someone's name by trying to recall people and events associated with that person.

Strategies are most clearly distinguishable from the two preceding categories when they are highly conscious, deliberate, and planful (at which point they unfortunately become harder to disentangle from the next category, metamemory). Brown (1975) spoke of the previous category as involving "knowing," and of this one as "knowing how to know." In its purest form, a memory strategy is a voluntary, purposeful move a person decides to make in an effort to enhance some desired mnemonic outcome.

The distinction between the first two and the last two of our four categories may be more apparent if we consider memory in animals (Flavell and Wellman, 1976). An adult horse surely has lots of memory hardware, e.g., mechanisms of recognition memory (basic processes category). It also certainly has acquired much practical knowledge of its world from years of experience that enormously influences what it will learn and remember (knowledge category). I doubt, however, if many psychologists would want to argue for the existence of intentional and planful equine memory strategies, let alone equine metamemory.

There have been far more developmental investigations of memory strategies than of basic memory processes, knowledge-memory relationships, or metamemory. In fact, it was the discovery of memory strategies as fruitful objects of developmental study about a decade ago that is largely responsible for the present-day good health of the area of memory development. Naturally, there is no shortage of useful secondary sources on this topic: Brown (1975), Flavell (1970*b*), Hagen *et al.* (1975), Meacham (1972), and especially chapters by Hagen, Kobasigawa, Moely, and others in Kail and Hagen (1976).

Rehearsal

There is an ill-defined group of memory strategies collectively referred to as "rehearsal". As we shall see, rehearsal is by no means the most effective mnemonic strategy available to a sophisticated and resourceful information processor. It does, however, make a good concrete example or vehicle within which to present some general conclusions about the development of memory strategies in children. Let us begin by examining two early studies of the development of verbal rehearsal as a mnemonic strategy.

Flavell, Beach, and Chinsky (1966) administered the following task to kindergarten, second-grade, and fifth-grade children (ages 5, 7, and 10, roughly). On each of several trials, seven pictures of common objects were displayed and an experimenter slowly pointed in turn to, say, three of them. The child understood that his task would subsequently be to point to those same three pictures in exactly the same serial order that the experimenter had. In the experimental condition of most interest here, the delay interval between the experimenter's pointing and the subject's recall was 15 seconds. The child wore a toy space helmet with a translucent visor. The visor was pulled down over the child's eyes during the delay interval, so the child could see neither pictures nor experimenters. One of the experimenters had been trained to lip read semicovert verbalization of these particular object names and carefully recorded whatever spontaneous verbal rehearsal he could detect. Of the 20 subjects at each age level, 2 kindergarteners, 12 second graders, and 17 fifth graders showed detectable verbal rehearsal on one or more trials. Thus, the study showed a clear increase with age in the spontaneous use of verbal rehearsal as a mnemonic strategy.

A subsequent experiment (Keeney, Cannizzo, and Flavell, 1967) used the same procedure with a group of first graders, a transitional age at which some children would be expected to have developed a tendency to rehearse and some would not. There were four major findings. First, children who spontaneously rehearsed the picture names, according to our lip-reading evidence, recalled the sequences of pictures better than those who did not. Second, the nonrehearsers were quite capable of rehearsing, and could be gotten to do so with only minimal instruction and demonstration by the experimenter. Third, once induced to rehearse, their recall rose to the level of that of the spontaneous rehearsers. Fourth, when subsequently given the option on later trials of rehearsing or not rehearsing, more than half of them abandoned the strategy, thereby reverting to their original, preexperimental status as nonrehearsers.

These studies typify the research literature on memory strategy development in two respects. First, they dealt primarily with strategies that are initiated during the storage rather than the retrieval phase of a memory problem. Rehearsal is something you start doing now, at storage, in hopes that starting it now will facilitate performance later, at retrieval. You know in advance you will have to remember something later, so you try to prepare for the recall test by rehearsing.

Suppose you did not know beforehand that you would later need to remember something, as in the earlier-mentioned examples of trying to recall a person's name or the location of your missing watch. In such instances, where the need to retrieve was unanticipated and came as a surprise, psychologists speak of *incidental* as opposed to *intentional* memory problems. The only strategies possible for solving incidental memory problems are of the retrieval versus storage variety. To be sure, the distinction between storage and retrieval strategies is not as clear as I am making it out to be. For instance, a storage strategy like rehearsal is likely to extend into the retrieval period and function as a retrieval strategy, and a retrieval strategy may involve trying to reconstruct and exploit the way the sought-for information was originally stored. The present point is that most developmental investigations to date have concentrated on storage strategies in intentional-memory task settings. As we shall see, however, interesting work is just now beginning on the equally important question of how retrieval strategies develop.

These two studies are also typical of the field in a second way. The task materials used were discrete, rote-type "items," as contrasted with the highly meaningful, connected discourse often used as memory input in research on knowledge-memory relationships (the knowledge category). Similarly, they presented the children with traditional, in-the-head storage and retrieval problems. In neither study could the children use the strategy of writing down the object names, for example, or of asking someone else to help them remember the names. In short, the tasks were definitely of the traditional laboratory-memory-experiment genre and, as such, were not wholly representative of the information storage and retrieval enterprises that children and adults undertake in the real world.

Table 6–1 presents a simplified overview of how memory strategies such as verbal rehearsal usually seem to develop (cf. Flavell, 1970*b*). Initially (left column), the component skills and skill integrations which

TABLE 6-1 Typical Course of Development of a Memory Strategy

	Major Periods in Strategy Development		
	Strategy Not Available	Production Deficiency	Mature Strategy Use
Basic Ability to Execute Strategy	Absent to Poor	Fair to Good	Good to Excellent
Spontaneous Strategy Use	Absent	Absent	Present
Attempts to Elicit Strategy Use	Ineffective	Effective	Unnecessary
Effects of Strategy Use on Retrieval	——	Positive	Positive

make up an act of verbal rehearsal are largely or wholly absent from the child's repertoire. These components might include: the ability to recognize and subvocalize stimulus names quickly and accurately; the ability to repeat (rehearse) words or word sequences to yourself in a fluent, rapid, well-controlled fashion; and the ability to keep constant track of where you have been and where you are going in the execution of your rehearsal plan. When you stop to think about it, it is apparent that verbal rehearsal entails a rather complex coordination and integration of skills. Needless to say, if a child is unable to rehearse at all, it follows that he or she will show no spontaneous rehearsal in a memory task context. We shall also assume, to simplify matters, that no significant amount of mnemonically-useful rehearsal can be elicited from the child in this earliest period, even with strenuous efforts at rehearsal training.

The second period in Table 6-1 (middle column) is much more interesting. As Hagen *et al.* (1975, p. 73) indicate: "Some of our most important insights have resulted from experiments that have focused on this transitional period." The experiment by Keeney *et al.* (1967) described above is only one of a number that testify to the existence of this curious transitional stage. Recall that some of their first-grade subjects did little or no spontaneous, deliberate rehearsing in that particular memory task setting. Nevertheless, these children proved to have good ability to rehearse, rehearsal was easily elicited by the experimenter, and its elicitation did have positive effects on their subsequent retrieval. A distinction frequently is made in memory development research between a *production deficiency* and a *mediational deficiency* (Flavell, 1970*b*). A child is said to have a production deficiency for a particular strategy if he fails to produce it on his own for reasons other than the sheer lack of ability or skill to enact it properly. A child is said to have a mediational deficiency if his execution of the strategy, whether spontaneous or elicited, does not facilitate his recall. The transitional pattern usually observed in research studies is the one shown in Keeney *et al.* (1967) and in Table 6-1, namely, a marked production deficiency coupled with no apparent mediational deficiency.

Why would a child exhibit a production deficiency? If he is equipped to carry out the strategy and if its production would benefit his memory performance, why on earth would he fail to produce it spontaneously? To say that he does not produce it because it does not occur to him to produce it sounds like a gross evasion of the question. Nevertheless, thinking about production deficiencies this way may point us toward some deeper explanations.

There are several possible reasons why it might not occur to him to produce it. One possibility is that he does not yet fully grasp the implicit demands of this or perhaps any storage-memorization task (Bem, 1970).

It may not be as obvious to him as it would be to you that he ought to do *something* special with those pictures now in order to enhance his memory of them later. He may not achieve or maintain, at storage time, a clear image of what is going to happen later, at retrieval time. In short, he may be insufficiently planful, foresighted, or goal-oriented, at least in this particular memory task situation. We will return to this interpretation of production deficiencies when we discuss metamemory development.

Another possibility is that he cannot spontaneously invoke and use this particular strategy—e.g., verbal rehearsal specifically—again, either in this particular task situation or more generally. One reason for this might be that the task situation tends to call forth some other mnemonic strategy instead. Another strategy might win out over rehearsal because it has been in the child's repertoire longer, is less difficult and effortful to execute, or for some other psychologically sensible reason. Such a strategy would, therefore, generally be an earlier-developing, more elementary-looking one than rehearsal. Examples from the Flavell *et al.* (1966) task might be simple one-time naming, or careful visual inspection, of each object as the experimenter points to it, but without any appreciable cognitive processing of the items during the 15-second delay period that follows. Such a child may be behaving more or less planfully and strategically with respect to the eventual mnemonic goal, unlike the possibility described in the previous paragraph, but the plan or strategy he has selected happens not to be rehearsal.

There may be yet other reasons why it "happens not to be rehearsal," however. A rather banal one is that this child simply has not yet learned that rehearsal can benefit recall (and indeed, there are circumstances in which some kinds of rehearsal probably do not). A less banal reason has been proposed by several Russian investigators (e.g., Smirnov and Zinchenko, 1969). They suggest that a skill must be fairly well developed in its own right before it can be effectively deployed as a strategic means to a memory goal:

> Before a cognitive operation . . . can become a means of remembering, it must be comparatively well formed. The initial use of a cognitive process for mnemonic ends becomes possible only when the individual can exercise a certain degree of freedom in operating with it. (Smirnov and Zinchenko, 1969, p. 469).

If a behavior pattern like verbal rehearsal is still rather effortful, challenging, and attention-demanding as an act in itself, the child may have trouble incorporating it as a subroutine within a larger cognitive program such as a memorization problem. His trouble could take the form of not readily thinking to use it that way in the first place, or of failing to maintain and continue its use without outside prompting. Recall that Keeney *et al.*'s (1967) first-grade nonrehearsers showed both kinds of trouble. Needless to say, such problems are likely to be more severe as we move leftward in Table 6-1, i.e., as the child we are considering has a fair rather than good or a poor rather than fair ability to execute the strategy. The child's production deficiency may be then coupled with a marked *production inefficiency,* i.e., an actual inability to carry out the strategy skillfully and efficiently (Flavell, 1970*b*). In summary, then, there are many reasons why a child might exhibit a production deficiency for a given strategy, and even the few I have suggested still lack adequate scientific documentation.

The rightmost column of Table 6-1 is almost self-explanatory. Production of the strategy can now occur spontaneously, without the experimenter's assistance. As already suggested, this spontaneity may be explainable partly by the child's increased ease and fluency in executing the strategy. There may now be enough space in his cognitive operating room to rehearse efficiently, *and* to monitor the progress of his memorization, *and* to keep the upcoming retrieval task firmly in mind—*and* perhaps even to worry about how well he will perform on it. With all that space available for strategy use, the likeliest reason for a failure to rehearse is the judicious selection of some better mnemonic strategy.

The course of strategy development shown in Table 6-1 is often illustrated experimentally by what is called an *age by treatment interaction.* Subjects of, say, three age levels are divided into two groups. One group at each age level is simply given the memory task. The second group is additionally provided with some sort of aid in using a certain strategy, for example, instruction or training in using it, or task conditions that favor its employment. Then the experiment may show that providing such aid greatly increases strategy use, but only in the intermediate (production deficient) age group. It does not significantly increase strategy use in either the youngest or the oldest groups because the former is unable to profit from it and the latter is already using the strategy spontaneously. The effects of the treatment vary with (statistically interact with) the age of its recipients, hence the age by treatment interaction effect.

As always, I have made things seem more straightforward than they really are. For example, the concept of production deficiency, while useful, is flawed by our inability to define "spontaneous production" unambiguously (Turnure, Buium, and Thurlow, in press). People "spontaneously" rehearse only in the context of some memory task environment. But this environment always contains stronger or weaker cues, more or less subtle prompts, as possible facilitators or elicitors of rehearsal activity. The specifics of the task and task setting play an important but as yet poorly understood role in determining whether a subject will or will not "spontaneously" think to rehearse. An important implication of this fact is that one cannot speak of *the* age when the child changes from being production deficient to spontaneously productive for a particular strategy because that age is likely to vary considerably within a single individual as a function of the exact task conditions in which strategy use-nonuse is assessed.

Ages of transition are also relative rather than absolute in other ways. In the first place, many possible types and patterns of rehearsal or rehearsal-like activity exist (Flavell, Friedrichs, and Hoyt, 1970), and there is reason to believe that each may have its own developmental timetable. Suppose, for example, you are to memorize a list of words. I present them to you by successively exposing the words on a screen, only one at a time but for several seconds each. One rehearsal strategy would be to say each word over and over again during its presentation period. A different rehearsal strategy would be to repeat several words rather than just one, e.g., to rehearse the first, second, and third words rather than just the third word alone during the third word's presentation interval. The second strategy appears to yield better recall than the first; in addition, the first is more likely to be elected by younger subjects, the second by older subjects (Cuvo, 1975; Ornstein, Naus, and Liberty, 1975). A related finding alluded to earlier is that children tend to verbalize stimulus names only while the stimuli are present perceptually before they develop the strategy of continuing to verbalize them after they are no longer present, e.g., during a Flavell *et al.* (1966) type pre-recall delay period (Flavell, Friedrichs, and Hoyt, 1970; Garrity, 1975; Hagen *et al.*, 1975).

Research by a number of investigators has shown that enormous variety exists in when, what, and how people rehearse in memory tasks (e.g., Butterfield, Wambold, and Belmont, 1973; Flavell, 1970*b*), and rehearsal strategies vary greatly in complexity and sophistication. Clearly, to ask when "rehearsal" develops as "a" mnemonic strategy is to ask a meaningless question.

Just as there are many rehearsal strategies, so also are there many memory strategies besides rehearsal. Their ages of acquisition are similarly relative—similarly variable between and within strategies.

Other Memory Strategies

Despite the fact that it can be quite complex and sophisticated, rehearsal is fundamentally a rather prosaic memory strategy. It is, after all, only a form of imitation or mimicry. Items are presented and the rehearser simply parrots them over and over, quite possibly adding little or nothing conceptual to the process. In particular, he may not be trying, as he rehearses, to discover or create meaningful relationships among the items that might cause groups of items to clump together at retrieval. Other memory strategies do go beyond the bare bones of the input by adding relationships.

Organization. One of the most frequently studied of these strategies is semantic grouping or categorization. The generic term often used is *organization.* The memorizer might automatically notice that the list of items contains a few articles of clothing and some things to eat. With a little more active search for interitem semantic connections, he might also discover that three other items could be construed as school-related objects, e.g., bus, desk, and book. Then he might think of the same-category items together during item presentation, and perhaps even rehearse them by category. If he did all these things his subsequent recall would tend to be strongly *clustered* by category, with most or all of the foods reported out together, as a string, and the same for the clothing and school-related items. Such clustering need not be and often would not be complete, and there are ways of measuring the amount or degree of clustering present in the subject's item recall sequence. The following recall sequence, for instance, is partially but not completely clustered, in terms of the categories just mentioned: desk, bus, bread, ice cream, book, apple, hat, shoes, dress.

The mere presence of clustering in a subject's recall does not prove that he had consciously and intentionally used a grouping strategy when storing and retrieving those items. Remember the finding of Goldberg *et al.* (1974) that recall of one item can cue the recall of a semantically-related item even in two year olds. Two year olds may have some impressive cognitive talents but conscious, intentional use of an organizational memory strategy is surely not one of them. Nevertheless, there is a developmental trend toward such deliberate use. If allowed to manipulate a randomly arranged but potentially categorizable set of object pictures during a study period, for instance, older subjects are likelier than younger ones to adopt the strategy of physically segregating the pictures into groups by category and then studying same-category items together (Moely, Olson, Halwes, and Flavell, 1969; Neimark, Slotnick, and Ulrich, 1971). Moreover, younger subjects exhibit the same kind of transitional production-deficiency pattern with respect to this strategy as they do in the case of rehearsal (see Table 6-1):

> (a) Except when assisted to do so by hints or instruction, they tended not to rearrange the pictures into spatial groups by class membership during the study periods, a study tactic which the oldest subjects tended to adopt spontaneously; (b) given such assistance, however, the resulting increase

in study period manual clustering was accompanied by a decided increase in subsequent recall. (Moely *et al.*, 1969, p. 26).

Elaboration. Another, closely-related type of strategy is called *elaboration* (e.g., Rohwer, 1973). It involves the identification of a common referent or a shared meaning between two or more things to be remembered. Elaboration strategies are usually studied in the context of a paired-associate learning task. In such tasks, the subject has to learn pairs of stimulus and response items (commonly words) so that when the stimulus (e.g., "elephant") is presented, he can recall the response (e.g., "pin"). You would be using an elaboration strategy here if you deliberately generated an absurd or otherwise memorable visual image linking the two members of the pair. You might, for example, create an image of an elephant delicately balanced on the head of a pin, modestly acknowledging the applause of the audience. Another elaboration strategy would be to think of a sentence that describes an event involving the two, e.g., "The elephant picked up the pin with his trunk." A lot of research shows that elaboration can be a very effective method of cementing items together in memory. Just try forgetting what object was paired with "elephant" in the above example.

As with organization and rehearsal, the older the subject, the less outside help he is liable to need in order to use elaboration strategies. This should not be taken to imply that deliberate organizing and elaborating are employed universally by adults in all memory problems where these strategies would be useful. As with formal-operational reasoning (Chap. 4), their use or nonuse will surely depend upon who the adult is and what the task situation is. It is probably correct to conclude, however, that both organization and elaboration are later-developing strategies than at least the simpler forms of rehearsal. I would also guess, from the available evidence, that most forms of conscious and deliberate elaboration are apt to appear later in ontogenesis than most forms of conscious and deliberate organization.

The acme of development here, however, undoubtedly is not the mere ability to invoke this or that strategy spontaneously. Rather, it is the ability to select the most effective strategy or strategies for the memory problem at hand, and then to alter or replace those strategies appropriately as the mnemonic situation changes, e.g., as one's learning progresses, or when changes appear in the nature of the information that has to be memorized (Butterfield and Belmont, 1975). But we are now clearly talking about metamemory, or more precisely, about the relation between metamemory and the deployment of memory strategies.

Retrieval strategies. So far, I have discussed only storage strategies, i.e., the kinds of mnemonically-oriented data processing an individual does now because he knows he will have to retrieve those data later. As indicated earlier, retrieval strategies refer to the resourceful moves an individual may make when actually trying to recover things from memory storage, whether he had previously known he would now be doing that (intentional memory) or not (incidental memory). Like storage strategies, retrieval strategies vary greatly in complexity and sophistication. A less sophisticated one is not to give up your memory search immediately just because the sought-for item does not come to mind immediately. Sticking with the problem a little longer does not always pay off, of course, but it certainly qualifies as an elementary retrieval strategy. More sophisticated strategies often involve a complex interplay between specific memory fragments, general knowledge of the world, and reasoning or inference: "I remember hearing the sound of waves outside (memory fragment), so it probably happened near an ocean (inference, general knowledge); but I've only been to the ocean once, in 1969 (memory fragment), so it must have been that summer, during vacation (inference)."

As also indicated earlier, developmental research on retrieval strategies has scarcely begun (Kobasigawa, 1976). An interesting study by Kobasigawa (1974) will illustrate the general nature of such research. His subjects were children in grades 1, 3, and 6. Each subject was initially presented with 24 items and told he would have to try to recall them later; they consisted of three items in each of eight categories (e.g., three zoo animals, three types of fruit). Also present were pictures that could later serve as retrieval cues for the items belonging to a given category. In the animal category, for instance, the items were small pictures of a monkey, a camel, and a bear, each mounted on a blue card, and the retrieval cue was a larger picture of a zoo with three empty cages, mounted on a white card. The items and cues were presented together, and the connection between them carefully pointed out: "Do you see that these big pictures [cues] go with the small ones [to-be-recalled items]? In the *zoo* [cue], you find. . . ."

One third of the subjects at each grade level (free-recall condition) were subsequently just asked to recall as many items as possible; the cue cards were not present. One third (cue condition) were given the set of cue cards, placed face down in their laps, and told: "When you try to remember the small blue pictures you can look at these cards if you think these cards will help your remembering." The remaining third (directive-cue condition) were handed the cue cards one by one and told: "There were three small blue pictures that went with this [*E* pointed to the first cue]. Can you remember those small blue pictures?"

The results showed the sort of age by treatment interaction pattern earlier said to be frequently encountered in research on memory strategy

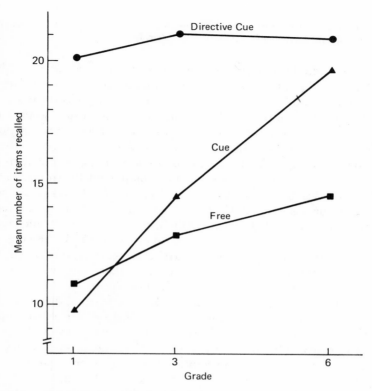

Figure 6-1. Mean number of items correctly recalled as a function of grade and recall condition. (From A. Kobasigawa, "Utilization of retrieval cues by children in recall," *Child Development*, 1974, 45, pp. 127-34. By permission.)

development. As Fig. 6-1 shows, item recall was very high in the directive cue condition, and about equally so at all three grade levels. It was much lower in the free-recall condition, and increased somewhat with grade. The increase across grades was much more pronounced in the cue condition. At grade 6—and only at grade 6—cue condition recall was statistically significantly better than free recall, and it was also not significantly poorer than directive-cue recall.

This pattern of results is partly explainable by the subjects' retrieval behavior under the various conditions, particularly the cue condition. As Kobasigawa analyzed the problem:

> A successful performance (high recall score) under the cue condition depends on S's ability to integrate spontaneously at least the following three task components: (1) to recall the small blue picture; (2) by looking at the

cue; and (3) to continue this process until all or most of the items related to that cue have been retrieved. . . . (1974, p. 132).

There are no doubt other strategy components involved here, e.g., knowing that one should go on to repeat components 1–3 with each and every cue card, but we will confine our attention to Kobasigawa's three.

The grade 1 subjects' difficulty in the cue condition seemed to lie in their inability to simultaneously focus attention on, and functionally integrate, components 1 and 2. They tended either to ignore the cues (focus on just component 1), or else to attend to the cues but then name them instead of the items (focus on just component 2). In contrast, the grade 3 subjects had good control of components 1 and 2 but would often falter on component 3. Often, they would look at a cue, retrieve only one item from that category, then go on to another cue, retrieve only one item from that category, and so on through all the cues. They would then frequently, but not always, cycle back again to the initial cue, perhaps retrieving a second item from that category, or perhaps instead re-retrieving (repeating) the first item again.

Whatever specific form of production inefficiency their use of the strategy took, the basic problem for the grade 3 subjects seemed to be a failure to make—or to think of making—a systematic, exhaustive search of each category. The directive-cue instruction and procedure may have helped them primarily by constantly reminding them that there were three items per category cue to be retrieved, and by implying that they should not terminate search until they had done their best to retrieve all three. Other research by Kobasigawa (1976) also suggests that young children may have some kind of difficulty with "termination rules" in memory search situations, but the precise nature of their difficulty is not yet clear. Like rehearsal, the strategic use of retrieval cues may also involve a complex integration of knowledge and skill components, even in a cue-use problem as simple as Kobasigawa's (1974). An obvious next research step in this area is to study the development of more elaborate, and perhaps more everyday-life-like retrieval strategies (Salatas and Flavell, 1975).

I have talked about memory as *Knowledge* in the preceding section and about memory as *Strategies* in this one. Is there any developmental theory and research linking the two? Not much as yet, but there should and probably will be in the next few years. That is, it is surely possible to apply voluntary, deliberate strategies to the storage and retrieval of complex, meaningful, and organized information as well as simple word lists and paired-associates (Brown, 1975). Learning to study effectively in school settings is a familiar and very important example of developing planful storage strategies for comprehending and retaining constructive-memory type, meaningful information. Just idly reading a passage about the complex and interrelated causes of World War II probably will yield some understanding and memory. But reading it very actively and "intelligently," taking really good notes, deliberately searching for relationships which are only implicit in the text—these are strategies that can yield much better understanding and memory. The same is true on the retrieval side. The above-mentioned sophisticated retrieval strategies, which interweave specific memories, general knowledge, and inferences, are equally applicable to highly meaningful material—to semantic as well as episodic memory. They can be used to reconstruct the causes of World War II as well as to reconstruct that single, isolated experience by the ocean mentioned earlier. It is obvious that a better understanding of the nature and development of these types of storage and retrieval strategies, and especially about how they might be solidly and permanently instilled through systematic training and instruction, would have considerable educational significance.

METAMEMORY

The subjects are kindergarteners, first graders, third graders, and fifth graders, and the investigation is an extensive interview study of children's metamemory, or knowledge about memory (Kreutzer, Leonard, and Flavell, 1975). In one of the interview items, the experimenter says to the child:

> Jim and Bill are in grade _____ (S's own grade). The teacher wanted them to learn the names of all the kinds of birds they might find in their city. Jim had learned them last year and then forgot them. Bill had never learned them before. Do you think one of these boys would find it easier to learn the names of all of the birds? Which one? Why? (Kreutzer *et al.*, 1975, p. 8).

It is obvious that this task does not fit under the Basic Processes or Knowledge headings of this chapter. It clearly does not fit under Strategies either, because the subject's method of learning bird names is not being studied. Rather it was meant to prove the child's intuitions about a specific memory phenomenon, namely, the advantage or "savings" involved in relearning something previously learned versus learning something for the first time. In short, it was intended to assess knowledge of memory, or metamemory.

Many of Kreutzer *et al.*'s subjects, even at the kindergarten and first grade levels, did, in fact, seem to intuit that the relearner would have the advantage. Moreover, a number of them gave reasonable justifications for their choice, e.g., "Because as soon as he heard the names, they would probably all come back to him" (an allusion to the process of recognition memory). That answer clearly testifies to some meta-memory. This third grader's answer clearly testifies to even more: the new learner would actually do better than the relearner, the subject said, "because the kid who learned them might think he knew them, and then he would get them wrong, but the kid who didn't learn them last year might study more than the kid who *thought* he knew them." (Kreutzer et al., 1975, p. 9).

If metamemory is knowledge about memory, what might such knowledge include? From a developmental standpoint, this amounts to asking what there might be for the growing child to acquire in this area of knowledge. The following is a classification scheme for describing possible varieties of metamemory.

One major category is *sensitivity* to the objective need for efforts at present retrieval or present storage, i.e., preparation for future retrieval. That is, one of the things the child presumably develops is a sense or attunement for when the situation calls for storage or retrieval efforts.

The other major category is knowledge of what *variables* or factors interact in what ways to affect how well an individual will perform on a retrieval problem. There are three classes of these variables or factors: (1) memory-relevant attributes of the *person* himself; (2) memory-relevant characteristics of the *task;* (3) possible *strategies* that the person could apply to the memory task. That is, how well an individual will remember jointly depends upon: (1) what he is like as a rememberer; (2) what the memory problem is like, e.g., the amount and kind of information to be remembered; (3) what behavior he engages in to remember it. The second major category of metamemory, then, includes a person's knowledge of these factors and of their interactive effects on memory performance.

Sensitivity

Perhaps the situation that most explicitly calls for intentional retrieval or storage effort on your part is another person's direct request that you try to recall or memorize something. As with strategy use, an individual would be likely to make deliberate mnemonic efforts in response to explicit instruction earlier in childhood than he would make them spontaneously, i.e., earlier than he would make them in response to a situation that only implicitly, rather than explicitly, calls for such efforts. We can thus ask when a child will first comprehend, and respond appropriately to, another's request to retrieve something from memory.

Similarly, when will he first do the same in response to a request to store something for future retrieval, i.e., memorize it?

As to the first question, it is apparent from casual observation that children will try to answer retrieval questions very early, e.g., attempt to respond appropriately to episodic-memory questions like "Who did we see at the store today?" Incredible though it may seem, however, that is about all we know about the beginnings of deliberate retrieval activity and associated metamemory; I am aware of no systematic research on the topic. We do not know, for instance, when (let alone how) children start learning that things which cannot be recalled instantly sometimes can be if one keeps trying a little longer, or sometimes will spontaneously come to mind at a later time.

There is, in contrast, some existing research evidence which bears on the second question, concerning deliberate storage or memorization efforts in response to instructions (cf. Flavell and Wellman, 1976). Russian and American investigators have hypothesized that the child initially does not distinguish or differentiate a request to memorize items from one that does not mention memory, e.g., a request simply to inspect the items perceptually. Deliberate memorizing seems an inherently more planful act than deliberate recalling, since it consists of present storage efforts in preparation for future retrieval efforts, rather than just those retrieval efforts themselves. Therefore, it would be expected to develop later than deliberate retrieving, and the available evidence suggests that it does. In at least some task situations, preschoolers do not seem to behave any differently (or recall any better) if asked to study a set of items for purposes of future recall than if asked only to look at them, with no mention made of any later recall requirement. It is as if they fail to grasp the essential structure and meaning of a memorization task, with its implicit mandate to try to do something special now that will enhance one's future performance.

Here as elsewhere, however, the age at which understanding emerges is partly dependent upon the task. For example, even three year olds may show some differentiated, memorization-like preparatory activity if the task is to remember where an object is hidden (Wellman, Ritter, and Flavell, 1975). Recalling where things are is undoubtedly a much more familiar and meaningful activity for a young child than recalling a set of picture names, and the idea of deliberately preparing for it may therefore be correspondingly more precocious. There is another reason why one should be cautious about concluding that a young child does not really understand what deliberate memorization means. It is possible that the child really does understand what it means, but cannot spontaneously generate any strategic, distinctively mnemonic-looking study behavior that mediates good retrieval performance. That is, if he can produce no detectable memorization strategy that yield good recall, we may erroneously conclude that he has no grasp of wha it means to try to memorize something.

We know next to nothing about the genesis of spontaneous a contrasted with instructed storage and retrieval efforts. On the storag side, older children have been shown to be more aware than younge ones that items you have just failed to recall on a test are more in nee of further study than ones you have just succeeded in recalling (Masu McIntyre, and Flavell, 1973). Similarly, older childen appear mor sensitive than younger ones to the usefulness of keeping written record of past solution attempts in a problem solving task, so as to avoid skip ping possible solution moves or repeating previous ones (Siegler an Liebert, 1975). The authors suggest (p. 402) that "the process underlyin 10-year-olds' failure to produce external memory aids may have bee a lack of foresight." This sort of "foresight" is an especially clear exampl of the present, Sensitivity category of metamemory.

There appear to be no comparable, clearly interpretable devel opmental studies of spontaneous, uninstructed retrieval efforts as ye (Flavell and Wellman, 1976).

Variables

Person. There is much that a growing child could come to sense o know about himself and others as mnemonic beings. Flavell and Well man (1976) distinguish between two related types of metamemory con cerning person variables. One type refers to knowledge of what the sel and others are generally like as storers and retrievers of information— their more or less enduring traits, abilities, and limitations in the area of memory functioning. The second type refers to the ability to monitor and interpret one's own immediate mnemonic experiences in specifi memory situations. The first thus has to do with knowledge of enduring mnemonic characteristics and capacities, the second with knowing how to detect and interpret transient mnemonic processes and states, i.e. with here-and-now memory monitoring.

With respect to the first type of person metamemory, Flavell and Wellman (1976) report three studies of person metamemory which show that older children tend to have a more realistic and accurate picture of their own memory abilities and limitations than younger ones do, at least on tasks of the following kind (e.g., Yussen and Levy, 1975). The experimenter briefly exposes a horizontal strip of two pictures of com mon objects and asks the subject if he or she could correctly name the objects in left-to-right serial order after the experimenter covers them up again. Subjects of all ages make the realistic judgment that they would. The subject is then asked the same question about a briefly-exposed strip of three pictures, then four, and so on. The process stops either when the subject says the series has now gotten too long for him to recall accurately or when a strip of 10 pictures has been presented (a series much too long for any subject to remember under these task conditions). The subject is then tested for his actual, as opposed to the foregoing predicted, memory span on this task. Younger children tend to overestimate their memory ability here; that is, their predicted memory span exceeds their actual memory span, often by a considerable amount. With increasing age the two come closer together, the predicted span realistically decreasing to meet an increasing actual span. For what little additional developmental evidence exists concerning this first type of person metamemory, see Flavell and Wellman (1976).

As for the second type of person metamemory, second- and fourth-graders seem to be considerably better than kindergarteners and first-graders at sensing when they have studied and learned a set of items well enough to remember them all (Flavell *et al.*, 1970; Markman, 1973). All subjects were carefully instructed to study the items until they were really sure they could recall them perfectly. The older subjects studied for a period of time, said they were ready, and usually were, i.e., remembered all the items correctly. The younger subjects studied for a period of time, said they were ready, and usually were not. Moreover, their feeling of recall readiness did not become more accurate over several study-test trials. As is true for most cognitive immaturities described in this book, the exact nature and source of young children's problems here have not yet been ascertained. But memory monitoring difficulties they do indeed seem to have, both in this task situation and others.

Probably the most searching developmental investigation of memory monitoring to date has been carried out by Wellman (1975). Kindergarten, first-grade, and third-grade children were presented with a variety of pictures of objects and asked to name them. For any object the child could not name, he was asked if he felt he knew its name anyway, and therefore, would later recognize it from among a set of alternatives if he heard it (called feeling-of-knowing or *FK* judgments). He also was asked if he had ever seen the object before (called *SEEN* judgments). Finally, he was subsequently tested to see whether he could, in fact, recognize the object's name when he heard it. Wellman found a strong age increase in the accuracy of children's *FK* judgments, i.e., in their ability to predict subsequent name recognition. In contrast, *SEEN* judgments proved to be highly correlated with subsequent name recognition at all three ages. Further analyses strongly supported the following conclusions. Children at all three ages have roughly equal potential access to the internal information they need in order to help themselves predict name recognition accurately, such as their awareness that they have or have not seen the object before (*SEEN* judgments). The older children do, in fact, usually attend to and exploit this information when predicting. For instance, if they feel they have never seen the object before, they seem to use this feeling as grounds for predicting that they will not recognize its name when they hear it. The younger ones usually do not exploit such information. It may be that they are not as aware as their elders of its predictive utility, are not as generally prone to search their inner world for useful clues, or both.

Task. There is a great deal for the developing child to learn about what makes some memory tasks more difficult than others. First, a memory task can be harder or easier because of the amount and kind of information to be learned and remembered. Second, for any given amount and kind of stored information, some retrieval demands or requirements are more severe and taxing than others. For example, the requirement merely to recognize, as previously encountered, something experienced earlier is usually much easier than the requirement to recall it from memory, i.e., without it being perceptually present. Therefore, task difficulty is a joint function of two things, what has to be stored and the nature of subsequent retrieval demands.

Certain memory-relevant properties of what is stored have to do with individual items of information, rather than with relationships among items. Some of Kreutzer *et al.*'s (1975) kindergarten and first-grade subjects seemed to believe that an individual item that was familiar or perceptually salient would be especially easy to learn and remember. Practically all of them knew that increasing the sheer number of individual items to be remembered made a memory task harder.

As implied in the earlier discussion of organization and elaboration strategies, items also become easier to remember if the learner discovers or creates meaningful connections among them. Several studies have documented the growing child's increasing awareness of the mnemonic value of various kinds of interitem relationships (Flavell and Wellman, 1976). For example, Moynahan (1973) found that third- and fifth-graders were more likely than first-graders to predict that a list of categorizable items (food items, items of clothing, etc.) would be easier to remember than a comparable list of unrelated items. Similarly, when asked to think of three words that would be very easy to remember along with the word "blue," say, older elementary-school children are much likelier than younger ones to think of three more color words (Tenney, 1975). Tenney's younger subjects could readily generate other words of the same category as the initial word (here, color) if explicitly asked to, but they did not spontaneously think of doing this under the above, "easy-to-remember" instruction. Kreutzer *et al.* (1975) also found developmental trends across the elementary grades in the child's knowledge that paired-associates composed of verbal opposites (e.g., "hard"—"soft") and a list of words that are meaningfully linked together by a story are easier to remember than pairs and lists without strong interitem relationships.

Kreutzer *et al.* (1975) found the same age trends with respect to two insights concerning retrieval demands. First their older subjects sensed that it may become harder to recall one set of words if, before the recall test, you also have to learn a second set of words that are easily confused with the first set; as you may know, students of memory call this phenomenon *retroactive interference*. Second, Kreutzer *et al.*'s (1975) older subjects knew that it is easier to retell a story in your own words than in the exact words it was told to you, i.e., memory for the semantic gist of a story is better than memory for its exact linguistic form.

Strategies. Since this topic has been discussed at length in the previous section, I shall only mention a few examples where the metamemory component is especially prominent. In several of Kreutzer *et al.*'s (1975) interview items, the subjects were presented with hypothetical storage (preparation for future retrieval) and retrieval problems and asked how they would solve them. In one storage problem, for instance, the child was asked how many things he could think of to do to make sure he would not forget to take his ice skates to school with him the next morning. The older subjects were able to think of more different things to do than the younger ones, and generally they seemed more strategic and planful in their approach to this real-world type memory problem. Nonetheless, a number of the kindergarten and first-grade subjects were able to describe appropriate strategies. Interestingly, for them as for the third- and fifth-graders, the most commonly mentioned strategies were not of the familiar, in-the-head variety, such as thinking again and again about bringing the skates (rehearsal). Rather, they involved external actions and the use of outside memory stores, such as putting the skates where you are sure to see them the next morning, asking your mother to remind you, and writing yourself a note. Possible literacy problems failed to deter a number of the younger subjects from proposing the note-writing strategy. This tendency to think of external versus internal mnemonic aids was also noted in children's response to other interview items in the same study.

Some of Kreutzer *et al.*'s (1975) subjects gave strategy descriptions that attested to some unexpectedly sophisticated intuitions about the nature of memory. The following is a prize example. The question was: "What do you do when you want to remember a phone number?" A third-grade girl replied:

> Say the number is 633–8854. Then what I'd do is—say that my number is 633, so I won't have to remember that, really. And then I would think now I've got to remember 88. Now I'm 8 years old, so I can remember, say, my age two times. Then I say how old my brother is, and how old he was last year. And that's how I'd usually remember that phone number. [Is that how you would most often remember a phone number?] Well, usually I write it down. (Kreutzer *et al.*, 1975, p. 11).

Questions About Metamemory

Metamemory is a new topic in the study of memory development, and consequently there are many things about it that are still unclear or unknown (Flavell and Wellman, 1976; Kreutzer *et al.*, 1975; Wellman, Drozdal, Flavell, Ritter, and Salatas, 1975). First of all, should metamemory be taken to mean only totally conscious and explicit, fully verbalizable ideas about memory phenomena? That would seem too restrictive a definition; metamemory also ought to be allowed to include inarticulate intuitions that *A* is easier to remember than *B,* largely unconscious feelings that *C* has now been studied well enough to be retrievable on a forthcoming test, and the like. Nevertheless, although one can point to clear and unambiguous examples of it, metamemory is not yet as well conceptualized as it ought to be.

We also know very little about children's developing understanding of the possible interactive effects of person, task, and strategy variables. An example would be your feeling that you had probably better adopt strategy *A* rather than *B*, given your estimate of which strategy would be better suited to this particular memory task plus your feeling about how efficiently and effectively you personally can use each.

Another question of interest is how the child acquires his knowledge of memory (the question of how he acquires memory strategies is, of course, equally interesting). Flavell and Wellman (1976) hypothesize that repeated informational feedback from the child's own actions and their outcomes in various memory situations might be one source of knowledge. Parents and teachers probably also play important roles in fostering metamemory development. There is, however, no research evidence on the matter as yet.

Finally, there is the key question of the possible relationships between metamemory and memory behavior, particularly strategies. About all we can say at present is that the connections between the two doubtless vary considerably from situation to situation and also from one developmental level to another (Flavell and Wellman, 1976). It is probably not the case, for instance, that metamemory invariably precedes, generates, and actively guides strategic behavior in either younger or older subjects. The strategic behavior might run off "mindlessly": a younger subject might engage in it without any knowledge that it could be mnemonically useful; an older one might engage in it automatically, out of long strategic habit, with no presently active knowledge or awareness of what he is doing and why. In the first example, there is no metamemory at all. In the second, we see only its fossilized remains, so to speak, barely discernable in what has now become an overlearned, almost reflexive response to a highly familiar memory situation. If you were to ask him what he was up to, his answers might reveal a lot of metamemory; but that metamemory is dormant during actual strategy use.

Nevertheless, metamemory simply must play a powerful, genuinely causal role in relation to some strategic memory behavior, as several writers have recently noted (Brown, 1975; Butterfield and Belmont, 1975; Hagen, *et al.*, 1975; Olson, 1976). As Wellman put it:

> . . . if the much used idea of "strategic" memory is analyzed in any detailed way, then clearly memory monitoring must be implicated in optimal, efficient strategy use. For example, in his model of a retrieval system, Shiffrin (1970) includes an "executive decision maker." For strategic retrieval a number of decisions must be made either purposefully or by default, such as whether to search, when to continue to search, when to terminate search, what strategy to use, when to continue with a strategy, when to modify a strategy, when to adopt a new strategy. For optimal, strategic search these decisions should be based on memory monitoring; if the item is not in memory do not begin search, continue to search if searching is having some effect on the accessability (state) of the item, etc.
>
> Memory monitoring plays a similar role in strategic storage (or the preparation for future retrieval), though it has not usually been analyzed as a factor. Consider strategy termination rules; when do you quit using a storage strategy? The optimum answer must be, when the state of the items you are storing matches the state required by the task. One might expect that even if young children were employing an effective strategy, poor preparation might result because they would not know when to terminate their preparation. (Wellman, 1975, pp. 7–8).

SUMMARY

Memory development became a popular field of inquiry when researchers turned their attention from the overt products of the child's memory to the underlying cognitive processes that generate these products. Several concepts are useful in analyzing memory development. *Memory in the strict sense* and *episodic memory* refer to memories for specific, personally experienced, past happenings, e.g., remembering that you saw a cup fall and break yesterday. *Memory in the wider sense* and *semantic memory* refer to acquired knowledge of all sorts, e.g., that cups are called "cups" in English and that cups exhibit Piagetian object permanence. Getting things into memory is called *storage;* getting them out again, *retrieval.* Retrieval may consist of: *recognition* of something that is already present in perception or thought; *recall* of something that is not present (often with the help of reminders or *retrieval cues*); *reconstruction* of wholes from memory, given only the parts; blends and mixtures of these three.

It is convenient to discuss memory development under four major headings: *basic processes, knowledge, strategies,* and *metamemory. Basic processes* refer to the "hardware" of the human memory system—its most fundamental operations and capabilities. Recognition and recall processes are two examples of particular interest. Even young babies show recognition memory, whereas the capacity for conscious recall seems to emerge only toward the end of the infancy period. We know virtually nothing about the genesis of recall capability, despite the real possibility that it is the only basic process that shows any significant childhood development.

In the *Knowledge* section, the argument was made that what a person knows (memory in the wider sense) greatly influences what he learns and remembers (memory in the strict sense). Consequently, developmental changes in the cognitive system should lead to developmental changes in what he or she stores and retrieves. Piaget and his associates have attempted to demonstrate such changes. Their most striking claim is that cognitive-structural development can lead to memory improvement. If a child sees a seriated array of sticks and over subsequent months develops an understanding of seriation, for instance, his later recall of that array may actually be more accurate than his initial recall of it. The scientific status of this claim is still uncertain at present, however.

A number of other students of memory share Piaget's view that storage is *construction* and retrieval is *reconstruction.* According to this view, we do not simply make a copy of information presented at storage and then simply reprint that copy when we retrieve. Rather, both storage and retrieval involve a great deal of active conceptual organization and reorganization, much gap-filling and inference, as the individual tries to achieve a meaningful representation of the information. There is considerable evidence that children as well as adults use constructive and reconstructive processes when they remember. There is also some beginning evidence that older children may be more spontaneously inferential, and perhaps use more complex and difficult inferences, in their mnemonic constructions and reconstructions than is true of younger children.

Strategies are potentially conscious activities that a person may use to facilitate memory. *Rehearsal* constitutes one frequently-studied class of storage strategies. Table 6-1 shows what may be the typical course of development of rehearsal and other memory strategies. Initially, the child is unable to execute the potentially-strategic activity at all, even under experimenter instruction or tuition. Subsequently, the child is likely to exhibit a pattern of *production deficiency* with respect to the strategy. That is, he can and will use it if explicitly directed to do so, and using it benefits his memory in the expected fashion, but he does not use the strategy spontaneously, on his own initiative. The causes of production deficiencies are not well understood, but some possible ones were suggested: (1) The child may not have the foresight to use any special cognitive activity now, in order to facilitate retrieval later. (2) The task situation may trigger the use of some other, better-developed strategy than the one under study. (3) The target strategy may not yet be well enough mastered—qua cognitive activity, as an end in itself—to be brought into service as a means to a mnemonic goal. In the final period shown in Table 6-1, such obstacles are no longer in force, and the child employs the strategy spontaneously.

There are other storage strategies that are more sophisticated and mnemonically effective than rehearsal. The learner would be using an *organization* strategy if he studied conceptually related items together, in groups by category membership, and then tended to *cluster* same-category items together in recall. *Elaboration* strategies also add meaning to what is presented. An example of elaboration would be the construction of a vivid visual image linking together two normally unrelated objects that are supposed to be remembered together, as in a paired-associate learning task. The ontogenetic pattern shown in Table 6-1 also appears to apply to these two types of strategies.

We know much less about the development of retrieval strategies than about the development of storage strategies. A study by Kobasigawa (1974) was described in some detail to illustrate how this topic is currently being investigated. Most developmental studies of storage and retrieval strategies entail purely mental, in-the-head memory for relatively meaningless, isolated "items." It is hoped that future research will examine children's acquisition of strategies for storing and retrieving more organized, meaningful bodies of information, and in task settings that permit the use of mnemonic resources other than just one's internal memory. Studying a subject matter like history (or cognitive development) with the aid of textbooks, notes, reference rooms, teachers, and fellow students is the sort of "memory task" I have in mind.

Metamemory means knowledge about anything concerning memory. Two major categories of metamemory were distinguished. The first is *sensitivity* to situations calling for efforts at information storage or retrieval. The call can be either explicit or implicit. For example, even very young children will try to answer questions that probe their memory. That is, they seem to comprehend, and will try to respond appropriately to, an explicit call for a retrieval effort. It is only later, however, that they seem to comprehend and respond appropriately to an explicit call for a storage effort, i.e., an instruction to memorize or remember something in preparation for a later recall test. The implicit counterparts of these would be spontaneously—without anyone instructing you to—thinking to store information you believe you will need to remember later, or spontaneously thinking to retrieve information that you believe you need to remember now. Almost nothing is known about the ontogenesis of these highly adaptive inner promptings.

The other major category of metamemory is knowledge of the *person, task,* and *strategy variables* that jointly affect one's memory performance. In the *person* case, studies have documented two kinds of development. First, the growing child becomes increasingly realistic and accurate in assessing his own memory capabilities, e.g., in estimating his memory span. Second, he becomes better able to monitor and interpret his immediate memory experiences and states, e.g., feel or sense that something he cannot now recall is nonetheless in memory and therefore would be recognized if encountered.

Evidence also exists that he comes to learn a great deal about what makes some memory *tasks* easier than others. He discovers that a set of items will be easier to recall if they are few in number, familiar, and meaningfully related to one another, e.g., categorizable. Similarly, he comes to appreciate the fact that some retrieval test requirements are more taxing than others. As an example, it is a more demanding test of memory to repeat a story word for word than to retell it in your own words.

Children also become better able to think of and articulate plausible storage and retrieval *strategies* in response to hypothetical memory problems. Younger and older children alike tend to favor the use of external memory aids over unaided internal memory. They think that written notes and other people make useful reminders, for example.

Finally, mention was made of some presently unanswered questions concerning metamemory and its development. How exactly should it be defined and conceptualized? How do children acquire it? How is metamemory related to actual memory behavior, especially the use of strategies?

7

questions and problems

Most textbooks fail to give the reader an insider's view of the field they cover. A field looks very different to an insider—a "pro"—than it does to an outsider. The insider continually lives with its numerous questions, problems, ambiguities, and uncertainties. He becomes used to, although never unconcerned about, its untidy, open-ended, no-problem-ever-seems-to-get-solved character. He knows how incredibly difficult it is even to think up a research study that will tell us something we really want to know.

Experiences like the following bring home the reality of this insider-outsider distinction. When I read in the popular press about some new medical claim or discovery, I nod approvingly at this Latest Advance in Our Understanding of Nature. When the claim or discovery is in the area of cognitive development, on the other hand, I usually have two reactions. The first is that, as always, the reporter has partly misunderstood what the developmental psychologist was trying to tell him. The second is that the developmental psychologist who told it to him is just old Bleatworthy, peddling *that* view again, and that Bleatworthy himself is probably just as conscious as I am of all the unresolved questions and problems that shroud it.

The aim of this chapter is to present some of the questions and problems you would live with if you were an insider in the field of cognitive growth. By implication, the aim is also to make you feel more insecure and skeptical about everything you have read in previous chapters. I can imagine two reactions that different readers might have to the content of this chapter, depending upon their backgrounds and interests. One is that finally, at long last, we are getting into the *real* issues. The author has finished describing all the different ways that kids get smarter as they grow older and will now get into more substantive matters. As the section headings indicate, he will now talk about how to assess or diagnose the child's cognitive level, how cognitive growth may be explained rather than just described, and the sorts of systematic patterns (stages, sequences) it exhibits. He will, in short, try to tie it all together, provide an overview and perspective, show us What It All Means. The other reaction is that things have suddenly gotten very abstract and hard to follow. The child's cognitive development is now populated with false positives, underlying processes, cognitive entities, structures, concurrences, qualitative changes, and other intangibles. Where did the child go?

Both reactions are perfectly understandable and reasonable. To those who have the first reaction I would suggest only that even the purely descriptive aspects of cognitive development are scientifically important, and also that—the insider's plight once again—those real issues and substantive matters are going to look very messy, very far from being resolved. To those with the second reaction, I would suggest that you either skip this chapter altogether (if that option is open to you) or else read it in a special way. The special way is to let it wash over you, trying only to get the main points. Above all, try to get a sense or feeling for how cognitive growth might proceed—or more accurately, for the *alternative* conceptions among which the insiders are struggling to decide of how cognitive growth might proceed. Try, in other words, to get some sort of wide angle view of the cognitive-developmental panorama, including the outstanding questions and problems concerning it. Regardless of which of the two reactions you may have, if either, providing you with such a view is one of the main objectives of this chapter.

DIAGNOSIS

What problems and issues do psychologists face in trying to diagnose or analyze children's developing knowledge and abilities? They are many, varied, and very, very troublesome. Discussions of these problems and issues can be found in, for example, Bortner and Birch (1970), Cole and Bruner (1971), Flavell (1970a, pp. 1032–1034; 1971a, pp. 429–

435), Flavell and Wohlwill (1969), Miller (1976), Smedslund (1969), and Zimiles (1971).

What is involved in cognitive-developmental diagnosis can best be communicated with reference to a specific example. Transitive inference is a concrete-operational acquisition within Piaget's theoretical system. As mentioned in Chap. 4 (*Consolidation and Solidification* section), one form of it is conceived by Piaget as consisting of this type of reasoning process: if $A > B$ (e.g., A is longer than B) and $B > C$, then it has to be true that $A > C$—no measurement is necessary. There are two sorts of questions developmental psychologists may ask about this or any other cognitive acquisition. They both involve "diagnosis," but in somewhat different senses. One has to do with our *conceptualization* of the acquisition itself, the other with its *assessment* in children.

Conceptualization questions ask what this ability or behavior we call "transitive inference" consists of, in psychological terms. What are the cognitive processes that actually underlie or comprise acts of so-called transitive inference? What, exactly, happens inside the individual's head when, given $A > B$, $B > C$, and A ? C, he responds $A > C$? In short, *what* develops when transitive inference develops?

There are several kinds of assessment questions. Some are more concrete and practical; others are more abstract and theoretical; all are related to one another and to the conceptualization questions. Here are some concrete and practical ones: Suppose we provisionally accept someone's (e.g., Piaget's) characterization of what "transitive inference" is. That is, we accept as a point of departure *some* answer to the conceptualization question. The practical assessment question then arises. How can we determine (diagnose) whether a given child has or has not acquired transitive inference? What assessment procedures should we use to test for its presence in the child's cognitive repertoire? These procedures should neither overestimate nor underestimate the child's capacity for transitive inference. Overestimation would lead to diagnostic errors of the *false-positive* variety: the child does not really have transitive inference, but your testing procedure wrongly leads you to conclude that he does. Underestimation would produce *false-negative* errors: the child does really have it, but your testing procedure wrongly leads you to conclude that he does not—your procedure is too insensitive. How do we find a method of diagnostic testing that decreases the likelihood of both kinds of errors? In order to find such a method, we would obviously have to know what could cause a child to appear to have transitive inference but not really have it (false positive) and vice-versa (false negative).

We cannot work on these concrete and practical assessment problems very long without being confronted with certain more abstract and theoretical questions. What, exactly, do we really mean to say about a child when we say he "has" or "does not have" transitive inference? Let us assume (contrary to actual fact) that we possess a completely valid test of transitive inference behavior, one that always will be right when it says that a child did or did not engage in transitive inference in any appropriate task situation. Suppose further that we discover that every child we test does one or the other of two things: (1) engages in transitive inference in all and only those situations where transitive inference can legitimately be made; (2) never engages in it. If every child did either 1 or 2, then "having" versus "not having" transitive inference would possess reasonably clear meanings. The child who does 1 definitely "has" it. The child who does 2 "does not have" it, but less definitely so. (It is theoretically possible that some capacity for it exists, but the capacity is too underdeveloped to be expressed even in the "easiest" transitive-inference task we have yet been able to devise.)

Suppose instead that, in addition to finding these two types of children, we also find some (3) who engage in transitive inference in only a few, very easy task situations, others (4) who do the same in all but a few, very difficult task situations, and (5) many children in between. I am sure you will not be surprised to learn that this additional supposition is well-founded in reality. That is, we definitely do find a whole gamut of 3's, 4's, and 5's between the two extremes of 1 and 2—not just in the case of transitive inference, but apparently for all sorts of Piagetian and non-Piagetian cognitive achievements. You may remember encountering similar developmental heterogeneities elsewhere in this book (e.g., the *Conclusions About Adolescent and Adult Thinking* section of Chap. 4).

What theoretical sense can we make of this untidy state of affairs? Will we need to distinguish several, or even many, different kinds or degrees of "having transitive inference"? If so, how should such distinctions be drawn? Perhaps the several or many we distinguish will line up nicely to form an orderly developmental sequence or progression. That is, we might theoretically define a "beginning" kind (degree? amount?) of capability for transitive inference, followed by a "more advanced" one (in what way?), and so on until a "completely mature" (in what sense?) capability is achieved. But if we think of transitive inference as more like a developmental succession of different things than like a unitary, unchanging cognitive entity, we find ourselves confronting the conceptualization form of the diagnosis question once again. The conceptualization question, you will recall, asks what cognitive processes actually make up or underlie "transitive inferences." However, if "transitive inference" changes with age, then those cognitive processes must also change with age.

To recapitulate, we begin with a preliminary, working notion of what transitive inference is (conceptualization questions). We then try to find ways to accurately diagnose its presence/absence in the child's task performance (concrete and practical assessment questions). The best available diagnostic procedures suggest that, for many children, it is present sometimes and absent sometimes, depending upon the specifics of the task situation and perhaps other factors. Then, we try to make developmental sense out of this lack of consistency (abstract and theoretical assessment questions), perhaps by hypothesizing an ontogenetic progression of different forms (degrees, or whatever) of transitive-inference-related capabilities. The existence of such a progression implies that these capabilities must change in some way from one point in that progression to another, and therefore, so also must the nature and/or organization of the cognitive processes underlying them (back to conceptualization problems again). Let us now examine this diagnostic cycle in more detail, beginning with the more concrete and practical sorts of assessment questions.

Assessment Questions

Concrete and practical aspects. We shall begin with the simplifying assumption that a child either does or does not possess the ability to make a transitive inference—with no gradations in between—and that our diagnostic goal is to find out which is the case for an individual child. Suppose the child really does possess this ability but gives no evidence of it in his performance on some test of transitive inference, leading us to make a false-negative diagnostic error. This could happen for a number of reasons. The child might fail to understand the task instructions, fail to attend to or comprehend the premises of the inference (i.e., the fact that $A > B$ and $B > C$), or forget either the instructions or the premises at the moment when the inference normally would be made (Smedslund, 1969). Also, as with production deficiencies for particular memory strategies (Chap. 6), for some reason the task may elicit from the child a problem-solving approach or strategy that is incompatible with transitive inference. For instance, having just learned through perception rather than inference that $A > B$ and $B > C$, he may assume that $A \ ? \ C$ must also be solved by perception rather than inference.

His true ability can also be masked by motivational and emotional factors, such as disinterest in your "game," or apprehension about you as an adult stranger. Some cognitive tasks require the child to generate a complex verbal response (e.g., an explanation) in order to demonstrate the cognitive ability the examiner is interested in; the child may be incapable of generating the verbal response and yet possess the cognitive ability. Recall the point made at the end of Chap. 3 in connection with the Gelman (1972*b*) study. Every task demands from the child knowledge and skills other than, and in addition to, the target concept or ability it was designed to tap. If the child does not or can not meet any of these additional, nontarget demands, a false-negative diagnostic error can result. It is small wonder that Bortner and Birch say that "performance levels under particular conditions are but fragmentary indicators of capacity" (1970, p. 735).

The chances of underestimating the child's capacity become especially great if his experiences and expectancies concerning cognitive tasks are markedly different from the examiner's, e.g., because he belongs to a different culture or subculture (Cole and Bruner, 1971; Cole and Scribner, 1974). Psychologists who attempt to do cross-cultural studies of cognitive growth have a particularly difficult problem avoiding false-negative errors of diagnosis.

False-positive diagnostic errors can also stem from several causes. Under certain task conditions, the child may get the right answer by guessing, by direct perception of $A > C$, or by using some irrelevant (i.e., nontransitive-inference) solution strategy which happens to yield the $A > C$ conclusion (Smedslund, 1969). One such strategy that has been identified stems from the young child's frequent tendency to think in absolute (e.g., "*A* is *long*") rather than relative or comparative terms (e.g., "*A* is *longer than B*"). He may code the premises $A > B$ and $B > C$ as something like "*A* is long, *B* isn't," and "*B* is long, *C* isn't," respectively. Since in this coding, *A* has been thought of as "long" once but *C* never has, for this reason the child may tend to choose *A* when asked which is "longer." The answer is, of course, correct, but it was not generated by transitive inference.

Researchers have thought of some clever ways to reduce the likelihood of such false-positive, nontransitive but correct solutions (Smedslund, 1969; Trabasso, 1975). It is possible, for instance, to show sticks *A* and *C* on a background of Müller-Lyer arrows, which creates the visual illusion that *C* is longer than *A* rather than vice-versa. We already have seen how transitivity of weight can appear to be violated by a rigged-scale balance (Miller's studies in Chap. 4, *Consolidation and Solidification* section). In both cases, the child is actually given false perceptual information about the A-C relation, which, of course, greatly reduces his chances of getting the right answer by processes other than transitive inference. Similarly, suppose we give the child this transitive-inference problem: given that $A > B$, $B > C$, $C > D$, $D > E$, what is the length relation between *B* and *D*? Since both *B* and *D* have been shown to be longer than one thing and shorter than another in this problem, the child cannot get the right answer by using the above-mentioned strategy of coding relative terms as absolutes; both B and D have had a chance to be coded as "long". Also, we can reduce markedly the chances of making a false-positive diagnostic error by requiring the child to explain or justify his $A > C$ conclusion. An answer like, "A *has* to be longer than C because it is longer than B, and even B is longer than C," could hardly emanate from a child who had no understanding of the transitivity rule.

But the reduction of false positives is very likely to result in an increase in false negatives. It is not hard to conceive of a child who would not fare at all well on these more stringent tests, while yet possessing at least some genuine capability for transitive inference. In the illusion condition, a young child might simply think that his direct perception of $C > A$ is a more trustworthy guide to decision making than logical inference. Give me a logical inference as novel and complex for me as transitive inference is for the young child, and I might feel the same way. The child may also not entertain the possibility that the adult experimenter could be deceiving him, although this is, of course, exactly what that authority figure is doing in using those Müller-Lyer arrows. You might not entertain it either, if the Pope or George Washington were testing you. The illusion could even lead him to misinterpret the problem altogether as one of determining which stick *looks* longer, rather than which one *really is* longer (cf. Chap. 3, *Perceived appearances versus inferred reality* section). The added complexity of five terms rather than three in the $A > B \ldots D > E$ task could overload the child's attention and memory capabilities, decreasing the likelihood that $B > C$ and $C > D$ will be front and center in his consciousness when B ? D has to be decided. Finally, of course it is possible that the child could have just solved the problem by transitive inference and yet lack the wherewithal—conceptual, linguistic, emotional, motivational—to generate a satisfactory verbal justification of his choice.

It should be apparent by now that the concrete and practical task of assessing transitive inference or any other cognitive acquisition is fraught with difficulties. As Smedslund put it: "The relationship between any set of behavioral indices and a mental process, therefore, is an uncertain one, and a diagnosis will always have the status of a working hypothesis" (1969, p. 247). This does not mean that diagnosis of a child's cognitive-developmental status is inherently impossible, incapable of being improved, or just generally not worth trying. "Uncertain" does not mean "unknown" or "unknowable," and "working hypotheses" are necessary and useful in all fields.

Abstract and theoretical aspects. It does mean, however, that we need to stand back a bit from our measurement efforts and examine the whole assessment enterprise in a more abstract and theoretical way. In particular, we have to ask what range and diversity of cognitive phenomena we may be tapping when we try to measure "transitive inference" in children of different cognitive-developmental levels. What *are* the different possible meanings and manners of "having," of "possessing," something like transitive inference? Does the growing child first "have" it in manner *A*, and later in manner *B*, and still later in manner *C*? The following is one way to think about these questions (Flavell, 1971*a*; Flavell and Wohlwill, 1969). It is not the only way, and it will not necessarily prove to be the best way. It is hard to overstress how unconfident most of us feel about these matters at the present time.

Let us suppose that one child may "have" transitive inference in a more advanced fashion than another child, in the specific sense of being able to call it into play more easily and being able to apply it successfully in more task situations. According to this view of how development might proceed, transitive inference is "in there somewhere" in both cases, but it is more readily and more generally available for use in the one case than in the other. What could cause this difference in availability? We have already mentioned a number of specific causes in our discussion of how false-negative diagnostic errors may arise, and there are no doubt many, many more. In some instances, the child may not use transitive inference because he does not think to. The task situation, for example, may evoke some other, competing solution strategy instead. In other instances, the task may evoke a transitive-inference strategy, but the inferential problem is so complex the child cannot successfully execute the strategy. In the first case, the problem is one of strategy *evocation;* in the second, it is one of strategy *utilization* (Flavell, 1971*a*, p. 429).

When the child begins to acquire transitive inference, first "has" it in some rudimentary sense, it may be both difficult to evoke, and if evoked, difficult to execute or utilize. We might have to evoke it directly, e.g., by actually instructing him to use it, and then we might also have to assist him a bit in its step-by-step utilization. If a great deal of such instruction and assistance were required, we might prefer to conclude instead that the child, in fact, did not "have" transitive inference in even the most rudimentary sense, prior to our intervention. That is, we might conclude instead that we had simply taught it to him outright—built it in from the ground up. Yet, it seems plausible to think that a newly developed cognitive form could be so fragile and unstable that a good deal of environmental support would be needed for its successful evocation and utilization. A cognitive training study might therefore be done for a somewhat unusual purpose, namely, to diagnose whether and how a child "has" transitive inference, based on his responsiveness to our training efforts. How much he can do as a function of how much training he is given may give us ideas as to what he "had" prior to training (Flavell, 1970a, p. 1043).

According to this scheme as so far presented, transitive inference itself, once in the repertoire at all, remains the same basic entity from then on; what changes with subsequent development is its evocability and utilizability. It is quite conceivable, however, that transitive inference itself may also change, and even that its own modifications are partly responsible for its increased evocability and utilizability. For instance, the child might think initially that, given $A > B$ and $B > C$, $A > C$ is only probable rather than certain—a good guess rather than a sure bet. There is at first, perhaps, no sense that A "has to be" longer than C, and hence no great confidence in the child's $A > C$ answer. Moreover, he may experience his $A > C$ response only as a tentative intuition of unknown origin. He may literally have no idea at all why $A > C$ should be concluded from $A > B$ and $B > C$; that conclusion just "feels right" to him on trial after trial. It is plausible to suppose that this kind of "transitive inference" could be highly vulnerable to all manner of countervailing factors. A child who "had" it that way would likely show it in one situation but not in another, when in this state of mind but not when in that, etc.

Conceptualization Questions

We now see why cognitive-developmental diagnosis is such a nettlesome venture. In addition to shortcomings in our diagnostic procedures, the very thing we are trying to diagnose undergoes changes as the child matures. We have just hypothesized that these changes may be of two interacting types. First, the target acquisition becomes more readily evoked and more effectively utilized over an ever-widening range of appropriate, applicable situations. It acquires good delivery services, so to speak. Second, it may itself undergo important alterations with age, some of which may also cause it to become more evocable and utilizable.

Suppose that cognitive capacities like transitive inference typically show this sort of developmental course. What more would we want to know? A great deal, actually, because we have not yet discovered what "transitive inference"—at any point in this developmental course—really is. We need to move on to what Smedslund (1969, p. 244) called "higher order inferences": "An even more complex diagnostic task is to determine the exact content and sequencing of the mental processes involved in solving a given task" (p. 244). What actually happens, in cognitive-process terms, between problem presentation and the subject's response? When confronted with the problem, he or she presumably assembles and executes cognitive processes of some sort, processes that are integrated and sequenced in some fashion. What are those processes and how are they organized, e.g., in the case of transitive inference? Also, why is some one particular structured set of processes assembled, rather than some other? That is, what abilities, limitations, biases, task representations, etc., within the child lead him to generate that particular set? Finally, how might the answers to these two questions—the what and the why of the child's process organization—change as the manner in which he "has" transitive inference changes with development?

Unfortunately, we know very little about the actual process organizations underlying transitive inference, or any other interesting cognitive acquisition, for that matter. However, recent research by Trabasso and his coworkers (Trabasso, 1975) represents an important beginning in the case of transitive inference. They have obtained evidence that people often—perhaps even typically—solve transitivity problems in the following way. The subject is repeatedly shown the adjacent pairs of a series of different length sticks, $A > B, B > C, C > D, D > E$, each stick identifiable by its color. Their data suggest that, in the course of these presentations, the subject gradually constructs from these adjacent pairs an internal, possibly image-like representation of the entire ordered array $A > B > C > D > E$. Essentially, the process is one of constructive memory, as described in the *Knowledge* section of Chap. 6.

When then asked to compare a pair of lengths he has never seen together before, e.g., B and D, the subject does not, as we had always thought, work out the answer through a step-by-step process of logical inference. Rather, he simply "reads" $B > D$ off his internal representation, much as though the five sticks were all lined up in order of length before his eyes. If logical inference were the solution process, questions about the relative lengths of widely-separated pairs that had never been experienced, e.g., $B ? D$ or $B ? E$, should certainly take longer to answer than questions about pairs that are adjacent and had been previously experienced, e.g., $A ? B$ or $C ? D$. But if the solution process were akin to comparing lengths perceptually, the opposite should be true since, for example, A and D are more different in length and are farther apart in the subject's internal $A \ldots E$ linear representation than are, say B and C. Trabasso (1975) found that the opposite is, in fact, true: the farther away one length is from another in the $A \ldots E$ series, the shorter the solution time. It is harder to achieve this sort of quasispatial internal representation in preschool children than in older subjects, e.g., more presentations of the adjacent pairs are required. Once achieved, however, preschool children can solve transitive inference problems, and they appear to solve them in this very same, essentially noninferential fashion.

Previously, most investigators had not found that children this young could solve transitive inference problems.

Trabasso (1975) has not shown that people never use inferential rather than quasiperceptual processes when dealing with transitivity problems, or that older children do not know anything about transitive inference that younger ones do not. Nevertheless, I believe that his work has irrevocably changed the way we must think about the nature and development of transitive inference. By identifying some plausible underlying processes, he has helped us understand what "transitive inference" might really refer to psychologically. Such a process-level understanding will ultimately be essential if we are ever to diagnose accurately and chart developmentally the important cognitive acquisitions of human childhood.

The Importance of Diagnosis

Let Y stand for any of these acquisitions—transitive inference or any other. We have said that the objectives of diagnosis include: (a) determining Y's psychological nature, or underlying process organization; (b) determining its typical developmental course, including sequential changes in its psychological nature, its evocability, and its utilizability; (c) determining what a particular child "has," or where he stands developmentally, with respect to (a) and (b). The successful achievement of all three diagnostic objectives is crucially important for several reasons.

One reason is that we cannot determine the relationship of Y to other cognitive acquisitions, e.g., X and Z, without accurate diagnosis. Suppose, for example, we hypothesize (erroneously) the existence of an invariant developmental sequence $X–Y–Z$, such that the acquisition of X makes possible and helps produce the subsequent development of Y, and Y does the same in relation to Z. There are at least two ways that inaccurate diagnosis could have led us to propose that erroneous hypothesis, and subsequent improvements in diagnosis lead us to abandon it. First, better diagnosis might show that the true temporal order of acquisition is not $X–Y–Z$ but, say, $Y–X–Z$. More sensitive and valid assessment procedures might reveal that Y really emerges considerably earlier in childhood than we had previously thought, thus making it logically impossible on purely temporal-sequential grounds for X to be its developmental progenitor. As Miller put it, "we cannot postulate mediating mechanisms that postdate the development that they supposedly explain" (1976). Second, a better analysis of the processes composing Y might make it clear that Y is an entirely different kind of cognitive creature than we had believed. Y might now appear to be utterly unrelated and unrelatable to X and Z either conceptually or logically, so much so that we just cannot conceive of how it could possibly be X's descendant and Z's ancestor. It would be like trying to imagine how hailstones could come from halberds and subsequently produce highbrows.

We might instead hypothesize (again contrary to fact, let us suppose) that X, Y and Z emerge together, synchronously or concurrently rather than sequentially or successively. X, Y, and Z might all be conceived as belonging to a common developmental stage, perhaps as integral parts of a common cognitive structure. We might believe, for instance, that they are three closely linked Piagetian concrete-operational acquisitions, and therefore they should develop together. It is easy to see that the same two points about diagnosis apply to stages and structures as apply to sequences. Better methods of assessment may show us that our developmental timetable was wrong: X, Y and Z really emerge at rather different ages rather than at roughly the same age. The greater the difference among their ages of emergence, the harder it would be to think of them as belonging to a common structure and stage (Miller, 1976). Similarly, drastic reconceptualizations of X, Y and/or Z, based upon deeper, process-oriented analyses, may make them look so conceptually unrelated to one another that we would again be unable to see how they could plausibly form part of the same cognitive-structural whole or be meaningfully assigned to the same cognitive-developmental stage. Trabasso's (1975) research might be a straw in the wind here. It suggests that transitive inference tasks are solved earlier, and by different cognitive processes, than we had believed. Such results may eventually force Piagetians and others to revise their ideas about any hypothesized sequences, structures, and stages containing transitive inference as a Y.

Other reasons why accurate diagnosis is important have to do with Y itself, considered more or less in isolation from other major acquisitions (cf. Miller, 1976). Educators as well as developmental psychologists may want to know when Y first emerges in rudimentary form and what its subsequent developmental course is likely to be. They may have reasons to want to help the child to acquire Y earlier or more adequately than he would without special training, or to teach him other things for which Y is an educational prerequisite. Accurate developmental diagnosis could help guide the nature and timing of their educational interventions. Among other things, a good diagnosis can help to define educational "readiness."

Some interventions are introduced more for theoretical-developmental than for practical-educational reasons. They are called "training studies" in the literature on cognitive development, and a great many of them have been done with reference to Piagetian acquisitions. The investigator theorizes that experience A may be important in the real-life acquisition of some Piagetian *Y*. He does a training study to test his theory. In skeletal form (omitting consideration of control groups, transfer tasks, delayed post-tests, etc.), a training study consists of an assessment of the child's initial, preexperimental grasp of *Y*, the introduction of the experience *A*, and a subsequent reassessment of his grasp of *Y*. (The educator may, of course, use a similar design to measure the effects of his more pedagogically-motivated intervention.) It is obvious that inaccurate pre- and post-intervention assessment of *Y* could yield quite erroneous conclusions about the role of *A* in the ontogenesis of *Y*.

Finally, diagnosis is central to all psychological study, cognitive-developmental or other. In the case of cognitive development, we absolutely must somehow penetrate to the processual heart of the acquisitions we call "transitive inference," "conservation," etc., and also we must be able to assess with precision where individual children stand in relation to these acquisitions. Good process analyses of cognitive functioning are exceedingly difficult to do, especially with child subjects. However, we are beginning to realize that they are indispensable if we are ever to make real progress in describing and explaining cognitive growth. My impression is that a trickle of good process-oriented developmental studies is appearing in the research literature. I hope it soon becomes a flood.

EXPLANATIONS

How is cognitive growth accomplished? What factors or variables play what roles in influencing the nature, rate of growth, and ultimate adult level of various forms of knowledge and cognitive ability? Possible variables here include: hereditary and maturational factors; diverse forms of social and nonsocial experience; developmental principles, processes, or mechanisms, such as differentiation, coordination, integration, and equilibrium. What do we really mean when we speak of "explaining" cognitive development, of finding its "causes?" How would human cognitive growth appear if viewed from a biological-evolutionary perspective? Would viewing it from such a perspective help us understand the meaning of developmental "explanations" and "causes?" Experience is obviously very important in the child's cognitive evolution, but how shall we conceptualize experience and its developmental effects? Are there a number of different types of experience, for instance? More generally, how shall we think about the "processes" of cognitive growth, those events taking place in the child's mind which cause his mind to exhibit developmental changes? How shall we model the process of cognitive development? In sum, how and to what extent can we *explain* the various changes we may have *diagnosed?*

Not surprisingly, accounting for cognitive growth is at least as problematic as diagnosing or describing it. Also predictable uncertainties and questions concerning diagnosis make for uncertainties and questions concerning explanation, and vice-versa. This topic is so broad and multi-faceted that it is hard to select a short list of useful references. The best single reference is probably Wohlwill's book (1973*a*, especially Chaps. 2 and 11), although it is not easy reading. Others include Beilin (1971), Cole and Scribner (1974), Flavell (1970*a*, pp. 1040–1043), Kuhn (1974), and especially, Scarr-Salapatek (1976) and Wohlwill (1973*b*).

Perspectives on the Explanation Problem

Why does the child develop cognitively at all? While this question is obviously fundamental, it is surprising how seldom it is raised and discussed in the literature in cognitive growth. Wohlwill's (1973*a*) thoughtful treatment is one of the few exceptions. He takes an interesting if somewhat extreme position on the problem of explaining psychological development. His arguments bear on noncognitive as well as cognitive aspects of ontogenesis, but I will present them as if he were talking only about cognitive growth:

We currently know nothing about the physiological events and processes underlying cognitive development. If we knew a great deal about these, it is conceivable—although not certain—that we could explain the basic fact that children's cognitive systems undergo important changes as they grow older. Limited as we presently are to the psychological plane, however, we might be better off conceptualizing this basic fact in the following way. Childhood cognitive growth is essentially inevitable, and it should be regarded as a given rather than as something to be explained. This growth is a process of change that human young, like those of other species, are simply destined and designed to undergo. Cognitive development has a sturdy, relentless, inexorable quality to it. Although Wohlwill does not say this, a sense of this intrinsic momentum towards growth becomes especially strong if we try to imagine what we would have to do to *prevent* a child from making any cognitive progress between the ages of 0 and 15 years. During the period of childhood, a human being is best construed as a device that is programmed to undergo marked changes over time. It is built to develop, and develop it will if given any reasonable opportunity to do so.

This sounds like a conception of cognitive growth that assigns no formative role at all to environmental and experiential factors, but Wohlwill's (1973*a*) position is not that extreme. He speaks of such factors as "variables which modulate or modify the course or character of these [inevitable developmental] changes" (p. 24), and thinks of them as "superimposed on an ongoing developmental process" (p. 318). Wohlwill believes that experience fuels and feeds this developmental process, and may also influence its direction and acquired content to an extent (to what extent is not made clear). More will be presented below on his ideas concerning the nature of experience. If I understand him rightly, however, he does not believe that experiential variables can actually generate, cause, or otherwise serve to explain the fundamental process of cognitive growth itself.

I think that Wohlwill's conception of cognitive development somewhat underestimates the contributions of environment and experience. His views deserve a hearing, nevertheless, because they serve to counterbalance the many developmental accounts which seem either tacitly or explicitly to overestimate the contributions of external factors. Wohlwill makes an important point when he says that there is an impetus to childhood cognitive growth that is not ultimately explainable by this environmental push or that experiential shove. The latter are indeed essential to development—there is no denying that. However, they operate within the context of a preexisting disposition towards growth and an ongoing developmental movement. They do not create that disposition and they do not generate that movement.

Some highly interesting speculations about sensory-motor development by Scarr-Salapatek (1976) also provide a useful perspective on the explanation problem. A specialist in behavior genetics and human development, she approaches this problem from an unusual point of view— that of evolutionary theory. Unlike later cognitive acquisitions, Scarr-Salapatek notes, normal human beings everywhere are virtually certain to complete Piagetian sensory-motor development. As she puts it: "Do you know anyone who didn't make it to preoperational thought?" (p. 185). This accords with the suggestion made in Chap. 4 *(Conclusions About Adolescent and Adult Thinking)* that earlier Piagetian stages are likely to be more universally-attained, more "panhuman," than later ones. She speculates that the sensory-motor ontogenetic pattern evolved earlier in our primate past than those that follow it in childhood cognitive development, e.g., concrete-operational thought.

The evolutionary selection pressures that led to the establishment of sensory-motor development ensured its species-wide universality in two ways: they acted on the infant *and* they acted on his environment, including the behavior of his caretakers. This important point needs elaboration.

On the infant's side, selection pressures are hypothesized to have produced an organism genetically predisposed or "canalized" towards the sequential acquisition of Piagetian sensory-motor schemes rather than other imaginable cognitive attainments. This organism's evolutionary history has powerfully biased it to develop in that direction, and we would presumably have to rear it in a highly deviant, "nonhuman" way to prevent that development or deflect its basic course.

So far, the emphasis is similar to Wohlwill's (1973a), except that the inexorable and constrained character of the child's developmental movement is given an evolutionary and genetic justification. What Scarr-Salapatek's account adds, however, is the idea that evolutionary selection pressures also have produced a species-typical, characteristically "human" rearing environment for this genetically-specialized organism. Moreover, it is just the sort of environment needed to promote sensory-motor development in this particular organism. Naturally, human environments differ in many ways, and these differences undeniably contribute to individual differences in cognition, especially in later childhood and adulthood. There are also some basic commonalities across human environments, however, and these are believed to constitute the essential psychological nutriments for the acquisition of sensory-motor intelligence. Despite their diversity within and between cultures, infant worlds are "functionally equivalent," as Scarr-Salapatek puts it, in their capacity to support this particular process of acquisition. They all provide social and nonsocial objects, events, and experiential opportunities of the kinds needed to allow a properly-designed organism to develop sensory-motor cognitive structures.

Notice that this view in no way denies the vital role of environment and experience in the process of cognitive growth. Environmental elements do not become any less essential to a particular form of development just because they are virtually certain to be available for its use. Their near-universality may make it difficult for us to detect them, but they are no less indispensable because of their low visibility. Scarr-Salapatek (1976) summarizes her position on these matters as follows:

> The ontogeny of infant intelligence has a distinctive pattern and timing. The species pattern, I would argue, is not an unfolding of some genetic program, but a dynamic interplay of genetic preadaptations and developmental adaptations to features of the caretaking environment. Individual variation is limited by canalization, on the one hand, and by common human environments, on the other (p. 166).

> I would argue that the genetic preadaptation in sensorimotor intelligence is a strong bias toward learning the typical schemes of infancy and toward combining them in innovative, flexible ways. What human environments do is to provide the materials and opportunities to learn. For the development of sensorimotor skills, nearly any natural, human environment will suffice to produce criterion level performance (p. 186).

Let us now examine more closely the environmental, experiential side of this organism-milieu developmental interaction. There are at least two general questions of importance here. First, in what ways can environments or experiences differ in the amount and kind of contribution they make to cognitive development? Second, what distinguishable varieties of such potentially contributory inputs or experiences are there? How might we classify them?

Environmental-Experiential Contributions To Cognitive Development

The concepts of *necessary* and *sufficient* contributions to development are useful in answering the first question (cf. Wohlwill, 1973*a*, Chap. 11). A type of experience or environmental input *A* could contribute to the development of cognitive knowledge or ability *X* at any one of four levels. First, *X* will develop if, and only if, *A* has occurred; *A* is both necessary and sufficient for *X's* development. Second, *A* must occur if *X* is to develop, but so must other things; *A* is a necessary but not a sufficient precondition for *X*. Third, *A* alone can mediate the development of *X* but other things can also do so in its stead; it is sufficient but not necessary. Finally, *A* need not occur for *X* to develop and cannot generate it unaided if it does occur. It can, however, assist the development of *X* in concert with other developmental factors; it can therefore be helpful and contributory, but it is neither necessary nor sufficient in itself.

We can make inferences about *A*'s level of contribution to *X* by seeing how *X* fares in children who have been provided with *A* versus those who have not. Such investigations are often called *enrichment* and *deprivation* studies, respectively. Piagetian training studies are enrichment studies; see Beilin (1971) Brainerd (1974) and Kuhn (1974) for more information on this extensive body of research. An investigator interested in explaining Piagetian acquisitions might hypothesize that a certain *A* is the usual developmental bridge to a certain *X* in everyday human ontogenesis. That is, children normally acquire *X* via *A*. He might believe, for example, that children gradually acquire conservation of number in the natural environment by gradually learning, through practice coupled with informational feedback, to attend to number-relevant information and disregard number-irrelevant information, such as length of row. He then does a training study to test his hypothesis. Children who do not yet conserve number are provided with such practice and feedback to see if it leads them to give conservation instead of nonconservation responses. In effect, he attempts to simulate or mimic development in the laboratory in order to explain how it proceeds in everyday life, much as other psychologists try to simulate human problem solving on the computer in hopes of explaining how it proceeds in human minds.

In neither case, however, is it possible for the researcher to conclude that nature has been faithfully imitated—that what happened in the training experience or in the computer is the same as what normally happens in real-life conservation development or problem solving. The same outcomes or products may have been achieved in both nature and its attempted simulation (although it is sometimes hard to be sure even of this). This is no guarantee, however, that the same processes were responsible for those outcomes or products. In the developmental case, it is unfortunately true that enrichment studies are just logically incapable of proving that a certain kind of experiential or milieu factor is a *necessary* contributor to any development. In real life, some or all children may acquire conservation of number with the aid of a wholly different factor, via some entirely different "developmental route." The investigator's enrichment study cannot rule out this possibility, no matter how effective his training regimen proved to be in that study.

Could his study at least prove that the *A* in question is *sufficient* to engender the development of *X*? Many developmental psychologists would argue that it could. Wohlwill (1973*a*, p. 319) argues that it could not, however. The reason is that, as already indicated, he conceives of all such factors as developmental modulators or "superimpositions," rather than as outright manufacturers of the developmental process. Therefore, he would probably interpret them as instances of the fourth type of contribution mentioned above, rather than of the third: a successful enrichment study may show that *A* can be an "assistant mediator" of *X*, but it cannot show that *A* is a necessary or even sufficient contributor to its achievement in everyday, extralaboratory development. Wohlwill states his position this way:

> Once we grant the existence of "normal developmental processes," that is, acting independently of particular specifiable external agents or conditions, there follows a much more far-reaching consequence. That is that we can only hope to isolate necessary rather than sufficient causes, i.e., those without which we can assert development does not take place, rather than those *thanks to which* it does take place. This would suggest, in other words, that the basic tool in the experimental study of development is the deprivation study, rather than the enrichment or special experience study (1973*a*, p. 319).

Even if one does not take quite this dim a view of enrichment studies, it is clear that their use in "explaining development" is inherently limited. At most, they can suggest how the development of something *could* proceed, and therefore how it *might* actually proceed in the real world of growing children. Knowing even this much is sometimes useful, to be sure. It is wholly incapable, however, of proving how this development *does* normally proceed in that world, and the latter is what we would most like to know. Enrichment studies, of course, are very valuable in educationally-oriented research. It is also only fair to add that many developmentalists have a higher opinion of their value for cognitive-developmental inquiry than is expressed here.

What of the deprivation study Wohlwill mentioned? Unlike the case with enrichment experiments, it would be highly unethical to do a deprivation experiment on children. One can, however, study the effects of deprivations that occur naturally. But there are problems in interpreting deprivation studies. It may be difficult, for example, to determine precisely what the child in question has and has not been deprived of. Deprivation studies can nevertheless be very useful, as Wohlwill points out.

What they have mainly shown us, in my opinion, is how well guaranteed or "canalized" (Scarr-Salapatek, 1976) many of our fundamental cognitive acquisitions are. Alternatively put, they show how many environmental inputs and experiences seem developmentally helpful or sufficient and how few seem developmentally necessary. As indicated in Chap. 2 *(More on the Semiotic Function* section), research by Furth (1971) and others on deaf children has shown that cognitive growth can progress surprisingly well in human beings who have little or no command of any sort of linguistic system. Similarly, case reports by Jordan (1972) and Kopp and Shaperman (1973) suggest that the ability to manipulate objects with hands or feet is not a necessary condition for normal cognitive development.

Jordan's "case" was a middle-aged woman living in an institution who had never had any functional use of her limbs. Despite this handicap: "She was one of the most popular and intelligent of the patients, serving as a regular discussion leader, and being of great help to both the other patients and the staff in filling out income tax returns" (Jordan, 1972, p. 380). As one who stands in awe of income tax consultants, I would be more than willing to credit her with full formal-operational competence.

What is significant here, as Jordan points out, is that she could never have had the motor half of ordinary, Piagetian sensory-motor experience and development. According to Piaget's theory, sensory-motor intelligence is constructed out of numerous sensory-motor interactions with the environment, and serves as an essential foundation for subsequent cognitive growth. Jordan believes that this woman's developmental history contradicts Piaget's theory; Piaget disagrees (Jordan, 1972, p. 380). I think Jordan is right (Flavell, 1970*a,* p. 1041), but that is not the major point here. Whatever its implications for Piaget's theory, this case clearly shows that a lot of normal, significant-looking infant experience may be helpful or even sufficient for a lot of important cognitive acquisitions, but yet not be necessary or essential for them. To be sure, this woman's massive handicap could have caused her to develop more slowly intellectually than she otherwise would have, even though it did not prevent her from reaching a normal (at least) adult level eventually. Experiential deficiencies and other adverse environmental circumstances sometimes can affect the *rate* at which something develops without necessarily affecting its *final level* of development (Scarr-Salapatek, 1976; Wohlwill, 1973a).

I believe that cases like Jordan's (1972) suggest an hypothesis about cognitive development and its explanation, one echoing ideas of Scarr-Salapatek (1976) and Wohlwill (1973a) described earlier. The hypothesis is that, when it comes to acquiring certain major kinds of cognition, human beings are amazingly *versatile*. They can often make do with whatever acquisitional machinery they possess and with whatever environmental content comes their way. If the usual, typical developmental route is blocked, the child may find an unusual, atypical one that somehow gets him to at least approximately the same cognitive destination.

Kagan and Klein (1973) report a case study which suggests that the growing child may also be *resilient,* as they term it, as well as versatile. An extremely nonstimulating, cognitively-impoverished early environment can, not surprisingly, seriously retard a young child's intellectual growth. If the child is then removed from that barren environment and subsequently reared in a more developmentally-hospitable one, however, the child may show accelerated, "catch-up" cognitive growth and even achieve a normal or near-normal final level.

There is a problem with these optimistic, Rousseauesque notions of developmental versatility and resiliency, however. The problem is that children do not always prove versatile and resilient in the face of organismic or environmental handicaps. Many writers of books on cognitive growth would emphasize and document this fact more than I have. What we need to know, and do not yet know, is what combinations of the relevant variables result in favorable versus unfavorable developmental outcomes: what kinds of children, what kinds of handicaps, when these handicaps are incurred and when removed, and what kind of cognitive acquisitions we are talking about. The importance of this last variable is sometimes overlooked. The ability to read and write and the ability to speak and understand oral language are both enormously significant cognitive accomplishments. The development of the latter seems much more "biological-evolutionary" than the former, however, and is much more certain to result from exposure to a normal human environment. Some forms of cognitive development clearly exhibit much more versatility and resiliency than others.

Varieties of Experience

Even though we may seldom know what level or kind of contribution to specific developments particular environmental and experiential factors may make, it is worthwhile trying to analyze and classify the types of potentially-formative experiences the child may undergo. This is the second general question about experiential aspects of development mentioned earlier. Wohlwill (1973*b*) has offered one such classification, on the grounds that: "The concepts of 'environment' and 'experience' have generally been used all too loosely by psychologists, subsuming under them what are in fact very disparate kinds of effects (pp. 105–6)." He distinguishes among four ideal types or models of experience:

I. *The hospital-bed model.* The individual is an essentially passive recipient of environmental stimuli, much like a totally paralyzed hospital patient. Wohlwill believes that the condition of the young infant approaches this extreme, although one could object that the baby is not wholly passive, since there is perceptual selectivity even at this age (Chap. 5).

I'. *The amusement-park model.* As in I, the individual is exposed to a variety of environmental inputs. In contrast to I, however, he can choose which aspects of the ambient stimulation he will and will not attend to and experience. Whatever is selected, however, will then affect him in ways he cannot significantly control: "Once he has decided to partake of the roller-coaster ride, there is little he can do to alter the experience he will derive from it" (Wohlwill, 1973*b*, p. 101).

II. *The swim-meet model.* In models I and I', the environment is a source of stimulation to which the individual can more (I') or less (I) selectively attend and respond. In models II and II', the environment serves rather as a context or medium for the individual's response. In I and I' the emphasis is on environmental stimuli and stimulation. In II and II' it is on organismic response and skill exercise. In II, the environment as behavioral vehicle and context versus behavioral elicitor and shaper is especially clear: "From the sound of the gun, the individual's behavior [at the swim meet] takes its course in virtual independence from environmental stimuli . . ." (Wohlwill, 1973*b*, p. 101).

II'. *The tennis-match model.* In this particularly interesting model, the individual's relation to the environment is more complex. On the one hand, his behavior is more strongly and specifically contingent upon variations in the environmental input (e.g., how his opponent returns his serve). On the other hand, the individual's behavior itself partly creates and shapes the very input to which he responds (e.g., once again, how his opponent returns his serve).

As Wohlwill (1973*b*) recognizes, there are many intermediaries within and between these four types. Moreover, complex and sustained experiential episodes undoubtedly contain numerous shifts from one type of organism-milieu interaction to another. There are other categories of developmentally relevant experiences which are often mentioned in the literature on development, learning, and education (e.g., Piaget, 1970*a*, pp. 719–722; Stevenson, 1972). These also blend and overlap with one another, as well as cross-cut Wohlwill's taxonomy in ways we need not try to spell out. There is classical and instrumental conditioning. There is Gibsonian perceptual learning, as described in Chap. 5. There is observational learning from social models, sometimes involving imitation of what is observed and subsequent practice of what is imitated. The child's mind can also be stretched with the aid of diverse types of formal and informal verbal instruction, and also through observation, exploration, experimentation, and practice vis-à-vis the nonsocial as well as the social milieu. The list could go on and on.

All of these are, of course, nothing but cover terms for organized psychological events, processes, and activities within the child. Naturally, we would like to be able to understand what lies beneath these covers. It is a reasonable beginning to propose imitation, say, as a possible developmental mechanism or learning process. However, we would then want to inquire into the "processes" which underlie this "process," just as we would in the case of transitive inference (Diagnosis section). That is, we would want to ask what the child is actually doing, cognitively, when he is performing a certain type of imitation, and also what cognitive equipment he must have developed in order to be able to do those things.

Processes or Principles of Cognitive Development

Another approach to the problem of explaining cognitive development is to attempt to identify a small number of processes or principles that seem to be operative in many or all cases where cognitive growth occurs. There have been relatively few systematic attempts to do this. Two major classes of these processes or principles seem to be distinguishable. One class generates distinctions within cognitive entities. The other relates one cognitive entity to one or more others. The first class of processes is almost always called *differentiation*. There is no satisfactory generic name for the second, because more than one kind of relationship among entities can be postulated. For example, the terms used to characterize various kinds of relationships among cognitive entities include *integration, hierarchic integration, subordination, coordination, regulation, conflict,* and *equilibration.*

We have already seen how E. J. Gibson (1969) uses the principle of differentiation in her theory of perceptual development. In another developmental theory which has not been described in this book (Werner, 1948, 1957), cognitive entities are also progressively differentiated as the child grows. Werner's theory further asserts that the products of this differentiation process, i.e., the new entities which result from it, become related to one another by a process of hierarchic integration. Differentiated entities or products that are lower in the hierarchy are said to stand in a subordinate or subordination relationship to those higher in the hierarchy. For example, thought, perception, motor action, and emotion are said to be relatively undifferentiated in the young child's experience. They become increasingly experienced as distinct and different from one another as the child grows older, and also mutually relatable in a hierarchically-integrated fashion, e.g., such that thought may direct or subordinate perception, emotion, or motor action in certain situations.

As indicated in Chap. 2, Piaget describes the progressive differentiation, coordination, and integration of sensory-motor schemes during infant development. For example, the hallmark of Stage 4 is the coordination or integration of two schemes into a means-end whole, with the means scheme becoming subordinated to the end or goal scheme. (Werner also uses the case of means-goal organization to illustrate his developmental principles.) In addition, Piaget has argued that a relationship of conflict or discrepancy between two cognitive entities leads to cognitive progress, and that cognitive development proceeds by coordination, self-regulation, and equilibration (e.g., Flavell, 1963, pp. 237–249; Langer, 1969; Piaget, 1970a, pp. 722–726). Piaget's "equilibration model", as it is called, is extremely influential in current thinking about the process of cognitive growth, and has stimulated a considerable amount of research (Beilin, 1971; Brainerd, 1974; Kuhn, 1974). As such, it warrants a brief summary and critical examination.

Piaget would use his equilibration model to explain the development of conservation of liquid quantity, for example, in roughly the following manner. Recall from Chap. 3 that the nonconserver usually focuses his attention only on the greater height of the liquid column in the taller, thinner glass, and therefore concludes that it has more liquid than the standard. His thinking about this problem is said to be in equilibrium, albeit at an immature, nonconservation level.

Suppose, however, that at some point he also notices that the new column is thinner, a fact that by itself would incline him to conclude that the new glass contains less liquid than the standard. If he finds both of these opposing conclusions plausible at the same psychological moment, his cognitive system has moved from a state of equilibrium to one of disequilibrium or cognitive conflict with respect to this problem. According to Piaget, states of cognitive conflict and disequilibrium impel the child to make cognitive progress. In this case, the child achieves a new, more intellectually advanced equilibrium state by conceptualizing both the height increase and the width decrease as predictable, mutually compensatory changes in a process of physical transformation that leaves liquid quantity unchanged. (A developmental advance has been made by means of a process of equilibration composed of these major steps: (1) cognitive equilibrium at a lower developmental level; (2) cognitive disequilibrium or conflict, induced by awareness of contradictory, discrepant, "nonassimilable" data not previously attended to; (3) cognitive equilibration (or reequilibration) at a higher developmental level, caused by reconceptualizing the problem in such a way as to harmonize what had earlier been seen as conflicting. Piaget argues that all significant cognitive-developmental advances are made through this kind of equilibration or self-regulation process. Notice that this process is essentially just an elaboration of the one described in Chap. 1 *(Assimilation-accommodation as a model of cognitive development* section).

There appear to be problems with Piaget's equilibration model (cf Flavell, 1971c). In order for equilibration to take place the child would seem to need the ability or disposition to do these four things in sequence: (1) attend to or notice both of the apparently conflicting elements in the situation; (2) interpret and appreciate them *as* conflicting and, therefore, problematic—something one cannot assume a young child would automatically do; (3) respond to the sensed conflict by progressing rather than regressing, e.g., by trying to explain it rather than by clinging defensively to his initial belief or refusing to have anything more to do with the problem; (4) come up with a better conceptualization of the situation that can resolve the apparent conflict and thereby "reequilibrate" his mental structure at a higher developmental level. It is not apparent how the emergence and subsequent development of these abilities and dispositions can themselves be accounted for by equilibration processes. Rather, the successful running off of an equilibration process is itself in need of explanation, and these abilities and dispositions would presumably figure importantly in that explanation.

Since a given child could lack one or more of these four prerequisite in relation to some specific cognitive problem, it is obvious that he may not be able to complete, or possibly even begin, a Piagetian process of equilibration with respect to it. In addition, however, it is hard to see how certain cognitive achievements could develop via an equilibration process at all, regardless of what the child possessed. Is it likely that many people hit on, say, systematic formal-operational methods for finding all possible combinations or permutations of a set of elements (Chap. 4, *Combinations and Permutations* section) through cognitive conflict or disequilibrium? Similarly, I find it hard to believe that children master seriation and certain other concrete-operational concepts through such a process.

In sum, I believe the equilibration process itself needs explaining when and where it does occur, and also that it does not occur in all instances of cognitive development. I think it likely, in fact, that there is no single, overarching process or principle sufficient to describe how all cognitive-developmental advances are made. Different sets of processes may typically be involved in different kinds of cognitive acquisitions. Different individuals may even use quite different processes to acquire the same things. Equilibration is probably one such process, and it may be a very important one, especially for certain kinds of acquisitions. It is worth noting in this connection that other process-oriented approaches to various aspects of cognitive development are now appearing in the literature (Baron, 1973; Klahr, 1973; Klahr and Wallace, 1973; Nelson, 1974; Schaeffer, 1975).

Finally, it remains to point out how matters of explanation ultimately hinge on matters of diagnosis. As indicated in the section on Diagnosis, a process analysis may change our ideas about what has actually developed when we say that X has developed. This reconceptualization of what X is then may suggest or force a reinterpretation of X's probable developmental history. As an example, Wohlwill (1973a, pp. 331–332) has suggested that the Piagetian conservations may not be acquired as such at all—at least not in the same sense one would say a specific vocabulary item or a specific motor skill had been acquired (see also Aebli, 1963). Rather, the child may acquire a variety of information and skills concerning quantitative dimensions, measurement, and the like, in the course of many and diverse everyday experiences. When confronted with a conservation task, these acquisitions are brought out of the cognitive stock room, so to speak, and used to assemble a conservation judgment. Unlike the case of the vocabulary item and the motor skill, the child had not actually formed or formulated a "conservation concept" per se before serving as an experimental subject, and probably never would if he steered clear of Piaget's conservation tasks. Does this way of conceptualizing what has developed when "conservation" has developed make sense? I'm not wholly sure it does. But if it does, Piaget's equilibration-process account of development in this area may also be awry. If the child does not really acquire what you thought he did, he probably also does not develop whatever he does acquire instead in the way you had originally hypothesized.

PATTERNS

A number of cognitive-developmental products or entities (concepts, skills, etc.) emerge during an individual's childhood. How and to what extent might these entities be related to one another in ontogenetic time? What patterns might be discernable in the developmental mosaic? Perhaps, during a certain period of childhood, a whole group of similar or related entities emerges synchronously or concurrently. Such an ensemble of concurrent, tightly-knit developments would probably be referred to as a major *stage* of cognitive growth. Thus, a stage would constitute one important type of developmental pattern.

A close look at the developmental mosaic might show that one stage regularly precedes another or, even if no major stages were evident, that one individual cognitive entity regularly develops prior to another. The pattern in this case is one of systematic asynchrony rather than systematic synchrony of acquisitions. The developments in question are temporally ordered rather than temporally concurrent, and the pattern thus is one of *sequence* rather than stage.

Stages

There are a number of unresolved issues concerning the meaning and possible existence of stage-like patterns in cognitive development. Useful sources on this topic include Brainerd (1975, 1976), Dagenais (1973), Feldman and Toulmin (1975), Flavell (1963, pp. 19–24; 1970a pp. 1037–1040), Flavell and Wohlwill (1969), Pinard and Laurendeau (1969), Toussaint (1974), and especially, Flavell (1971a) and Wohlwill (1973a, Chap. 9). It is useful to focus on Piaget's stage of concrete operations when discussing this topic, since it has been the subject of more theoretical and experimental attention than any other. Our tentative conclusions about stages will extend beyond that particular one, however. Most of what needs discussing in this area falls under the headings of *structures, qualitative change, abruptness,* and above all, *concurrence* (cf Flavell, 1971a).

Structures. Piaget has argued that what we actually acquire when we acquire, say, concrete operations is a unified set of cognitive *structures* not just an accumulation of mutually isolated and independent, psycho logically unconnected cognitive entities. In fact, the presence of such unified structures—*structures d'ensemble* he calls them—is one of Piaget's major criteria for asserting that a given set of developments constitutes a stage.

There are two questions we can ask concerning cognitive-developmental structures. First, when a given body of knowledge, cognitive skills, etc. has been acquired, might cognitive structures of any sort have been acquired? Do at least some of the products of cognitive growth become interrelated in our heads, get linked together into organized functional wholes, or do they tend to remain unorganized, unintegrated, and unconnected? There are good reasons to think that they do become interrelated (Flavell, 1971a, pp. 443–450), both in the area of concrete-operational thinking and elsewhere. I doubt if a serious case could be made that the various processes and concepts inhabiting our cognitive systems do not interact with or otherwise link up with one another—do not exhibit "structure".

Piaget does not just assert that concrete-operational thinking is structured. Rather, he argues that it posseses a definite, specific type of structure or organization. As mentioned in Chap. 4 (*Inversion and Compensation* section), Piaget has proposed a logical-mathematical model of how cognition is structured in that stage. It was also suggested in that chapter section that Piagetian structural models are coming under heavy critical attack these days. It seems reasonable, then, to conclude that, in fact, there is considerable organization in the area of concrete-operational thinking, as there undoubtedly is in other areas, but that the specific formal structures Piaget has proposed may not capture it very well.

Qualitative change. One is not tempted to talk about developmental stages in the case of age changes that are purely quantitative in nature. Consider the digit span memory test mentioned at the beginning of Chap. 6. It would sound silly to say that Mary was in the "three-digit stage" last year but has now entered the "four-digit stage." A stage-type characterization perhaps would not sound so silly if she had used a rehearsal strategy to memorize things last year but then switched over to a wholly different strategy this year, e.g., elaboration. A quantitative change from little apples to big apples is never called a stage change; a qualitative change from apples to oranges might be. If there are no qualitative changes in cognitive development, there are no "stages" of cognitive development in any meaningful sense.

Are there any such qualitative changes? The answer depends on what one means by "qualitative" and on one's level of analysis or universe of discourse (Werner, 1957). I personally find it easy to think of the substitution of one memory strategy for another, or a switch from a perceptually-based nonconservation answer to a conceptually-based conservation one, as qualitative developmental changes; they seem like apples-to-oranges type transformations to me. Another developmental psychologist might disagree (e.g., Brainerd, 1976). We could both agree, however, that the developmental processes—whatever they are—that underlie these behavioral changes may not exhibit any real qualitative transformations, any significant discontinuities. What looks like a qualitative change at one level of analysis may not at another.

Abruptness. Cognitive development would look very stage-like if the transition from one cognitive level to another were abrupt rather than gradual. Consider as an example conservation of weight, a concrete-operational acquisition. Suppose that acquisition typically occurred very abruptly. One day, the child shows no signs of weight conservation. The next day, it is present in fully mature form: the child can adequately explain his conservation judgment, the experimenter cannot extinguish it by rigging the scale balance, etc. If the emergence of weight conservation and other concrete-operational accomplishments occurred in such an abrupt, metamorphosis-like fashion, it would seem wholly natural to speak of stages. Indeed, even that abrupt a *quantitative* change would seem somewhat stage-like.

The truth of the matter, however, is that most important cognitive developments appear to proceed slowly and gradually rather than abruptly (Flavell, 1971a, pp. 425–435). As indicated in Chap. 4 (*Consolidation and Solidification* section), conservation of weight may continue to mature, in the sense of becoming further consolidated and solidified, well after the end of the concrete-operational period. Once again, there are more and less mature ways of "having" weight conservation and other cognitive-developmental products. Research evidence suggests that the period in the child's life between initial, minimal possession and fully mature, maximal command of many of these products can be a matter of years.

Such evidence changes the meaning of "stage" in an interesting way. For a major stage like concrete operations, we might have expected a very brief period of change and transition, during which concrete operations emerge and mature, followed by several years of relative stasis and quiescence, during which the child is more or less stably and unchangeably concrete-operational in his thinking. If, instead, the child actually continues to perfect, generalize, and solidify his grasp of weight conservation throughout most of middle childhood and perhaps also well into adolescence, the stage of concrete operations is all change and transition, with little or no stasis and stability. Thus the stage itself, and not the transition to it, becomes the period of continuous growth and change.

Because of this continuous growth and change, one cannot predict the child's responses to concrete-operational tasks merely from the knowledge that he is in the concrete-operational stage, as one could have if being in that stage meant continuing to have essentially the same mental structure for a period of years. This loss of predictability reduces the scientific value of the stage concept, but I do not think it makes it valueless. Suppose that all concrete-operational skills developed concurrently in an interdependent, mutually facilitative fashion. The fact that all these synchronous, closely interacting developments took a long rather than a short time to be completed would not mean that the term "stage" could not be applied meaningfully and usefully to this developmental pattern. We simply would have a more dynamic concept of stage, one that refers to an extended process of concurrent, interdependent developmental changes. Wohlwill thinks the concept of stage is theoretically useful, and the sort of stage he has in mind is of this dynamic sort (Wohlwill, 1973a, Chap. 9).

Concurrence. In fact, most developmental psychologists believe that just this kind of tightly-interlocked, concurrent growth must obtain in an area of cognitive development if the term "stage" is to be usefully applied to that area. If concrete-operational entities do not really develop concurrently, for instance, they would say that the concept "concrete-operational stage" is theoretically vacuous. (For a dissenting view on this point, however, see Wohlwill, 1973a, Chap. 9). The following excerpt from a recent experimental study of the concrete-operational stage probably expresses the majority opinion on this point:

> The structuring or *structure d'ensemble* criterion, one of Piaget's defining characteristics of the stage construct, postulates that mutual connections and reciprocal interdependencies exist between the logical operations, and that it is these interrelationships which create the unified system of the logical structures that characterize a given period of development. . . . Two important consequences that follow from this postulate are: (a) that the acquisition or development of a family of related concepts should be expected to occur at about the same time, and consequently (b) that solutions to tasks of related logical structure should be expected to be of equivalent difficulty. (Toussaint, 1974, p. 992).

Unfortunately, it is very difficult to determine whether two or more cognitive entities do or do not develop concurrently and interdependently (Flavell, 1971a, pp. 435–443). As indicated earlier in this chapter, much of the difficulty stems from diagnostic uncertainties. Suppose that, without our knowing it, our test x for development X had extraneous but very taxing performance demands not present in our test y for development Y. That is, test x is harder and less sensitive than test y because of heavy information-processing requirements or other task factors that have nothing intrinsically to do with the cognitive acquisition the test was designed to measure. Accordingly, test x will underestimate the child's level of development of X much more than y will with respect to Y, since it will yield more false-negative type misdiagnoses. This difference in the sensitivities of the two tests could cause developments X and Y to look concurrent when X actually occurs earlier in ontogenesis than Y; conversely, it could make a true developmental concurrence look sequential, with Y seeming to emerge before X.

A number of investigators have tried to find out if concrete-operational attainments develop concurrently. Some of them have attempted to equate their developmental measures for information-processing demands and related sources of differential test sensitivity (e.g., Brainerd, 1972: Dagenais, 1973; Smedslund, 1964; Toussaint, 1974; Weinreb and Brainerd, 1975). Some of these attempts appear to have been more successful than others. I say "appear" because there really is no way one can be sure that two tests have equivalent sensitivities in this respect, and therefore no way to be absolutely sure that the concurrence hypothesis is receiving a valid assessment.

Despite these problems, I think it is possible to make an educated guess about concurrence-nonconcurrence, based on the general drift of the existing evidence. My guess is that nonconcurrence is the rule and concurrence the exception. Two types of relationships among concrete-operational entities are perhaps most commonly "seen" (albeit through a murky diagnostic lens). In one type, a pair of these entities may develop at roughly the same age, on the average, but their levels of development are not highly correlated with one another within individuals. One may be developmentally more advanced than the other in this child; the opposite may be true in that child. There is little evidence, in other words, that their developments are interdependent or mutually facilitative in any way. In the other type, one entity regularly develops prior to another in most or all individuals tested, suggesting that the earlier one might play some facilitative role in the genesis of the later one. In this latter case, the investigator looked for synchronous development, which would suggest a stage, and found instead systematically asynchronous development which suggests a fixed sequence. Neither of these two types of relationships testifies to the psychological reality of a concrete-operational "stage," as the term is generally taken to mean.

Conclusions about stages. I think it is fair to conclude that developmental psychologists are currently becoming increasingly skeptical of the theoretical use of the construct of "cognitive-developmental stage" (many, indeed, never thought much of it). In particular, Piaget's concrete-operational and formal-operational "stages" are coming under heavy fire. The structures used to model concrete- and formal-operational thinking may be inadequate; the stage-to-stage developmental changes not quite so exclusively qualitative if you look at underlying processes; the within-stage changes more gradual, important, and long-lasting than originally believed; and the same-stage developments less concurrent than Piagetian theory seemed to require. This is not to say that stages no longer have able advocates. In addition, of course, to numerous Piagetians the world over, we have already seen (Chap. 4) that Kohlberg, Selman, and their associates have proposed stage theories of social-cognitive development. Wohlwill (1973a, Chap. 9) has also suggested that it would be premature to abandon a stage approach to cognitive development. He accepts "the undeniable fact of asynchrony" (p. 239), and agrees that it is damaging to the concept of stage as traditionally conceived. Wohlwill suggests, however, that alternative, more developmentally realistic conceptualizations of stage are possible, and goes on to propose several. While I personally do not find his proposals either very clear or very convincing, they do show that novel approaches to this old problem are possible.

My own hunch is that the concept of stage will not, in fact, figure importantly in future scientific work on cognitive growth. This does not imply a disbelief in the existence of unidirectional and bidirectional developmental dependencies, wherein one development assists another and perhaps conversely (see *Sequences* section below). Nor does it imply that there is no unity or consistency in cognitive functioning across situations. But it does imply that there may be less unity, consistency, and developmental interdependence than theories like Piaget's would have us believe. Wohlwill seems to accept as self evident "that behavioral development does not take place in isolated packages or along neatly separated, independent tracks, but along a variety of fronts in close interaction with one another" (1973a, p. 240). While I find this conception of development intuitively appealing and would like to believe in it, I do not think the existing evidence supports it. Students of personality are also becoming disenchanted with a concept in that area that is reminiscent of the stage notion, namely, that of the stable, consistent-across-situations personality disposition or trait (e.g., Mischel, 1973). Mischel's (1971) comment about traits might well be heeded by cognitive-developmentalists:

> Perhaps, as Daryl Bem . . . notes . . . it is time to abandon the assumption (so prevalent till now) that everything is glued together; perhaps it is time instead to seriously entertain the hypothesis that nothing is glued together unless proven otherwise (p. 23).

Sequences

The following discussion of cognitive-developmental sequences is largely based on Flavell (1972). Other useful sources include Gagné (1968a, 1968b), Glaser and Resnick (1972, pp. 210–213), Resnick (1970),

Van den Daele (1969), and Wohlwill (1973*a*, Chaps. 4, 8, and especially 6).

As we have already seen, diagnostic problems may make it difficult to be sure that two cognitive entities, *X* and *Y*, really develop in the sequence *X–Y*. In addition, sequences are interesting to us only if *X* and *Y* seem to be importantly related to one another. For instance, the fact that sensory-motor secondary circular reactions (*X*) always develop before concrete-operational weight conservation (*Y*) is not very interesting, because we cannot imagine how the former could figure directly and importantly in the ontogenesis of the latter. Suppose, however, that we could be sure that *X* and *Y* usually do or always do emerge in the sequence *X–Y* and can also imagine an interesting developmental relationship between the two. What might that relationship be? I have previously (Flavell, 1972) suggested that there are five major types or categories of such relationships: *addition, substitution, modification, inclusion* and *mediation*.

Addition. In most addition sequences, *X* and *Y* are alternative cognitive means to the same goal. *Y* does not replace *X* once it develops; it is simply added to the active repertoire of routes to that goal. For example (Chap. 6), children learn to use simple rehearsal strategies (*X*) before acquiring organizational ones (*Y*) in memory situations, but the former continue to be used in many of these situations after the latter are developed.

Substitution. *X* and *Y* again represent possible alternatives, but here *Y* more or less completely replaces or substitutes for *X* once it is acquired. Younger children respond to number conservation problems by comparing row lengths and concluding that the longer row has more. When they get older they will abandon that strategy completely, substituting for it an inferential approach that will yield a conservation conclusion.

Modification. In addition and substitution sequences, *X* and *Y* are clearly two different cognitive entities. Here, as the name suggests, there is instead some sort of developmentally-progressive modification of a single entity. *Y* is clearly continuous with and derived from *X*, as woman from girl or man from boy. Three types of modifications are distinguished: *differentiation, generalization, and stabilization.* Initially, a child may rehearse items to be remembered in only one way, for example, but in subsequent years he or she may differentiate several different rehearsal patterns. Likewise, any given way of rehearsing may with development become progressively generalized to more and more different memory problems. Finally, as any rehearsal pattern continues to be practiced, it stabilizes as a skill—becomes more readily initiated in appropriate circumstances, more skillfully and effortlessly carried out, etc. As an additional example, sensory-motor schemes differentiate, generalize, and stabilize during infancy.

Inclusion.   At some point in X's development, X becomes interconnected or coordinated with one or more other cognitive entities to form part of (become included in) a larger cognitive unit Y. The processes or principles of hierarchic integration, subordination, and coordination described earlier in this chapter generate inclusion sequences, e.g., the progressive coordination of two sensory-motor schemes to form a means-end whole. In the area of memory development, the earlier-developing ability to name objects becomes integrated into a later-developing rehearsal strategy.

Mediation.   In these sequences, X serves as a bridge, facilitator, or mediator with respect to the subsequent development of Y. Unlike inclusion sequences, however, X does not become an actual part or component of Y; once developed with the help of (mediation by) X, Y functions independently of X. The inversion and compensation forms of concrete-operational reversible thinking (Chap. 3, *Irreversibility versus reversibility* sections) could conceivably help the child achieve conservation solutions to various conservation problems. These forms of thinking do not become integral parts of conservation concepts as, say, a means scheme becomes an integral part of a means-end whole. If I present an adult with a liquid quantity conservation problem, he surely does not need to go through a whole train of reasoning about how height changes might compensate for width changes in order to reach a conservation conclusion.

Each of these five types of sequences illustrates something about how cognitive growth occurs. The cognitive repertoire is enriched by addition sequences: the child used to have only one approach (X) to a problem but now has two (X and Y). Substitution sequences serve to replace less (X) with more (Y) mature cognitive approaches to problems. A cognitive entity (X) develops to a higher, more mature level (Y) via a modification sequence. Inclusion sequences illustrate the fact that developmental change often occurs, neither by modifying old cognitive entities nor by adding or substituting new ones, but by coordinating or integrating existing ones to form larger wholes. Finally, mediation sequences show that the development of one cognitive entity can substantially assist the development of another, distinct and independent entity. It should also be mentioned that the sequencing of cognitive acquisitions is a topic of great interest to educational theorists and researchers (e.g., Gagné, 1968*a*, 1968*b*; Glaser and Resnick, 1972; Resnick, 1970; Wang *et al.*, 1971) as well as to developmental psychologists.

An image of cognitive development.   When I doff my parent/layman hat and don my developmental psychologist hat, I sometimes try to understand the child and his cognitive growth by means of images. One of these images depicts the child as an arena in which a large number of sequential changes of these diverse types are all taking place at once. There are psychological interdependencies among some of the developments going on in the arena: within individual sequences, certainly; between sequences, sometimes. There is also probably bidirectional or reciprocal as well as unidirectional mediation (Flavell, 1972, pp. 336–344). That is, X may not only facilitate the development of Y, but Y may also, once partly developed, facilitate the further evolution of X. A possible example of such mutual facilitation was given in Chap. 3 (*Possible developmental interactions between number skills and number knowledge* section).

As indicated earlier, I would like to believe with Wohlwill (1973*a*), but cannot on present evidence, that there is enough developmental interdependence and coherence across sequences to warrant a Piagetian style stage-by-stage account of what happens in the arena over ontogenetic time. The present evidence suggests that something more like a three-ring circus than like a chamber-music trio is performing in that arena. There appears to be some of the aforementioned Bem-Mischel glue within each ring, binding successive portions of that ring's act together, but not much across rings. Perhaps what the field needs is another genius like Piaget to show us how, and to what extent, all those cognitive-developmental strands within the growing child are really knotted together.

SUMMARY

Psychologists who work in the area of cognitive development see it as replete with difficult questions and problems. Many of these can be subsumed under the headings of *diagnosis, explanations,* and *patterns.*

There are three closely related types of questions and problems in the area of diagnosis, namely, those concerning (1) *concrete and practical aspects of assessment,* (2) *abstract and theoretical aspects of assessment,* and (3) *conceptualization.* A useful cognitive-developmental acquisition to illustrate these is transitive inference concerning length relations, e.g., if $A > B$ and $B > C$, then $A > C$ can be inferred.

A concrete and practical type of assessment problem is to find ways to minimize *false-negative* and *false-positive* diagnostic errors. A false-negative error consists of falsely concluding, based on one's testing results, that a particular child has not yet acquired a capability for, say, transitive inference. Even though he does really possess this capability, he fails to show it in his test performance because of information-processing, linguistic, motivational, emotional, or other problems. All tasks demand more from the child than the target cognitive entity the experimenter is interested in assessing. If the child fails to respond appropriately to any of these nontarget demands, a false-negative diagnostic error can result. Conversely, a false-positive error consists in falsely concluding, based on test performance, that a child does possess the target capability. For example, the child may conclude that $A > C$ simply because A had been called "longer than" something else (i.e., B) whereas C had not; he therefore reaches the correct conclusion, but not by means of transitive inference. It is often possible to design a cognitive task in such a way that the probability of making a false-positive diagnostic error is greatly reduced. Unfortunately, these very same changes may increase the risk of false-negative errors.

Such facts suggest that there may be developmental changes in how the child "has" cognitive entities like transitive reasoning, and this possibility leads us to examine the diagnosis problem in a more abstract and theoretical fashion. A younger child may exhibit such reasoning only under the most favorable and facilitative task conditions, whereas an older one may exhibit it in almost all appropriate task situations. How can we characterize the difference in the way these two children "have" transitive inference? One possibility is that the older child may be better than the younger one in recognizing those task situations that call for a transitive-inference solution strategy; more task situations appropriately evoke an attempt to use that strategy *(evocation)*. The older child may also be better at utilizing or executing the strategy successfully when it is evoked *(utilization)*. An additional possibility is that the psychological nature of transitive inference itself may change as the child matures, and that this change may be partially responsible for its increased evocability and utilizability.

Consideration of these possibilities in turn raises the fundamental question of how cognitive entities like transitive inference are to be conceptualized. What is the nature and organization of the cognitive processes involved in an act of transitive inference? What psychological events are actually taking place in the child's head as he solves a transitive-inference problem? Recent process-oriented studies suggest that the underlying processes here may be quite different from those previously assumed.

Good diagnosis is essential for determining which cognitive entities regularly emerge in sequence, and which ones regularly develop synchronously or concurrently. Adequate conceptualizations of the process organizations which compose these entities are also needed to tell us whether these entities could plausibly be developmentally interdependent. Finally, diagnosis plays a crucial role in all intervention studies.

How is cognitive growth to be explained? Not entirely by environmental factors, according to two recent writings summarized in this chapter. The first stresses the essentially inevitable, inexorable quality of human cognitive growth. While environmental factors certainly modulate and modify its course, they do not generate it and cannot explain the basic fact that growth occurs. The second argues that selection pressures during the evolutionary history of our species have contributed two things which virtually guarantee that children the world over will acquire sensory-motor intelligence. One contribution is an organism (the human infant) which is strongly biased, genetically, to acquire sensory-motor schemes. The other is a normal human caretaking environment which supplies just the kinds of inputs and experiential opportunities that an organism of that design needs to acquire sensory-motor schemes.

Environments or experiences differ in the amount and kind of contribution they could potentially make to cognitive development. A particular type of experience could conceivably be both *necessary* and *sufficient* for a particular type of development, necessary but not sufficient, sufficient but not necessary, or helpful without being either necessary or sufficient. The results of *enrichment* and *deprivation* studies are often used to make inferences about environmental-experiential contributions. Piagetian training experiments are instances of enrichment studies, whereas investigations of individuals born with sensory or motor handicaps, or reared in psychologically impoverished circumstances, would be examples of deprivation studies. An enrichment study can show that experience A is capable of facilitating the development of cognitive skill X, but it cannot show that A is necessary to X's acquisition, nor even that it normally plays a formative role in the real-world, extralaboratory ontogenesis of X. In contrast, a deprivation study is potentially capable of showing that A is or is not necessary to X's real-world ontogenesis. Several deprivation studies illustrate how *versatile* and *resilient* a developing child can be: if the usual development route is blocked, he may find an unusual route to the same destination (versatility); if his cognitive growth is initially arrested because he has been reared in an abnormal environment, there may be pronounced "catch-up" growth if he is subsequently reared in a normal environment (resilience). Developmental versatility and resilience are not always in evidence, however, and we still know very little about the circumstances under which a child will and will not exhibit them.

Several varieties of experience can be distinguished. In some, the environment functions as a source of stimulation, eliciting certain more or less fixed responses or reactions by the child: the child may selectively expose himself to a particular one of these environments (the *amusement-park model* of experience), or he may not (the *hospital-bed model*). In others, the environment functions more like a setting or context for the child's actions: it may shape his behavior relatively little (the *swim-meet model*), or quite a lot, with his own behavior also producing part of the environment to which he responds (the *tennis-match model*).

Some theorists have proposed general processes or principles to explain the course of cognitive development. For example, Werner argued that development always proceeds by means of *differentiation* and *hierarchic integration*. Piaget's *equilibration model* of cognitive growth has been especially interesting to contemporary researchers. The process of development via equilibration takes place in three basic steps. Initially, the child's cognitive system with respect to some problem or conceptual domain is in equilibrium at a lower developmental level. Subsequently, the child detects something that conflicts or is discrepant with his present system, something that the system cannot assimilate or accommodate to, and therefore something which puts it in a state of disequilibrium. Finally, equilibrium is reestablished at a higher developmental level by modifying the cognitive system so that what was formerly perceived as discordant is now readily assimilable. There appear to be two difficulties with Piaget's equilibration model: (1) certain prerequisite skills seem to be needed in order to develop via an equilibration process, and the theory does not explain how the child develops these prerequisites; (2) not all major cognitive acquisitions look like they would have developed through a process of equilibration.

Two possible types of cognitive-developmental patterns are *stages* and *sequences*. The concepts of *structures, qualitative change, abruptness,* and especially, *concurrence* are relevant to the question of whether cognitive growth is stage-like. Tentative conclusions were made about each: Cognitive structures develop, but Piaget's structural models may not accurately characterize them. Many of the major cognitive-developmental changes appear to be qualitative rather than quantitative, at least at some level of analysis. Cognitive growth is gradual—perhaps very gradual—rather than abrupt. Same-stage cognitive acquisitions (e.g., concrete-operational ones) ought to develop in a closely-interdependent, temporally concurrent fashion, according to most interpretations, if Piaget's concept of stage-by-stage development is to have any real meaning or validity. While diagnostic problems make it difficult to tell for sure, it does not appear that they do normally develop in this tightly-knit, concurrent fashion. The existing evidence suggests to me that cognitive growth is not as stage-like a process as Piaget's theory claims it is. It should be added, however, that a number of developmental psychologists would not agree with this conclusion.

Five types of $X-Y$ development sequences can be distinguished, where X and Y represent cognitive entities: Y develops after X and constitutes an additional, alternative cognitive means to the same goal (*addition* sequence). Later-developing Y replaces earlier-developing X as an approach to a given problem *(substitution)*. Y is derived from X by *differentiation, generalization,* or *stabilization (modification)*. X becomes a component part of a larger cognitive unit Y *(inclusion)*. X serves as a developmental facilitator of, or bridge to Y *(mediation)*.

bibliography

Aebli, H. *Über die geistige Entwicklung des Kindes*. Stuttgart: Klett, 1963.

Amsterdam, B. Mirror self-image reactions before age two. *Developmental Psychobiology*, 1972, *5*(4), 297–305.

Aronson, E. & Rosenbloom, S. Space perception in early infancy: Perception within a common auditory-visual space. *Science*, 1971, *172*, 1161.

Aronson, E., & Tronick, E. Perceptual capacities in early infancy. In J. Eliot (Ed.), *Human development and cognitive processes*. New York: Holt, Rinehart, & Winston, 1971.

Banks, M. S., Aslin, R. N., & Letson, R. D. Sensitive period for the development of human binocular vision. *Science*, 1975, *190*, 675–77.

Baron, J. Semantic components and conceptual development. *Cognition*, 1973, *2*(3), 299–317.

Bates, E. *Language and context: Studies in the acquisition of pragmatics*. Unpublished doctoral dissertation, University of Chicago, 1974.

Bearison, D. J. Role of measurement operations in the acquisition of conservation. *Developmental Psychology*, 1969, *1*, 653–60.

Beilin, H. The training and acquisition of logical operations. In M. F. Rosskopf, L. P. Steffe, & S. Taback (Eds.), *Piagetian cognitive-development research and mathematical education*. Washington: National Council of Teachers of Mathematics, 1971.

Bell, S. M. The development of the concept of object as related to infant-mother attachment. *Child Development*, 1970, *41*, 291–311.

BEM, S. The role of comprehension in children's problem-solving. *Developmental Psychology,* 1970, *2,* 351–58.

BERNDT, T. J. The development of person perception. Unpublished paper, University of Minnesota, 1973.

BERNDT, T. J., & BERNDT, E. G. Children's use of intentions in person perception and moral judgment as assessed with films and with stories. Unpublished study, University of Minnesota, 1974.

BLAKEMORE, C. Developmental factors in the formation of feature extracting neurons. In F. O. Schmitt & F. G. Worden (Eds.), *The neurosciences (third study program).* Cambridge, Mass.: M.I.T. Press, 1974.

BOND, E. K. Perception of form by the human infant. *Psychological Bulletin,* 1972, *77,* 225–45.

BORKE, H. Interpersonal perception of young children: Egocentrism or empathy? *Developmental Psychology,* 1971, *5,* 263–69.

BORKE, H. The development of empathy in Chinese and American children between three and six years of age: A cross-culture study. *Developmental Psychology,* 1973, *9,* 102–108.

BORTNER, M., & BIRCH, H. G. Cognitive capacity and cognitive competence. *American Journal of Mental Deficiency,* 1970, *74,* 735–44.

BOWER, T. G. R. *Development in infancy.* San Francisco: Freeman, 1974.

BOWER, T. G. R., & PATERSON, J. G. Stages in the development of the object concept. *Cognition,* 1972, *1,* 47–55.

BOWLBY, J. *Attachment and loss* (Vol. 1): *Attachment.* New York: Basic Books, 1969.

BRAINE, M. D. S., & SHANKS, B. L. The development of conservation of size. *Journal of Verbal Learning and Verbal Behavior,* 1965, *4,* 227–42. (a)

BRAINE, M. D. S., & SHANKS, B. L. The conservation of a shape property and a proposal about the origin of the conservations. *Canadian Journal of Psychology,* 1965, *19,* 197–207. (b)

BRAINERD, C. J. Structures of thought in middle-childhood: Recent research on Piaget's concrete-operational groupements. Paper presented at the Third Interdisciplinary Meeting on Structural Learning, Philadelphia, March-April, 1972.

BRAINERD, C. J. Neo-Piagetian training experiments revisited: Is there any support for the cognitive-developmental stage hypothesis? *Cognition,* 1974, *2,* 349–70.

BRAINERD, C. J. The role of structures in explaining cognitive development. Unpublished paper, University of Alberta, 1975.

BRAINERD, C. J. "Stage," "structure," and developmental theory. In G. Steiner (Ed.), *The psychology of the twentieth century.* Munich: Kindler, 1976.

BRAINERD, C. J., & BRAINERD, S. H. Order of acquisition of number and quantity conservation. *Child Development,* 1972, *43,* 1401–1406.

BRANSFORD, J. D., & FRANKS, J. J. The abstraction of linguistic ideas. *Cognitive Psychology,* 1971, *2,* 331–50.

BRONSON, G. The postnatal growth of visual capacity. *Child Development,* 1974, *45,* 873–90.

BRONSON, W. A. The growth of competence: Issues of conceptualization and measurement. In H. R. Schaffer (Ed.), *The origins of human social relations.* New York: Academic Press, 1971.

BROWN, A. L. Judgments of recency for long sequences of pictures: The absence of a developmental trend. *Journal of Experimental Child Psychology,* 1973, *15,* 473–80.

BROWN, A. L. The development of memory: Knowing, knowing about knowing, and knowing how to know. In H. W. Reese (Ed.), *Advances in child development and behavior* (Vol. 10). New York: Academic Press, 1975.

BRUNER, J. S. Origins of mind in infancy. Paper presented at the meeting of Division 8 of the American Psychological Association, Washington, D.C., September, 1967.

BRUNER, J. S., & KOSLOWSKI, B. Visually preadapted constituents of manipulatory action. *Perception,* 1972, *1,* 3–14.

BRUNER, J. S., OLVER, R. R., & GREENFIELD, P. M. *Studies in cognitive growth.* New York: John Wiley & Sons, 1966.

BRUSH, L. R. *Children's conceptions of addition and subtraction: The relation of formal and informal notions.* Unpublished doctoral dissertation, Cornell University, 1972.

BUTTERFIELD, E. C., & BELMONT, J. M. Assessing and improving the executive cognitive functions of mentally retarded people. In I. Bialer & M. Sternlicht (Eds.), *Psychological issues in mental retardation.* Chicago: Aldine-Atherton, 1975.

BUTTERFIELD, E. C., WAMBOLD, C., & BELMONT, J. M. On the theory and practice of improving short-term memory. *American Journal of Mental Deficiency,* 1973, *77,* 654–69.

BYNUM, T. W., THOMAS, J. A., & WEITZ, L. J. Truth-functional logic in formal operational thinking. *Developmental Psychology,* 1972, *7,* 129–32.

BYRNE, D. F. *The development of role-taking in adolescence.* Unpublished doctoral dissertation, Harvard University, 1973.

CASE, R. Structures and strictures: Some functional limitations on the course of cognitive growth. *Cognitive Psychology,* 1974, *6,* 544–74.

CHARLESWORTH, W. R. Development of the object concept: A methodological study. Paper presented at the meeting of the American Psychological Association, New York, September, 1966.

CHARLESWORTH, W. R. Cognition in infancy: Where do we stand in the mid-sixties? *Merrill-Palmer Quarterly,* 1968, *14,* 25–46.

CHASE, W. G., & SIMON, H. A. Perception in chess. *Cognitive Psychology,* 1973, *4,* 55–81.

COHEN, L. B., & GELBER, E. R. Infant visual memory. In L. B. Cohen & P. Salapatek (Eds.), *Infant perception: From sensation to cognition.* New York: Academic Press, 1975.

COHEN, L. B., & SALAPATEK, P. (Eds.) *Infant perception: From sensation to cognition.* New York: Academic Press, 1975.

COIE, J. D., COSTANZO, P. R., & FARNILL, D. Specific transitions in the development of spatial perspective-taking ability. *Developmental Psychology,* 1973, *9,* 167–77.

COLE, M., & BRUNER, J. S. Cultural differences and inferences about psychological processes. *American Psychologist,* 1971, *26,* 867–76.

COLE, M., & MALTZMAN, I. (Eds.), *A handbook of contemporary Soviet psychology.* New York: Basic Books, 1969.

COLE, M., & SCRIBNER, S. *Culture and thought: A psychological introduction.* New York: John Wiley & Sons, 1974.

COLLINS, W. A., BERNDT, T. J., & HESS, V. L. Observational learning of motives and consequences for television aggression: A developmental study. *Child Development,* 1974, *45,* 799–802.

COOK, N. L. *Attachment and object permanence in infancy: A short-term longitudinal study.* Unpublished doctoral dissertation, University of Minnesota, 1972.

COOPER, C. R. *Training inquiry behavior in young disadvantaged children.* Unpublished doctoral dissertation, University of Minnesota, 1972.

CORDES, M. J. A study of search skill in the Piagetian task for object concept in infants. Unpublished honor's thesis, University of Minnesota, 1970.

CUVO, A. J. Developmental differences in rehearsal and free recall. *Journal of Experimental Child Psychology,* 1975, *19,* 265–78.

DAEHLER, M. W. Children's manipulation of illusory and ambiguous stimuli, discriminative performance, and implications for conceptual development. *Child Development,* 1970, *41,* 225–41.

DAGENAIS, Y. *Analyse de la cohérence opératoire entre les groupements d'addition des classes, de multiplication des classes et d'addition des relations asymétriques.* Unpublished doctoral dissertation, Université de Montréal, 1973.

DALE, P. S. *Language development: Structure and function.* Hinsdale, Ill.: Dryden Press, 1972.

DAMON, W. The development of the child's conception of justice. Paper presented at the meeting of the Society for Research in Child Development, Philadelphia, March, 1973.

DASEN, P. R. Cross-cultural Piagetian research: A summary. *Journal of Cross-Cultural Research,* 1972, *3,* 23–39.

DEMBER, W. N., & JENKINS, J. J. *General psychology: Modeling behavior and experience.* Englewood Cliffs, N.J.: Prentice-Hall, 1970.

DE VILLIERS, P. A., & DE VILLIERS, J. G. On this, that, and the other: Non-egocentrism in very young children. *Journal of Experimental Child Psychology,* 1974, *18,* 438–47.

DE VRIES, R. Constancy of generic identity in the years three to six. *Society for Research in Child Development Monographs,* 1969, *34*(3, Serial No. 127).

DORE, J. *The development of speech acts.* The Hague: Mouton, in press.

EIMAS, P. D. Information processing in problem solving as a function of developmental level and stimulus saliency. *Developmental Psychology,* 1970, *2,* 224–29.

EIMAS, P. D. Speech perception in early infancy. In L. B. Cohen & P. Salapatek (Eds.), *Infant perception: From sensation to cognition.* New York: Academic Press, 1975.

ELKIND, D. Egocentrism in adolescence. *Child Development,* 1967, *38,* 1025–1034.

ERVIN-TRIPP, S. The comprehension and production of requests by children. In E. V. Clark (Ed.), *Papers and reports on child language development* (Vol.

6). Stanford, Calif.: Committee on Linguistics, Stanford University (mimeo), 1974.

EVANS, W. F., & GRATCH, G. The stage IV error in Piaget's theory of object concept development: Difficulties in object conceptualization or spatial localization? *Child Development,* 1972, *43,* 682–88.

FEFFER, M., & GOUREVITCH, V. Cognitive aspects of role-taking in children. *Journal of Personality,* 1960, *28,* 383–96.

FELDMAN, C. F., & TOULMIN, S. Logic and the theory of mind: Formal, pragmatic and empirical considerations in a science of cognitive development. In *Nebraska Symposium on Motivation* (Vol. 23). Lincoln: University of Nebraska Press, 1975.

FESHBACH, N. D. Empathy: An interpersonal process. Paper presented at the meeting of the American Psychological Association, Montreal, August, 1973.

FITZGERALD, H. E., LINTZ, L. M., BRACKBILL, Y., & ADAMS, G. Time perception and conditioning of an autonomic response in young infants. *Perceptual and Motor Skills,* 1967, *24,* 479–86.

FLAPAN, D. *Children's understanding of social interaction.* New York: Teachers College Press, 1968.

FLAVELL, J. H. *The developmental psychology of Jean Piaget.* Princeton, N. J.: Van Nostrand, 1963.

FLAVELL, J. H. Concept development. In P. H. Mussen (Ed.), *Carmichael's manual of child psychology* (Vol. 1). New York: John Wiley & Sons, 1970. (a)

FLAVELL, J. H. Developmental studies of mediated memory. In H. W. Reese & L. P. Lipsitt (Eds.), *Advances in child development and behavior* (Vol. 5). New York: Academic Press, 1970. (b)

FLAVELL, J. H. Stage-related properties of cognitive development. *Cognitive Psychology,* 1971, *2,* 421–53. (a)

FLAVELL, J. H. First discussant's comments: What is memory development the development of? *Human Development,* 1971, *14,* 272–78. (b)

FLAVELL, J. H. Comments on Beilin's "The development of physical concepts." In T. Mischel (Ed.), *Cognitive development and epistemology.* New York: Academic Press, 1971. (c)

FLAVELL, J. H. An analysis of cognitive-developmental sequences. *Genetic Psychology Monographs,* 1972, *86,* 279–350.

FLAVELL, J. H. The development of inferences about others. In T. Mischel (Ed.), *Understanding other persons.* Oxford, England: Blackwell, Basil, and Mott, 1974.

FLAVELL, J. H., BEACH, D. H., and CHINSKY, J. M. Spontaneous verbal rehearsal in a memory task as a function of age. *Child Development,* 1966, *37,* 283-99.

FLAVELL, J. H., BOTKIN, P. T., FRY, C. L., WRIGHT, J. W., & JARVIS, P. E. *The development of role-taking and communication skills in children.* New York: John Wiley & Sons, 1968. (Reprinted by Robert E. Krieger Publishing Company, Huntington, New York, 1975).

FLAVELL, J. H., FRIEDRICHS, A. G., & HOYT, J. D. Developmental changes in memorization processes. *Cognitive Psychology,* 1970, *1,* 324–40.

FLAVELL, J. H., & WELLMAN, H. M. Metamemory. In R. V. Kail & J. W. Hagen

(Eds.), *Memory in cognitive development.* Hillsdale, N. J.: Lawrence Erlbaum Associates, 1976.

FLAVELL, J. H., & WOHLWILL, J. F. Formal and functional aspects of cognitive development. In D. Elkind & J. H. Flavell (Eds.), *Studies in cognitive development: Essays in honor of Jean Piaget.* New York: Oxford University Press, 1969.

FRIJDA, N. H. Simulation of human long-term memory. *Psychological Bulletin,* 1972, *77,* 1–31.

FURTH, H. G. *Piaget and knowledge: Theoretical foundations.* Englewood Cliffs, N. J.: Prentice-Hall, 1969.

FURTH, H. G. On language and knowing in Piaget's developmental theory. *Human Development,* 1970, *13,* 241–57.

FURTH, H. G. Linguistic deficiency and thinking: Research with deaf subjects 1964-1969. *Psychological Bulletin,* 1971, *76,* 58–72.

GAGNÉ, R. M. Contributions of learning to human development. *Psychological Review,* 1968, *75,* 177–91 (a).

GAGNÉ, R. M. Learning hierarchies. *Educational Psychologist,* 1968, November. (b)

GALLUP, G. G. Chimpanzees: Self-recognition. *Science,* 1970, *167,* 86–87.

GANZ, L. Conjunctive neural gating as a mechanism mediating the development of object recognition. In A. D. Pick (Ed.), *Minnesota symposia on child psychology* (Vol. 9). Minneapolis: University of Minnesota Press, 1975.

GARDNER, H. *The arts and human development.* New York: John Wiley & Sons, 1973.

GARDNER, J., & GARDNER, H. A note on selective imitation by a six-week-old infant. *Child Development,* 1970, *41,* 1209–13.

GARRITY, L. I. An electromyographical study of subvocal speech and recall in preschool children. *Developmental Psychology,* 1975, *11,* 274–81.

GARVEY, C., & HOGAN, R. Social speech and social interaction: Egocentrism revisited. *Child Development,* 1973, *44,* 562–68.

GELMAN, R. The nature and development of early number concepts. In H. W. Reese (Ed.), *Advances in child development and behavior* (Vol. 7). New York: Academic Press, 1972. (a)

GELMAN, R. Logical capacity of very young children: Number invariance rules. *Child Development,* 1972, *43,* 75–90. (b)

GELMAN, R., & WEINBERG, D. H. The relationship between liquid conservation and compensation. *Child Development,* 1972, *43,* 371–83.

GIBSON, E. J. *Principles of perceptual learning and development.* New York: Appleton-Century-Crofts, 1969.

GIBSON, E. J., & LEVIN, H. *The psychology of reading.* Cambridge, Mass.: The M. I. T. Press, 1975.

GIBSON, J. J. *The senses considered as perceptual systems.* Boston: Houghton-Mifflin, 1966.

GINSBURG, H., & OPPER, S. *Piaget's theory of intellectual development: An introduction.* Englewood Cliffs, N.J.: Prentice-Hall, 1969.

GLASER, R., & RESNICK, L. B. Instructional psychology. *Annual Review of Psychology,* 1972, *23,* 207–76.

GLEITMAN, L. R., GLEITMAN, H., & SHIPLEY, E. F. The emergence of the child as grammarian. *Cognition,* 1972, *1,* 137–64.

GLUCKSBERG, S., KRAUSS, R. M., & HIGGINS, T. The development of communication skills in children. In F. Horowitz (Ed.), *Review of child development research* (Vol. 4). Chicago: University of Chicago Press, 1975.

GOLDBERG, S., PERLMUTTER, M., & MYERS, N. Recall of related and unrelated lists by 2-year-olds. *Journal of Experimental Child Psychology,* 1974, *18,* 1–8.

GOODNOW, J. J. The role of modalities in perceptual and cognitive development. In J. P. Hill (Ed.), *Minnesota symposia on child psychology* (Vol. 5). Minneapolis: University of Minnesota Press, 1971.

GRATCH, G. A study of the relative dominance of vision and touch in six-month-old infants. *Child Development,* 1972, *43,* 615–23.

GRATCH, G. Recent studies based on Piaget's view of object concept development. In L. B. Cohen & P. Salapatek (Eds.), *Infant perception: From sensation to cognition.* New York: Academic Press, 1975.

GRATCH, G., & LANDERS, W. F. Stage IV of Piaget's theory of infant's object concepts: A longitudinal study. *Child Development,* 1971, *42,* 359–72.

GREEN, D. R. Retrospect and prospect. In D. R. Green, M. P. Ford, & G. B. Flamer (Eds.), *Measurement and Piaget.* New York: McGraw-Hill, 1971.

GRUBER, H. E., GIRGUS, J. S., & BANUAZIZI, A. The development of object permanence in the cat. *Developmental Psychology,* 1971, *4,* 9–15.

GUARDO, C. J., & BOHAN, J. B. Development of a sense of self-identity in children. *Child Development,* 1971, *42,* 1909–21.

HAGEN, J. W., & HALE, G. A. The development of attention in children. In A. D. Pick (Ed.), *Minnesota symposia on child psychology* (Vol. 7). Minneapolis: University of Minnesota Press, 1973.

HAGEN, J. W., JONGEWARD, R. H., & KAIL, R. V. Cognitive perspectives on the development of memory. In H. W. Reese (Ed.), *Advances in child development and behavior* (Vol. 10). New York: Academic Press, 1975.

HAGEN, M. A. Picture perception: Toward a theoretical model. *Psychological Bulletin,* 1974, *81,* 471–97.

HALE, G. A., & TAWEEL, S. S. Age differences in children's performance on measures of component selection and incidental learning. *Journal of Experimental Child Psychology,* 1974, *18,* 107–16.

HALLIDAY, M. A. K. Early language learning: A sociolinguistic approach. Paper presented at the Ninth International Congress of Anthropological and Ethnological Sciences, Chicago, August-September 1973.

HENLE, M. On the relation between logic and thinking. *Psychological Review,* 1962, *69,* 366–78.

HILL, J. P., & PALMQUIST, W. J. Social cognition and social relations in adolescence: A precursory view. Paper presented at the meeting of the Eastern Psychological Association, Philadelphia, April 1974.

HOCHBERG, J. E. Nativism and empiricism in perception. In L. Postman (Ed.), *Psychology in the making.* New York: Knopf, 1962.

HOFFMAN, M. L. Toward a developmental theory of prosocial motivation. Paper presented at the National Institute of Child Health and Human Development Workshop, "The Development of Motivation in Childhood," Elkridge, Maryland, May 1972.

HOROWITZ, F. D. (Ed.). Visual attention, auditory stimulation, and language discrimination in young infants. *Monographs of the Society for Research In Child Development,* 1974, *39* (5, Serial No. 158).

HUNT, E. B. The weakness of negative thinking. *Contemporary Psychology,* 1974, *19,* 233–35.

HUNT, J. McV. The impact and limitations of the giant of developmental psychology. In D. Elkind & J. H. Flavell (Eds.), *Studies in cognitive development: Essays in honor of Jean Piaget.* New York: Oxford University Press, 1969.

INHELDER, B., & PIAGET, J. *The growth of logical thinking from childhood to adolescence.* New York: Basic Books, 1958.

INHELDER, B., & SINCLAIR, H. Learning cognitive structures. In P. H. Mussen, J. Langer, & M. Covington (Eds.), *Trends and issues in developmental psychology.* New York: Holt, Rinehart, & Winston, 1969.

JORDAN, N. Is there an Achilles heel in Piaget's theorizing? *Human Development,* 1972, *15,* 379–82.

KAGAN, J. The determinants of attention in the infant. *American Scientist,* 1970, *58,* 298–306.

KAGAN, J., & KLEIN, R. E. Cross-cultural perspectives on early development. *American Psychologist,* 1973, *28,* 947–61.

KAIL, R. V., & HAGEN, J. W. (Eds.) *Memory in cognitive development.* Hillsdale, N.J.: Lawrence Erlbaum Associates, 1976.

KATZ, P., & ZIGLER, E. Self-image disparity: A developmental approach. *Journal of Personality and Social Psychology,* 1967, *5,* 186–95.

KEENEY, T. J., CANNIZZO, S. R., and FLAVELL, J. H. Spontaneous and induced verbal rehearsal in a recall task. *Child Development,* 1967, *38,* 953-66.

KELLEY, H. H. The processes of causal attribution. *American Psychologist,* 1973, *28,* 107–128.

KESSEN, W., HAITH, M. M., & SALAPATEK, P. H. Infancy. In P. H. Mussen (Ed.), *Carmichael's manual of child psychology* (Vol. 1). New York: John Wiley & Sons, 1970.

KING, M. The development of some intention concepts in young children. *Child Development,* 1971, *42,* 1145–52.

KLAHR, D. An information-processing approach to the study of cognitive development. In A. D. Pick (Ed), *Minnesota symposia on child psychology* (Vol. 7). Minneapolis: University of Minnesota Press, 1973.

KLAHR, D., & WALLACE, J. G. The role of quantification operators in the development of conservation of quantity. *Cognitive Psychology,* 1973, *4,* 301–27.

KNIFONG, J. D. Logical abilities of young children—two styles of approach. *Child Development,* 1974, *45,* 78–83.

KOBASIGAWA, A. Utilization of retrieval cues by children in recall. *Child Development,* 1974, *45,* 127–34.

KOBASIGAWA, A. Retrieval strategies in the development of memory. In R. V. Kail & J. W. Hagen (Eds.), *Memory in cognitive development.* Hillsdale, N.J.: Lawrence Erlbaum Associates, 1976.

KOHLBERG, L. A cognitive-developmental analysis of children's sex-role concepts and attitudes. In E. E. Maccoby (Ed.), *The development of sex differences.* Stanford, Calif.: Stanford University Press, 1966.

KOHLBERG, L. Stage and sequence: The cognitive-developmental approach to socialization. In D. A. Goslin (Ed.), *Handbook of socialization theory and research*. New York: Rand McNally, 1969.

KOPP, C. B., & SHAPERMAN, J. Cognitive development in the absence of object manipulation during infancy. *Developmental Psychology*, 1973, *9*, 430.

KREUTZER, M. A., & CHARLESWORTH, W. R. Infants' reactions to different expressions of emotion. Paper presented at the meeting of the Society for Research in Child Development, Philadelphia, March 1973.

KREUTZER, M. A., LEONARD, C., & FLAVELL, J. H. An interview study of children's knowledge about memory. *Monographs of the Society for Research in Child Development*, 1975, *40* (1, Serial No. 159).

KUHN, D. Inducing development experimentally: Comments on a research paradigm. *Developmental Psychology*, 1974, *10*, 590–600.

KURTINEZ, W., & GREIF, E. B. The development of moral thought: Review and evaluation of Kohlberg's approach. *Psychological Bulletin*, 1974, *81*, 453–70.

LANDERS, W. F. Effects of differential experience on infants' performance in a Piagetian stage IV object-concept task. *Developmental Psychology*, 1971, *5*, 48–54.

LANGER, J. Disequilibrium as a source of development. In P. Mussen, J. Langer, & M. Covington (Eds.), *Trends and issues in developmental psychology*. New York: Holt, Rinehart, & Winston, 1969.

LeCOMPTE, G. K., & GRATCH, G. Violation of a rule as a method of diagnosing infants' levels of object concept. *Child Development*, 1972, *43*, 385–96.

LEMPERS, J. D., FLAVELL, E. R., & FLAVELL, J. H. The development in very young children of tacit knowledge concerning visual perception. *Genetic Psychology Monographs*, in press.

LESKOW, S., & SMOCK, C. D. Developmental changes in problem solving strategies: Permutations. *Developmental Psychology*, 1970, *2*, 412–22.

LIBEN, L. S. Piagetian investigations of the development of memory. In R. V. Kail & J. W. Hagen (Eds.), *Memory in cognitive development*. Hillsdale, N.J.: Lawrence Erlbaum Associates, 1976.

LIVESLEY, W. J., & BROMLEY, D. B. *Person perception in childhood and adolescence*. London: John Wiley and Sons, 1973.

LOEVINGER, J. The meaning and measurement of ego development. *American Psychologist*, 1966, *21*, 196–206.

LUNZER, E. A. Formal reasoning. In E. A. Lunzer & J. F. Morris (Eds.), *Development in human learning*. New York: American Elsevier, 1968.

LURIA, A. R. The directive function of speech in development and dissolution. *Word*, 1959, *15*, 341–52.

LURIA, A. R. *The role of speech in the regulation of normal and abnormal behaviour*. New York: Pergamon Press, 1961.

MACCOBY, E. E. The development of stimulus selection. In J. P. Hill (Ed.), *Minnesota symposia on child psychology* (Vol. 3). Minneapolis: University of Minnesota Press, 1969.

MACCOBY, E. E., & MASTERS, J. C. Attachment and dependency. In P. H. Mussen (Ed.), *Carmichael's manual of child psychology* (Vol. 2). New York: John Wiley & Sons, 1970.

MACNAMARA, J. Cognitive basis of language learning in infants. *Psychological Review*, 1972, *79*, 1–13.

MARATSOS, M. P. Nonegocentric communication abilities in preschool children. *Child Development*, 1973, *44*, 697–700.

MARKMAN, E. *Factors affecting the young child's ability to monitor his memory.* Unpublished doctoral dissertation, University of Pennsylvania, 1973.

MARTORANO, S. C. *The development of formal operational thought.* Unpublished doctoral dissertation, Rutgers University, 1974.

MASANGKAY, Z. S., McCLUSKEY, K. A., McINTYRE, C. W., SIMS-KNIGHT, J., VAUGHN, B. E., & FLAVELL, J. H. The early development of inferences about the visual percepts of others. *Child Development*, 1974, *45*, 357–66.

MASUR, E. F., McINTYRE, C. W., & FLAVELL, J. H. Developmental changes in apportionment of study time among items in a multitrial free recall test. *Journal of Experimental Child Psychology*, 1973, *15*, 237–46.

McGHEE, P. E. The role of operational thinking in children's comprehension and appreciation of humor. *Child Development*, 1971, *42*, 733–44. (a)

McGHEE, P. E. Cognitive development and children's comprehension of humor. *Child Development*, 1971, *42*, 123–38. (b)

McGURK, H., & LEWIS, M. Space perception in early infancy: Perception within a common auditory-visual space? *Science*, 1974, *186*, 649–50.

MEACHAM, J. A. The development of memory abilities in the individual. *Human Development*, 1972, *15*, 205–28.

MENIG-PETERSON, C. L. The modification of communicative behavior in pre-school-aged children as a function of the listener's perspective. *Child Development*, 1975, *46*, 1015–18.

MILLER, D. J., COHEN, L. B., & HILL, K. T. A methodological investigation of Piaget's theory of object concept development in the sensory-motor period. *Journal of Experimental Child Psychology*, 1970, *9*, 59–85.

MILLER, P. H., KESSEL, F. S., & FLAVELL, J. H. Thinking about people thinking about people thinking about . . . : A study of social cognitive development. *Child Development*, 1970, *41*, 613–23.

MILLER, S. A. Contradiction, surprise, and cognitive change: The effects of disconfirmation of belief on conservers and nonconservers. *Journal of Experimental Child Psychology*, 1973, *15*, 47–62.

MILLER, S. A. Nonverbal assessment of Piagetian concepts. *Psychological Bulletin*, 1976.

MILLER, S. A., & LIPPS, L. Extinction of conservation and transitivity of weight. *Journal of Experimental Child Psychology*, 1973, *16*, 388–402.

MILLER, S. A., SCHWARTZ, L. C., & STEWART, C. An attempt to extinguish conservation of weight in college students. *Developmental Psychology*, 1973, *8*, 316.

MILLER, S. A., SHELTON, J., & FLAVELL, J. H. A test of Luria's hypotheses concerning the development of verbal self-regulation. *Child Development*, 1970, *41*, 651–65.

MISCHEL, W. The construction of personality: Some facts and fantasies about cognitive and social behavior. Paper presented to Division 12 of the American Psychological Association, Washington, D.C., September 1971.

MISCHEL, W. Toward a cognitive social learning reconceptualization of personality. *Psychological Review,* 1973, *80,* 252–83.

MISCHEL, W., EBBESEN, E. G., & ZEISS, A. R. Cognitive and attentional mechanisms in delay of gratification. *Journal of Personality and Social Psychology,* 1972, *21,* 204–18.

MOELY, B. E., OLSON, F. A., HALWES, T. G., & FLAVELL, J. H. Production deficiency in young children's clustered recall. *Developmental Psychology,* 1969, *1,* 26–34.

MOYNAHAN, E. D. The development of knowledge concerning the effect of categorization upon free recall. *Child Development,* 1973, *44,* 238–46.

MULLENER, N., & LAIRD, J. D. Some developmental changes in the organization of self-evaluations. *Developmental Psychology,* 1971, *5,* 233–36.

MUSSEN, P. H., CONGER, J. J., & KAGAN, J. *Child development and personality* (4th Ed.). New York: Harper & Row, 1974.

NEIMARK, E. D. Model for a thinking machine: An information-processing framework for the study of cognitive development. *Merrill-Palmer Quarterly,* 1970, *16,* 345–68.

NEIMARK, E. D. Intellectual development during adolescence. In F. D. Horowitz (Ed.), *Review of child development research* (Vol. 4). Chicago: University of Chicago Press, 1975. (a)

NEIMARK, E. D. Longitudinal development of formal operations thought. *Genetic Psychology Monographs,* 1975, *91,* 171–225. (b)

NEIMARK, E. D., & LEWIS, N. The development of logical problem-solving strategies. *Child Development,* 1967, *38,* 107–17.

NEIMARK, E. D., SLOTNICK, N. S., & ULRICH, T. Development of memorization strategies. *Developmental Psychology,* 1971, *5,* 427–32.

NELSON, K. Some evidence for the cognitive primacy of categorization and its functional basis. *Merrill-Palmer Quarterly,* 1973, *19,* 21–39.

NELSON, K. Concept, word, and sentence: Interrelations in acquisition and development. *Psychological Review,* 1974, *81,* 267–85.

NELSON, K. E. Accommodation of visual tracking patterns in human infants to object movement patterns. *Journal of Experimental Child Psychology,* 1971, *12,* 182–96.

NELSON, K. E., & EARL, N. Information search by preschool children: Induced use of categories and category hierarchies. *Child Development,* 1973, *44,* 682–85.

O'BRYAN, K. G., & BOERSMA, F. J. Eye movements, perceptual activity, and conservation development. *Journal of Experimental Child Psychology,* 1971, *12,* 157–69.

ODOM, R. D., & GUZMAN, R. D. Development of hierarchies of dimensional salience. *Developmental Psychology,* 1972, *6,* 271–87.

OLSON, D. R., & PAGLIUSO, S. M. (Eds.) From perceiving to performing: An aspect of cognitive growth. *Ontario Journal of Educational Research,* 1968, *10,* 155–210.

OLSON, G. M. An information processing analysis of visual memory and habituation in infants. In T. J. Tighe & R. N. Leaton (Eds.), *Habituation: Perspectives from child development, animal behavior, and neurophysiology.* Hillsdale, N.J.: Lawrence Erlbaum Associates, 1976.

ORNSTEIN, P. A., NAUS, M. J., & LIBERTY, C. Rehearsal and organizational processes in children's memory. *Child Development*, 1975, *46*, 818–30.

OSHERSON, D. N. *Logical abilities in children* (Vols. 1 & 2). Hillsdale, N.J.: Lawrence Erlbaum Associates, 1974.

OSHERSON, D. N., & MARKMAN, E. Language and the ability to evaluate contradictions and tautologies. *Cognition*, in press.

PAPANDROPOULOU, I., & SINCLAIR, H. What is a word? Experimental study of children's ideas on grammar. *Human Development*, 1974, *17*, 241–58.

PARIS, S. G. Integration and inference in children's comprehension and memory. In F. Restle, R. Shiffrin, J. Castellan, H. Lindman, & D. Pisoni (Eds.), *Cognitive theory* (Vol. 1). Hillsdale, N.J.: Lawrence Erlbaum Associates, 1975. (a)

PARIS, S. G. Developmental changes in constructive memory abilities. Paper presented at the meeting of the Society for Research in Child Development, Denver, April 1975. (b)

PARIS, S. G., & LINDAUER, B. K. Constructive processes in children's comprehension and memory. In R. V. Kail & J. W. Hagen (Eds.), *Memory in cognitive development*. Hillsdale, N.J.: Lawrence Erlbaum Associates, 1976.

PARIS, S. G., & MAHONEY, G. J. Cognitive integration in children's memory for sentences and pictures. *Child Development*, 1974, *45*, 633–42.

PEEVERS, B. H., & SECORD, P. F. Developmental changes in attribution of descriptive concepts to persons. *Journal of Personality and Social Psychology*, 1973, *27*, 120–28.

PIAGET, J. *The language and thought of the child*. New York: Harcourt, Brace, 1926.

PIAGET, J. *The child's conception of number*. New York: Humanities Press, 1952.

PIAGET, J. Introduction. In P. Gréco, J-B. Grize, S. Papert, & J. Piaget, *Problèmes de la construction du nombre*. Paris: Presses Universitaires de France, 1960. (Vol. 11 of the *Etudes d'Epistémologie Génétique series*.)

PIAGET, J. *On the development of memory and identity*. Barre, Mass.: Clark University Press and Barre Publishers, 1968.

PIAGET, J. Piaget's theory. In P. H. Mussen (Ed.), *Carmichael's manual of child psychology* (Vol. 1). New York: John Wiley & Sons, 1970. (a)

PIAGET, J. *Genetic epistemology*. New York: Columbia University Press, 1970. (b)

PIAGET, J. Intellectual evolution from adolescence to adulthood. *Human Development*, 1972, *15*, 1–12.

PIAGET, J., GRIZE, J.-B., SZEMINSKA, A., & VINH BANG. *Epistémologie et psychologie de la fonction*. Paris: Presses Universitaires de France, 1968. (Vol. 23 of the *Etudes d'Epistémologie Génétique* series)

PIAGET, J., & INHELDER, B. *The psychology of the child*. New York: Basic Books, 1969.

PIAGET, J., & INHELDER, B. *Memory and intelligence*. New York: Basic Books, 1973.

PIAGET, J., SINCLAIR, H., & VINH BANG. *Epistémologie et psychologie de l'identité*. Paris: Presses Universitaires de France, 1968. (Vol. 24 of the *Etudes d'Epistémologie Génétique* series)

PICK, A. D., CHRISTY, M. D., & FRANKEL, G. W. A developmental study of visual selective attention. *Journal of Experimental Child Psychology,* 1972, *14,* 165–75.

PICK, A. D., & FRANKEL, G. W. A developmental study of strategies of visual selectivity. *Child Development,* 1974, *45,* 1162–65.

PICK, A. D., FRANKEL, D. G., & HESS, V. L. Children's attention: The development of selectivity. In E. M. Hetherington (Ed.), *Review of child development research* (Vol. 5). Chicago: University of Chicago Press, 1975.

PICK, H. L. Perceptual development of children. *Encyclopedia of Education,* 1971, *7,* 69–76.

PICK, H. L., & PICK, A. D. Sensory and perceptual development. In P. H. Mussen (Ed.), *Carmichael's manual of child psychology* (Vol. 1). New York: John Wiley & Sons, 1970.

PINARD, A., & LAURENDEAU, M. "Stage" in Piaget's cognitive-developmental theory: Exegesis of a concept. In D. Elkind & J. H. Flavell (Eds.), *Studies in cognitive growth: Essays in honor of Jean Piaget.* New York: Oxford University Press, 1969.

POLLACK, R. H. Perceptual development: A progress report. In S. Farnham-Diggory (Ed.), *Information processing in children.* New York: Academic Press, 1972.

POTTER, M. C., & LEVY, E. I. Spatial enumeration without counting. *Child Development,* 1968, *39,* 265–72.

PUFALL, P. B., & SHAW, R. E. Precocious thoughts on number: The long and the short of it. *Developmental Psychology,* 1972, *7,* 62–69.

PUFALL, P. B., SHAW, R. E., & SYRDAL-LASKY, A. Development of number conservation: An examination of some predictions from Piaget's stage analysis and equilibration model. *Child Development,* 1973, *44,* 21–27.

REITMAN, W. R. *Cognition and thought: An information-processing approach.* New York: John Wiley & Sons, 1965.

RESNICK, L. B. Issues in the study of learning hierarchies. Paper presented at the meeting of the American Educational Research Association, Minneapolis, March 1970.

REST, J. R. The cognitive developmental approach to morality: The state of the art. *Counseling and Values,* 1974, *18,* 64–78.

RICCIUTI, H. N. Object grouping and selective ordering in infants 12–24 months old. *Merrill-Palmer Quarterly,* 1965, *11,* 129–48.

ROHWER, W. D. Elaboration and learning in childhood and adolescence. In H. W. Reese (Ed.), *Advances in child development and behavior* (Vol. 8). New York: Academic Press, 1973.

ROSENBACH, D., CROCKETT, W. H., & WAPNER, S. Developmental level, emotional involvement, and the resolution of inconsistency in impression formation. *Developmental Psychology,* 1973, *8,* 120–30.

ROTHENBERG, B. B. Children's social sensitivity and the relationship to interpersonal competence, intrapersonal comfort, and intellectual level. *Developmental Psychology,* 1970, *3,* 335–50.

SALAPATEK, P. Stimulus determinants of attention in infants. In *International Encyclopedia of Neurology, Psychiatry, Psychoanalysis and Psychology.* New York: Van Nostrand Reinhold, in press.

SALATAS, H., & FLAVELL, J. H. Perspective-taking: The development of two components of knowledge. *Child Development,* 1976, *47,* 103–9.

SALATAS, H., & FLAVELL, J. H. Retrieval of recently learned information: Development of strategies and control skills. Unpublished study, University of Minnesota, 1975.

SAVITSKY, J. C., & IZARD, C. E. Development changes in the use of emotion cues in a concept-formation task. *Developmental Psychology,* 1970, *3,* 350–57.

SCARR-SALAPATEK, S. An evolutionary perspective on infant intelligence: Species patterns and individual variations. In M. Lewis (Ed.), *The origins of intelligence: Infancy and early childhood.* New York: Plenum, 1976.

SCHAEFFER, B. Skill integration during cognitive development. In R. A. Kennedy & A. Wilkes (Eds.), *Studies in long term memory.* New York: John Wiley & Sons, 1975.

SCHAEFFER, B., EGGLESTON, V. H., & SCOTT, J. L. Number development in young children. *Cognitive Psychology,* 1974, *6,* 357–79.

SCHAFFER, H. R. Cognitive structure and early social behavior. In H. R. Schaffer (Ed.), *The origin of human social relations.* New York: Academic Press, 1971.

SCHAFFER, H. R., GREENWOOD, A., & PARRY, M. H. The onset of wariness. *Child Development,* 1972, *43,* 165–75.

SELMAN, R. L. A developmental approach to interpersonal and moral awareness in young children: Some theoretical and educational perspectives. Paper presented at the National Seminar of the American Montessori Society, Boston, June 1974.

SELMAN, R. L. Stages of role-taking and moral judgment as guides to social interaction. In T. Lickona (Ed.), *A handbook of moral development.* New York: Holt, Rinehart, & Winston, 1976.

SELMAN, R. L., & BYRNE, D. F. Manual for scoring social role-taking stages in moral dilemmas. Unpublished Moral Education and Research Foundation Report No. RS1A, Harvard University, December 1972.

SELMAN, R. L., & BYRNE, D. F. Manual for scoring social role-taking in social dilemmas. Unpublished Moral Education and Research Foundation Report No. RS1B, Harvard University, March 1973.

SELMAN, R. L., & BYRNE, D. F. A structural-developmental analysis of levels of role taking in middle childhood. *Child Development,* 1974, *45,* 803–06.

SELMAN, R., DAMON, W., & GORDON, A. The relation between levels of social role taking and stages of justice conception in children ages four to ten. *Merrill-Palmer Quarterly,* in press.

SHANTZ, C. U. The development of social cognition. In E. M. Hetherington (Ed.), *Review of child development research* (Vol. 5). Chicago: University of Chicago Press, 1975.

SHAPIRO, B. J., & O'BRIEN, T. C. Logical thinking in children ages six through thirteen. *Child Development,* 1970, *41,* 823–29.

SHATZ, M., & GELMAN, R. The development of communication skills: Modifications in the speech of young children as a function of listener. *Monographs of the Society for Research in Child Development,* 1973, *38* (5, Serial No. 152).

SHIFFRIN, R. Memory search. In D. A. Norman (Ed.), *Models of human memory.* New York: Academic Press, 1970.

SHULTZ, T. R. An attribution theory analysis of precausal explanations. Unpublished paper, McGill University, 1974. (a)

SHULTZ, T. R. Development of the appreciation of riddles. *Child Development,* 1974, *45,* 100–105. (b)

SIEGLER, R. S., & LIEBERT, R. M. Acquisition of formal scientific reasoning by 10- and 13-year-olds: Designing a factorial experiment. *Developmental Psychology,* 1975, *11,* 401–402.

SIMON, H. A., & NEWELL, A. Human problem solving: The state of the theory in 1970. *American Psychologist,* 1971, *26,* 145–59.

SMEDSLUND, J. Concrete reasoning: A study of intellectual development. *Monographs of the Society for Research in Child Development,* 1964, *29* (2, Serial No. 93).

SMEDSLUND, J. Psychological diagnostics. *Psychological Bulletin,* 1969, *71,* 237–48.

SMIRNOV, A. A., & ZINCHENKO, P. I. Problems in the psychology of memory. In M. Cole & L. Maltzman (Eds.), *A handbook of contemporary Soviet psychology.* New York: Basic Books, 1969.

SNYDER, M. The self-monitoring of expressive behavior. *Journal of Personality and Social Psychology,* 1974, *30,* 526–37.

Social Science Research Council. *Annual report: 1971–1972.* New York: Social Science Research Council, 1973.

SPIVACK, G., & SHURE, M. B. *Social adjustment of young children: A cognitive approach to solving real-life problems.* San Francisco: Jossey-Bass, 1974.

STEVENSON, H. W. *Children's learning.* New York: Appleton-Century-Crofts, 1972.

STROMMEN, E. A. Verbal self-regulation in a children's game: Impulsive errors on "Simon says." *Child Development,* 1973, *44,* 849–53.

TAGIURI, R. Person perception. In G. Lindzey & E. Aronson (Eds.), *The handbook of social psychology* (Vol. 3). Reading, Mass.: Addison-Wesley, 1969.

TAPP, J. L. (Ed.) Socialization, the law, and society. *Journal of Social Issues,* 1971, *27* (2).

TAPP, J. L. The psychological limits of legality. In J. R. Pennock & J. W. Chapman (Eds.), *The limits of law (Nomos XV).* New York: Lieber-Atherton, 1974.

TENNEY, Y. J. The child's conception of organization and recall. *Journal of Experimental Child Psychology,* 1975, *19,* 100–114.

TOUSSAINT, N. A. An analysis of synchrony between concrete-operational tasks in terms of structural and performance demands. *Child Development,* 1974, *45,* 992–1001.

TRABASSO, T. Representation, memory and reasoning: How do we make transitive inferences? In A. D. Pick (Ed.), *Minnesota symposia on child psychology* (Vol. 9). Minneapolis: University of Minnesota Press, 1975.

TULKIN, S. R., & KONNER, M. J. Alternative conceptions of intellectual functioning. *Human Development,* 1973, *16,* 33–52.

TULVING, E. Episodic and semantic memory. In E. Tulving & W. Donaldson (Eds.), *Organization of memory.* New York: Academic Press, 1972.

TURNURE, J., BUIUM, N., & THURLOW, M. The effectiveness of interrogatives for promoting verbal elaboration productivity in young children. *Child Development,* in press.

VAN DEN DAELE, L. D. Qualitative models in developmental analysis. *Developmental Psychology,* 1969, *1,* 303–10.

VAUGHTER, R. M., SMOTHERMAN, W., & ORDY, J. M. Development of object permanence in the infant squirrel monkey. *Developmental Psychology,* 1972, *7,* 34–38.

VURPILLOT, E. The development of scanning strategies and their relation to visual differentiation. *Journal of Experimental Child Psychology,* 1968, *6,* 632–50.

WANG, M. C., RESNICK, L. B., & BOOZER, R. F. The sequence of development of some early mathematics behaviors. *Child Development,* 1971, *42,* 1767–78.

WASON, P. C., & JOHNSON-LAIRD, P. N. *Psychology of reasoning: Structure and content.* Cambridge, Mass.: Harvard University Press, 1972.

WEBB, R. A., MASSAR, B., & NADOLNY, T. Information and strategy in the young child's search for hidden objects. *Child Development,* 1972, *43,* 91–104.

WEINREB, N., & BRAINERD, C. J. A developmental study of Piaget's groupement model of the emergence of speed and time concepts. *Child Development,* 1975, *46,* 476–85.

WELLMAN, H. M. *The development of memory monitoring: The feeling of knowing experience.* Unpublished doctoral dissertation, University of Minnesota, 1975.

WELLMAN, H. M., DROZDAL, J. G., FLAVELL, J. H., RITTER, K., & SALATAS, H. Metamemory development and its possible role in the selection of behavior. In G. A. Hale (Chair), *The development of selective processes in cognition.* Symposium presented at the meeting of the Society for Research in Child Development, Denver, April 1975.

WELLMAN, H. M., RITTER, K., & FLAVELL, J. H. Deliberate memory behavior in the delayed reactions of very young children. *Developmental Psychology,* 1975, *11,* 780–87.

WENAR, C. Executive competence and spontaneous social behavior in one-year-olds. *Child Development,* 1972, *43,* 256–60.

WERNER, H. *Comparative psychology of mental development.* Chicago: Follett, 1948.

WERNER, H. The conception of development from a comparative and organismic point of view. In D. Harris (Ed.), *The concept of development.* Minneapolis: University of Minnesota Press, 1957.

WERNER, H., & KAPLAN, B. *Symbol formation: An organismic developmental approach to language and the expression of thought.* New York: John Wiley & Sons, 1963.

WHITEMAN, M. Children's conceptions of psychological causality. *Child Development,* 1967, *38,* 143–55.

WISE, K. L., WISE, L. A., & ZIMMERMAN, R. R. Piagetian object permanence in the infant rhesus monkey. *Developmental Psychology,* 1974, *10,* 429–37.

WOHLWILL, J. F. A study of the development of the number concept by scalogram analysis. *Journal of Genetic Psychology,* 1960, *97,* 345–77.

WOHLWILL, J. F. *The study of behavioral development.* New York: Academic Press, 1973. (a)

WOHLWILL, J. F. The concept of experience: S or R? *Human Development*, 1973, *16*, 90–107. (b)

WOZNIAK, R. H. Verbal regulation of motor behavior—Soviet research and non-Soviet replications. *Human Development*, 1972, *15*, 13–57.

*YARROW, L. J., & PEDERSON, F. A. Attachment: Its origins and course. In W. W. Hartup (Ed.), *The young child: Reviews of research* (Vol. 2). Washington, D.C.: National Association for the Education of Young Children, 1972.

YONAS, A., & PICK, H. L. An approach to the study of infant space perception. In L. B. Cohen & P. Salapatek (Eds.), *Infant perception: From sensation to cognition*. New York: Academic Press, 1975.

YUSSEN, S. R., & LEVY, V. M. Developmental changes in predicting one's own span of short-term memory. *Journal of Experimental Child Psychology*, 1975, *19*, 502–508.

ZIMILES, H. An analysis of methodological barriers to cognitive assessment of preschool children. Paper presented at the International Society for Study of Behavioral Development, Nijmegen, Netherlands, July 4–8, 1971.

name index

subject index